Embodying Women's Work

Embodying Women's Work

Caroline Gatrell

 Open University Press

Open University Press
McGraw-Hill Education
McGraw-Hill House
Shoppenhangers Road
Maidenhead
Berkshire
England
SL6 2QL

email: enquiries@openup.co.uk
world wide web: www.openup.co.uk

and Two Penn Plaza, New York, NY 10121-2289, USA

First published 2008

A catalogue record of this book is available from the British Library

ISBN-13: 978-0-335-21990-2 (pb) 978-0-335-21991-9 (hb)
ISBN-10: 0-335-21990-X (pb) 0-335-21991-8 (hb)

Library of Congress Cataloging-in-Publication Data
CIP data applied for

Typeset by RefineCatch Limited, Bungay, Suffolk
Printed in the UK by Bell and Bain Ltd., Glasgow

Fictitious names of companies, products, people, characters and/or data that may
be used herein (in case studies or in examples) are not intended to represent any
real individual, company, product or event.

The **McGraw·Hill** Companies

For my beautiful daughters

Anna and Emma

Contents

Acknowledgements

It has taken me four years to write this book, and there are many people to whom I owe thanks. First, I would like to thank my colleague and friend Dr Imogen Tyler, with whom I jointly organized two conferences, 'Maternal Bodies' (2005) and 'Birth' (2006), as part of a research series entitled 'Hard Labour: The Cultural Politics of Reproduction'. The work with Imogen has been a wonderful experience which has allowed both of us to extend and develop networks of other women scholars, also interested in maternal bodies and women's labour. I would also, in this regard, like to thank the Lancaster University Institute of Advanced Studies for awarding us the funding for the Hard Labour conferences, making possible the sharing of ideas and views at Lancaster University.

Through 'Maternal Bodies' and 'Birth', I met Dr Lisa Barraitser and Dr Tina Miller. I would like to thank Lisa and Tina, and other members of the MAMSIE group, for opening up new opportunities to consider and debate issues of maternal subjectivities with like-minded scholars.

At Lancaster, special thanks are due to colleagues who have shared with me the highs and lows of this book, provided feedback and fantastic support over the last four years, and kept me going when I never thought I would finish it. They are: Dr Ellie Hamilton, Dr Valerie Stead and Dr Elaine Swan. *Very* special thanks are owed to Elaine, who generously read an earlier draft of the whole manuscript, and provided the most detailed and constructive, thoughtful comments.

I should also like to thank my good friend Professor Tony Watson, with whom I discussed ideas at an early stage and who, as always, has offered encouragement and support.

Thanks, too, to Rowena Murray, whose writing workshops and techniques have been an inspiration and have spurred me on when I did not feel like it!

Many thanks are also due to the team at Open University Press, past and present. Shona Mullen, Mark Barratt, Chris Cudmore and Jack Fray have all helped me in shaping the ideas for this book, and encouraged the move from general ideas about agency and choice to the more specific focus on women's bodies and women's work. Thanks also to the Open University Press team for their forbearance – this book has been rather a long time coming!

Finally, my deepest gratitude is due to my family. I would like to thank my parents, Pam and Max, and my step-dad Mike, for their support which is always there. I would like especially to express my indebtedness to my husband, Tony, and my daughters, Anna and Emma, all of whom have been incredibly patient and kind as I have progressed this book, particularly towards the end as I sat at the table writing it while everyone worked around me, making the tea, doing homework and writing their own books! Tony, Anna and Emma, thank you.

1   Introduction

All work is gendered and all work is embodied.

(Morgan *et al.* 2005: 1)

I begin this book by recounting a conversation which took place in one of my classes on the sociology of childbirth, which I teach to undergraduate medical students. I am not a medic but a sociologist, working in a management school. What my students learn about childbirth relates to the social, emotional and embodied aspects of giving birth, rather than the biomedical aspects of bearing children. My course is an 'elective', meaning that students study it by choice. It is probably no coincidence that over the years my students have, with only one exception, been exclusively female.

In 2005, as I was drafting the first chapters of this book, I asked my student group how they saw their future careers. I wondered why they had chosen my course. Would they specialize in obstetrics and gynaecology, or would they choose something else? Did they see themselves as surgeons, physicians or research scientists? They all gave the same response, and I was shocked by what they said. One student explained to me:

> We can't be obstetricians, and we won't be surgeons either. These might be fields in which we have an interest, but we have been told that women shouldn't choose them as a career if they want children. We have been advised to train as GPs because we might want a family. You can combine being a GP with having children because it's accepted that women GPs can have families and work part-time, which you can't do as an obstetrician. So we will never be surgeons. We will almost certainly be GPs, because it's possible that we might have children.

The average age of my students was 21. At the time this incident occurred, none of them was a mother, none was pregnant and none, apparently, was actively seeking to be a single mother or to settle down with a life partner. Babies, if they were ever to be considered, were a far-off prospect. Yet already, at this early stage in their lives, certain career options had been closed down for these women because of what I will argue is their embodied potential for maternity. Of course, I could not (and did not) leave the matter there. 'Well what about the male students?' I asked. 'Have they been told to choose between having a family and being an obstetrician or a surgeon?' They replied:

> Oh no. The bright ones are encouraged to enter the surgical special-ties, and they will probably have families too. But it is different for them, because they will have wives to look after their children.

Two years later, as I was writing the closing chapters of this book, I taught the same module to a new group of women medical students. On this occa-sion, I was asking the students to investigate the issue of Caesarean section and maternal request. The conversation was different, but the idea that women doctors were unlikely to be obstetricians had not changed since 2005. The group of students were able to imagine women doctors in the role of general practitioner, but *not* as hospital consultants. Despite their own obvious interest in obstetrics, group members continually defined antenatal consultations between doctor and patient in gendered terms, referring to the obstetrician, always, as 'he' – 'he' advises the patient, 'he' will tell her what to do, 'he' must consider her needs.

How can this be explained? The year was 2007 – over 30 years after the Sex Discrimination Act became law. Yet young women were still being excluded (or at least, invited to exclude themselves) from certain areas of medicine due to the possibility that they might, at some point, have children. No matter that these are some of the brightest and most privileged young women in con-temporary society. No matter that (assuming they follow national trends) a significant minority of female doctors may never have a child at all. And no matter that, as obstetricians or surgeons, they would be earning large salaries and able to fund good childcare, or that they might be with partners who were prepared to share childcare responsibilities.

For the young women in my classes in 2005, and 2007, what I define as their embodied capacity for reproduction or 'maternal bodies' appeared still to mean that they were guided away from the most prestigious roles within their profession well before they had even graduated. In contrast to the male stu-dents on their degree programme and long before the prospect of a potential live birth, the 2005 group had been asked to make a choice between childbirth and career. The most recent 2007 group – although they were themselves training to be doctors – could not visualize the notion of a woman-to-woman consultation between obstetrician and patient. The students had, apparently, neither questioned nor challenged these issues (though I hope they might have done so by the time they reached the end of my course). They simply accepted it as women's 'lot' – the way of the world.

Of course, it is possible that my students are not representative of the majority of women in medicine. However, statistical evidence of the career paths of women in medicine in the UK suggests otherwise. Helen Fernandes, a neurosurgeon at Addenbrooke's Hospital in Cambridge, is also chair of the research group Women in Surgical Training. Fernandes has pointed out that, although the number of women entering medicine is now higher than the number of men (a ratio of 60 : 40 women to men), only 5% of surgeons are women. This number is even lower in some specialties – only around 2% of neurosurgeons and heart surgeons are women (Fernandes 2007). Fernandes observes:

> For some reason, by the time the long medical training is over, the figure [of 60 : 40 women to men] has been completely reversed, with the number of male consultants accounting for the vast majority of jobs. Although many more women are entering the profession, many will drop out or become stranded at a lower point – and no one seems to know why . . . Something has happened to all those bright, brilliant female medical students along the way and that should be recognised by all of us for the loss it is.
>
> (Fernandes 2007)

In this book, I shall claim that there *are* explanations for the loss of 'brilliant female students', not only in medicine but also in other professions. I argue that these explanations relate to the gendered nature of medical, and other, professional careers and the problem that, despite their increased entry to higher education, women still experience restricted career opportunities on the basis of their potential for maternity. For the women whom I was teaching, the 'choices' on offer were focused not upon which area of medicine to specialize in, but upon the idea that women should 'choose' between motherhood and a career as a hospital consultant, this decision being imposed upon them at a point before they were ready to make decisions about childbearing. This level of inequity, in medicine and in other professional and managerial occupations, which can occur before women's careers have even begun, might be so subtle that young women themselves fail to notice it. However, it suggests that the choices offered to women are defined on a different basis than what is on offer to young men.

The aims of this book

The above example serves as an illustration of the key issues which I address in this book, in which I explore the gendered nature of women's work through the lens of the body, from a feminist perspective. My purpose is to investigate the relationship between women's reproductive bodies (i.e. their potential for maternity), and women's productive work, both paid and unpaid. I take an inclusive approach to the definition of 'work' and I analyse ideas about women's work from the perspective of reproductive and productive labour, both paid and unpaid, and with regard to formal and informal labour markets.

At the heart of this research is the idea that women's bodies are central to gendered power relations and remain a negotiated site of power between men and women within contemporary society. By this, I mean that whether they are labouring in the birthing room, in the home, or within the workplace, and whether or not they have children, women are identified principally through their reproductive characteristics in a way that men are not. This belief shapes my own understanding of bodies, of work, and of the relationship between the two.

The book has three main aims which I summarize here and describe in more detail below. First, I seek to extend the definition of 'women's work' beyond the conventional contexts of paid work and productive (but unremunerated) domestic and care work, to encompass the labour of reproduction. Second, I analyse women's reproductive labour in the context of women's paid employment, surfacing the tensions between social narratives of 'good' motherhood and the expectations of employers. Finally, I examine women's embodied position in relation to productive work, both paid and unpaid and in relation to formal and informal labour markets. In this respect I evaluate the blurring of the boundaries between home and the workplace and between policy and practice. I observe how employed women are theoretically afforded equality of opportunity but are often subordinate to, and paid less than, men. I suggest that women's labour market 'choices' are more tightly circumscribed than those on offer to men, and that these differences are caused by social attitudes to what I describe as women's 'maternal bodies' (Gatrell and Tyler 2005).

'Choice' is a theme which runs throughout the book. I examine how far women are able to 'choose', and to maintain, their own embodied boundaries in relation to work and working practices. My question relates not only to what *are* the boundaries in relation to women's bodies and women's work, but how are these established, and by whom? To what extent are women constrained by social norms and/or standards which are set by others in relation to the performance of, for example, motherhood? And what is 'counted' as women's work? For example, in Chapter 9, I query how much agency sex workers may have in setting boundaries with regard not only to their individual bodies, but also more widely in terms of their position within the labour market.

The notion of 'women's work' could encompass a wide range of issues and the examples chosen here are strategic, and intended to facilitate the analysis of the relationship between women's bodies and women's paid and unpaid labour. The women featured in the discussions are mainly those living in Anglo-American societies, though examples from Europe and other countries are included. The approach of the book is interdisciplinary, and I draw upon sources from past and present across a range of subjects as I review the position of women's labouring bodies in the context of contemporary social attitudes and practices.

As background to these discussions, I now set out in more detail the aims of the book relating to the labour of reproduction, the positioning of women's bodies within the labour market, and the analysis of women's labour market opportunities in relation to policy. I then provide some background and context in relation to my own understandings of women's bodies and women's work, and how women's work is measured, as these themes feature throughout the book. At the end of the chapter, I explain my own position as a writer and as a feminist.

Reconceptualizing the labour of reproduction as work

As summarized above, the first aim of this book is to reconceptualize, and to redefine, the labour of reproduction as 'work'. In particular, I focus on the labour involved in having children in late modern society, especially if childbirth is combined with employment. Thus, the social requirement for women to manage what Gatrell and Tyler (2005) have described as their 'maternal bodies', in accordance with 'the expectations and demands of . . . the contemporary form of western capitalism in which we live' (Evans 2002: 10), is a principal element of this research. The labour of pregnancy, birth and new motherhood (especially breastfeeding) thus forms the basis of the discussions in Chapters 4 and 5. In relation to reproductive labour, I suggest that women are subject to managerialist or 'Taylorist' approaches involving the measurement of women's performance against standards and targets which are imposed upon them by others, and which involve forms of labour which may be difficult to reconcile with contemporary lifestyles and employment.

The maternal body

In addition to reconceptualizing the labour of reproduction as 'work', I seek to acknowledge, and to surface, the work involved in being a reproductive body which may be childless, but which appears to have the potential for maternity. As I explain in Chapter 3, I see the 'maternal body' and the work involved in conforming to, or resisting, a set of deeply ingrained social expectations around child-bearing, as a concept which extends beyond the specific boundaries of 'motherhood'. In this book, therefore, the notion of the 'maternal body' is used not only to encompass motherhood *per se* – as in the work of, for example, Walker (1998) and Davis (2004) – but also includes the ways in which women are allocated social roles in relation to their actual, potential or non-maternity. Thus the notion of the 'maternal body' is extended to include menstruation, non-motherhood and menopause (Gatrell and Tyler 2005).

In my consideration of maternal bodies, and in reconceptualizing reproductive labour as 'women's work', I revisit some of the key ideas propounded by radical feminists such as Rich (1977) and Oakley (1981), who foregrounded women's bodies as central to feminist debate, and argued for a changed world order which fully accommodated the maternal body (as opposed to the expectation that women should fit in with traditional social structures, seeking only changes at the margins to enhance their social standing in comparison with men).

The relationship between women's productive and reproductive work

The revisiting of radical feminist ideas from a contemporary perspective has assisted with my second aim, which is to investigate the social and economic relationships between women's reproductive and women's productive (paid and unpaid) work, in the context of the close interrelationship between women's productive and reproductive bodies. Although there is a growing and innovative literature on bodies and work (e.g. Puwar 2004; Wolkowitz 2006), there remain unanswered questions about how women manage their reproductive bodies within the workplace. In the 1960s and 1970s, feminist analyses of women's work began to reshape the way productive and reproductive labour was socially defined. Writers such as Oakley (1974) and Friedan (1965) sought to highlight previously hidden aspects of women's work, seeking for example to define the 'private' unpaid, physical labour of housework as a form of productive labour (undertaken by women in their own homes) which should be publicly acknowledged. I suggest that contemporary attitudes towards women's role in the workplace, and with regard to women's reproductive labour, mean that the boundaries between 'public' and 'private' work are becoming increasingly blurred and require rearticulation. For example, there are expectations that 'good' mothers should breastfeed their infants as part of the labour of motherhood. However, the requirements of breastfeeding are difficult to combine with employment, due to expectations that breastfeeding work should be confined to the private realm.

This suggests a need to expose the chasm between expectations that mothers in the workplace should conform to 'male embodied norms' (Hausman 2004) while simultaneously undertaking the complex, demanding and embodied work of pregnancy and new motherhood, as defined by health agencies and professionals. In Chapters 4 and 5, I seek to highlight the tensions, for employed pregnant women, between notions that they should conceal their pregnant bodies and be 'sparky', 'perky' and present at all times within the workplace, while concurrently following complicated diets, attending health appointments and, after birth, breastfeeding babies into toddlerhood. I observe how employers' fear of the 'leaky' pregnant body, both in the literal and metaphorical sense, underlines women's sexual difference from the male 'norm' at work. It has already been established how, in the workplace, men are defined in relation to solidity, predictability and rationality, both physically and psychologically (Edwards and Wajcman 2005). In this context, I observe how the actuality of a pregnant or breastfeeding body brings into the open explicit discriminatory practices which may have existed, but which were previously hidden from view.

Given the tensions between the conflicting demands of women's productive and reproductive work, I suggest that traditional attempts to define women's work on the basis of divisions between 'the home' and 'the workplace' are no longer tenable. This is because, despite the wealth of policies deploying the language of equality, women are often are accepted as members of the paid workforce *only* on the basis that they conceal their 'leaky', maternal bodies when they are 'at work'. Furthermore, while feminist considerations of women's work have acknowledged women's reproductive capacity as key to understanding women's social and economic situation, many arguments continue to focus on *either* the gendering of paid work (but not necessarily from the perspective of the body) *or* on social attitudes towards, and women's experiences of, pregnancy and birth. It is important to point out that there are notable exceptions to this trend – among others, Martin (1989), Hausman (2004), Mullin (2005), Longhurst (2008) and Tyler (2000). Nevertheless, research which explicitly considers women's reproductive bodies and functions in the context of employment, which foregrounds the interrelations between the maternal body and women's productive work, and which seeks to redefine how we think about women's productive and reproductive labour remains limited. In Chapters 3–5, I seek to contribute to this gap through exploring the relationship between women's bodies and women's work in the context of the gendered and social power relations of non-motherhood, and also of birth and employment.

Women's position in the labour market

The third aim of this book is to consider women's productive work, with reference to paid and unpaid work, within both formal (or 'legitimate') and informal labour markets, in the case of the latter focusing specifically on 'illegal' sex work. In relation to formal paid work, I consider the social and economic consequences of being an employee with a maternal body and I explore the relationship (and the disparities) between policy and practice, looking at such issues as the lack of women in leadership roles, occupational segregation and the gender pay gap.

I begin the discussion of women's productive work in Chapter 6 with a short overview of the history of women's position in the labour market. This provides background to present-day practices and helps to explain how perceptions about women's labour have always been closely intertwined with ideas about embodiment and heterosexuality. In Chapter 7, I observe how women in the formal labour market, who seek high-status jobs previously associated with male bodies (such as Members of Parliament) are either blocked or persuaded to exclude themselves on grounds of their reproductive status. I consider how women are obliged to make 'choices' between motherhood and career, even when this directly contravenes policy, and I attempt to analyse why this is the case. I also note how men continue to receive more money than women for doing equivalent jobs, and argue that women's performance at work is measured and interpreted negatively through the lens of the maternal body, while men's workplace performance is less likely to be viewed in health-related terms.

I then explore, in Chapter 8, the relationship between women's reproductive status and gendered expectations about women's productive labour as carers and domestic workers. I observe how, despite women's increased participation in the formal labour market, the unpaid productive labour of housework continues to be regarded as principally women's responsibility, with women in heterosexual relationships especially doing consistently more housework than men. In the context of paid domestic and care work, I consider how forms of women's productive (but often unremunerated) labour such as cleaning and care work have transferred into the contemporary jobs market. I suggest that these intensive forms of physical work are undervalued in the labour market and are often poorly paid.

In Chapter 9, I move on to explore the notion of women's sexuality and work, both in the context of the formal labour market and in relation to women who work within the 'informal' labour market as prostitutes or sex workers. In particular, I explore the notion of women's 'choice' in relation to their bodies and paid work. This is a recurrent theme in the book, and I make the argument that employment opportunities for women, especially at the low-skilled end of the jobs market, are very limited. Thus, a woman's decision to be a sex worker may be her 'choice', but this decision may be made in the face of few other viable options within the formal labour market.

How do I understand women's bodies?

Having outlined the main purposes and structure of this book, it seems helpful to offer a sense of my own perspective on women's bodies, and women's work, and to try and make explicit the concepts upon which I am basing my ideas about embodiment and work. For me, the metanarrative, or lens, of 'embodiment' provides a means of exploring three important themes: the relationship between women's bodies and women's labour; the blurring of the boundaries between women's paid and unpaid work; and the impact of social conventions on women's productive and reproductive labour. As I discuss in Chapter 2, women's bodies form the basis of debate from a range of perspectives in research on the health, social and employment status of women. Some views conceive women's bodies as biologically determined. Others argue, conversely, that bodies are socially and culturally defined (Evans 2002). In this text, I seek to balance, with the notion that the maternal body is a fluid and negotiable site, the idea that a woman's body is inhabited, an ever present, material part of daily life which cannot (and should not) be disentangled from debates about gender and work. I thus investigate notions of social control in relation to reproduction, and concepts of fear and disgust in relation to women's bodies in the workplace. In relation to productive and reproductive labour, I observe how far women's social experience is influenced by demands that they should achieve what Evans (2002: 10) describes as 'bodily conformity'.

On this basis, I consider women's embodied labour from the perspective of what Iris Marion Young (2005: 9) describes as 'lived' bodily experience. By this I mean the day-to-day sense of living in a reproductive body; of going 'out' to work and doing domestic chores, of being a woman without children; of being pregnant, giving birth and being a mother. These ideas are fundamental to this book, and thus, as I attempt to analyse and review the social positioning of the maternal body, the idea of 'women's experience as lived and felt in the flesh' (Young 2005: 9) is foregrounded.

I therefore draw upon, and draw together, views from a range of feminist scholars from the 1960s to the present. Second-wave radical feminist texts such as *The Dialectic of Sex*, (Firestone 1970), *Of Woman Born* (Rich 1977) and *From Here to Maternity* (Oakley 1981) are reread and reviewed in the context of twenty-first-century practices. In addition to these texts, I also draw upon more recent feminist works which focus on the social and medical management of women's lived and 'leaky' bodies, for example, Martin (1989), Grosz (1994), Shildrick (1997), Tyler (2000), Puwar (2004), Young (2005), Kitzinger (2005) and Nettleton (2006).

In keeping with the views of these writers, I conceptualize the female body as negotiated, and restricted more by social and gendered expectations about female bodily comportment than by biology. I suggest that the notion of constraint is particularly relevant when women's bodies are considered in the context of employment, and I draw upon ideas of revulsion and abjection in relation to women's reproductive functions. Notions of leakage and seepage are especially relevant to my discussions of women's paid work because women's propensity to 'leak' has been seen to signify women's 'otherness', their 'inherent lack of control of [their] bodies' and consequently of themselves (Shildrick 1997: 34). This does little to enhance women's subject position in the workplace.

Judith Butler's (1993) work is relevant to the discussion on the relationship between female embodiment and women's work because, while I seek principally to understand women's work through materialist concepts of women's embodied experience, it is not my intention to provide an essentialist explanation for gendered inequalities and work. Thus, Butler's concept of performativity, and the idea that the body is 'culturally coded and socially constructed' (Anleu 2006: 359), are acknowledged, particularly in Chapter 7, in relation to gendered practices and work.

What do I mean by 'women's work'?

There are many different approaches to, and definitions of, women's work. There are also key differences between early sociological and managerial classifications of 'work', which were developed in relation to men's paid employment, and later feminist understandings of 'work', which are broader and include women's unpaid labour (e.g. housework). In her discussion of feminism and work, Carole Truman (1996: 36) focuses on the need to highlight women's unpaid work, arguing that the analysis of the relationship between women's paid and unpaid labour is central to understanding gender inequalities. According to Truman (1996: 36),

> a major difference between men's work and women's work is around what actually constitutes 'work' ... for women, the term 'work' includes waged labour and also [various] forms of unwaged labour associated with households ... domestic labour, care of young and elderly dependents are features of many women's working lives.

Truman argues for the development of new and more inclusive descriptions of work, which foreground gendered inequalities and may be a catalyst for change – a desire which accords with the key aims of this book. Miriam Glucksmann (2005) has made similar observations to those of Truman. In her work on women assembly workers, Glucksmann (1990) observed how, although women were expected to develop manual dexterity, this skill was discounted and classified as an essentialist and inherently female characteristic.

Over the past two decades, Glucksmann has continued to focus on the classification and articulation of 'work' and has developed a framework which describes the 'total social organization of labour' (Glucksmann 2005). I briefly describe the total social organization of labour here because it complements my own interest in boundaries, in relation to the understanding of women's work.

Glucksmann (2005: 21) describes the total social organization of labour as an 'inclusive' concept which

> acknowledges as work many forms of labour that are not remunerated or . . . differentiated out, or recognised as activities separate from the relationships . . . within which they are conducted. It is concerned with . . . the shifting and permeable character of boundaries and the formation and dissolution of boundaries.

The concept of work as fluid and negotiable accords with my own approach, which seeks to extend definitions of women's work, surfacing and including aspects of women's labour which have previously been hidden. The total social organization of labour is described by Glucksmann in terms of four dimensions, each of which offers a different perspective.

Dimensions 1 and 4 reflect changing processes of production such as new technologies which affect the spaces and temporalities of work. New technologies are mentioned briefly in Chapter 9, as the advent of the internet has altered both the temporalities and the manner in which some sex workers source and contact clients.

Dimensions 2 and 3 are more relevant here, because they focus on the way in which work and non-work activities are defined, and on the boundaries between paid and unpaid labour. Glucksmann (like Truman) underlines the importance of taking an 'inclusive' approach to work, to encompass unpaid as well as paid work, acknowledging the fluidity of some types of work (e.g. care work) which may be unpaid but may also be transferred into paid labour markets. Glucksmann (2005: 19) describes Dimension 2 as moving 'across the boundaries between paid and unpaid work, market and non-market, formal and informal sectors'. She suggests a continued need to 'unpack the different dimensions of work and non-work that are intertwined in the performance of particular forms of labour'. In this respect, Dimension 3 (Glucksmann 2005: 19) is described as enabling 'the articulation of work activities and relations with non-work activities and relations' and is seen to 'address the . . . boundaries and articulation between work and non-work processes.' Dimension 3 addresses three research areas: 'embeddedness' in which 'work' such as mothering and housework is discounted due to social expectations about women's familial roles (as observed by Truman 1996); 'consumption work', which involves choosing and operating complex and demanding household items such as dishwashers; and 'aesthetic and emotion work'. Emotion work, in which women workers are required to provide emotional support to others, has been for many years an important topic in key feminist research by, for example, Hochschild (2003), writing in 1983, Adkins (1995) and Bolton (2001).

Dimensions 2 and 3 of the total social organization of labour are pertinent due to their focus on some themes which are central to this discussion: namely boundaries, the relationship between paid and unpaid work, and the definition of 'work'. However, while the articulation of work activities through the lenses of embeddedness, consumption, and emotion work assists in surfacing some 'hidden' aspects of women's work, these frameworks do not specifically analyse women's labour via the lens of the body. Together with Truman's desire to highlight women's unpaid labour, Glucksmann's Dimensions 2 and 3 are thus positioned as helpful descriptions which facilitate the consideration of boundaries and of relationships between different types of labour. However, as recommended by Truman (1996), I further extend and explore notions of boundaries in relation to women's work and choice by attempting to reconceptualize women's reproductive and productive labour from a fresh perspective – via the lens of the body.

Measuring women's work

Having outlined how I intend to approach my analysis and reconceptualization of 'women's work', I conclude this discussion with a short note about how women's work is measured, which is relevant in relation to the surfacing of hidden aspects of women's work.

As Truman (1996: 36) suggests, 'If women's work is open to a variety of different definitions then it follows that it is difficult to measure'. The notion of the 'measurement' of women's work is, however, important in relation to embodying women's work. This is because the setting of goals, targets and standards, and the measuring of human achievement against these, is an integral feature of late modern society (Morgan 1986). Thus, standards are set in relation to women's work not only in the workplace but also in the context of reproductive labour – how, when and where women should give birth, how they should behave during pregnancy and how they should nourish their infants. According to Gareth Morgan (1986), many contemporary systems of measurement and management derive from Taylorism, a concept which has been described as a 'science' of management. Taylorism has for decades been used to measure individual levels of human productive labour (usually the physical work involved in making or operating things) against particular benchmarks or standards in order to improve organizational efficiency. The philosophy behind Taylorism involves the belief that it is acceptable and desirable for those in power (employers, managers or institutions) to keep workers under surveillance and to use this surveillance (and the standards against which the surveilled are measured) as a form of control. Systems of measurement based on Taylorism were designed around the male working norms of the early twentieth century (Truman 1996; Grint 2005). Morgan (1986) argues that although contemporary management practices are rarely described as 'Taylorist', the *ideas* behind Taylorism continue to influence, pervade and measure both our economic and our personal lives.

There may be good arguments as to why Taylorism is unreasonably constraining for any worker, male or female. However, there is an even greater issue about the appropriateness of applying, to women's work, methods which were developed around men's embodied labour. Nevertheless, Taylorism remains central to the measurement and surveillance of women's work in late modern society. I suggest that the application to women (especially in relation to reproductive labour) of a system of measurement built around men's paid work has several undesirable consequences. The first of these relates to the concern that women's work, while it may be measured, often goes unrecognized and is thus undervalued (Truman 1996). The consequence of applying a management science approach to women's reproductive labour is that Taylorist forms of measurement are employed by health services in order to demand particular forms of social bodily conformity on the part of women, but the work *involved* for women in achieving these goals is hidden behind essentialist discourses of good motherhood. So, for example, the labour of initiating and maintaining breastfeeding is measured, but is at the same time discounted on the basis that breastfeeding is 'natural' and part of the job of a 'good' mother, therefore it does not count as 'work'.

The second implication of measuring women's work against goals and standards deriving from studies and research based on men relates to the workplace, where women may be required to subordinate the material needs of the 'leaky' female body to 'embodied male norms', but are also expected to retain a sense of femininity, even if most of their colleagues are men. Thus, for example, women managers are expected to wear clothing which emphasizes their femininity, while simultaneously conforming to dress codes based on masculine conventions (Longhurst 2001; Puwar 2004).

Keeping the feminist debate firmly open

If the boundaries between different forms of women's work are hard to define (but are set by others) and if women's reproductive and productive labour is measured using systems designed around men's work, the extent of women's 'choice', in comparison with what is available to men, is brought into question. Central to my research is the notion that women's bodies remain a negotiated site of power. In an era which professes equality of opportunity between women and men, we must accompany debates about how women's work is defined and measured in *theory* with feminist assessments of how women experience choice and opportunity in practice. In this respect I suggest that, despite the promises of the past thirty years to deliver to women more social freedoms and improved employment opportunities, women's 'choice' remains limited. For example, in relation to the labour of reproduction, as I shall explain in Chapter 4, women's situation remains in some ways just as oppressive now as it was in the past. Taylorism is alive and well, with many women finding themselves subject to goals and targets relating to weight, diet and infant feeding. And in the workplace, while economists such as Catherine Hakim (1996, 2000) may claim that women now have choice about whether to enter the formal labour market, the gender pay gap and occupational segregation remain problematic, with women often clustered in poorly paid, low-status jobs. The perpetuation of male domination continues to be maintained via the body, because social roles and responsibilities are assigned on the basis of reproductive function. As a result, women's identities as individual agents are often subsumed by their collective identities as reproductive and sexualized bodies, in a manner which does not apply to men. Society continues to allocate to male bodies power and privileges which are not available to women – and which may, indeed, be afforded to men at women's expense.

Thus, despite well-established feminist debates on gender, women's paid work and child-bearing, changes in women's circumstances have been limited. Furthermore, there remain prominent figures within society who resent the concept of female emancipation. Powerful individuals can be observed attempting to close down the feminist debate – perhaps because they seek to preserve men's rights and/or wish to to claw back social gains on women's part, by foregrounding women's reproductive identities. Women, in relation to their maternal status and their labour market participation, may consequently be variously represented in popular debate as selfish (Scott and Duncombe 1991) incompetent (McIntyre *et al.* 2002), uncommitted to their paid work (Hakim, quoted in Moorhead 2004), and as a threat to men. In 2005, for example, senior advertising executive Neil French allegedly made the public claim that women are 'crap' and undeserving of promotion because they will inevitably 'wimp out and go suckle something' (Hopkins 2005). A later statement by French, recorded in the UK *Times* newspaper (Hopkins 2005), confirmed his essentialist views about women's bodies. French suggests that women should be disqualified from opportunities in the advertising industry because of their potential to bear children which, he infers, renders all female advertising professionals less dedicated than men. French states that seniority in advertising 'requires 100 per cent commitment. People who have babies to look after can't do that.' On the basis of such restrictions on women's productive and reproductive opportunities, it appears that twenty-first-century women continue to be constrained by the values conventionally associated with heterosexual masculinity. This is the case in the home, in relation to reproductive labour, and in the workplace. In many workplace situations women are regarded primarily as potential mothers (or as menopausal or post-menopausal), and secondarily as productive individuals, even if they have achieved 'success' in a professional or economic context.

The apparent desire of men such as French to close down women's labour market options suggests that there is an urgent need to ensure that the feminist debate remains firmly open. Thus, an important part of the motivation for writing this book has been the wish to keep challenging social attempts to oppress women. In particular, I focus on how the 'maternal body' continues to be used as a vehicle for reducing and restricting the opportunities that are available to women.

A feminist position

In research which defines itself as 'feminist', a desire to contribute to what Frances (2002: 52) describes as the advancement of 'the values and principles which lie at the heart of the feminist project' must be central. Given, however, that scholarly feminist 'values and principles' are themselves the subject of intense debate, and may be interpreted differently depending on the situation and politics of those who pursue 'feminist' research, I attempt below to define my own approach. The task of articulating my own 'values and principles' is not straightforward. As Frances (2002: 49) argues, 'there can never be one "true" perspective on justice and value or an holistic feminist account that speaks for all women'. Ramazanoğlu and Holland (2002: 5) have observed, similarly, that the meaning of 'feminism' is difficult to capture because 'Feminism covers a diversity of beliefs, practices and politics . . . For every generalization that one can make about feminism, it is possible to find "feminists" who do not fit, or who do not want to fit.' Furthermore, as Olesen (1994: 158) suggests, 'feminism' and 'feminist research' do not stand still because the 'context and contours of feminist research are shifting' in accordance with politics, economics, new ideas and the voices and experiences of younger generations.

So where does this place me and this book? Despite the difficulties of defining feminism as a project, I agree with Frances's contention that feminist inquiry requires researchers to be political. My own understanding of feminism and of feminist research derives from the notion that feminist research should relate to practice, policy and decision-making. In the words of Skeggs (1995: 11), feminist researching is more than just 'a job to be done, work to be accomplished, a publication achieved'. My interpretation of feminist research is to provide a 'framework for political action' (Skeggs 1995: 19), with feminist researchers seeking to enhance the situation of women in society, while acknowledging that feminist 'dreams of resistance' (Holland

and Ramazanoğlu 1994: 3) might mean different things to different women. Thus, I seek to undertake feminist research which is political and which is 'for, rather than merely about, women' (Olesen 1994: 169). This fits with Skeggs's (1995: 12) notion of research which is 'motivated by . . . political aspirations. Behind each contribution stands a clear desire . . . for change . . . to challenge categories of common knowledge and to deconstruct the representations which damagingly position women.'

This does not imply what Bryson (1999: 29) describes as 'an . . . unworkable view of [all] men as "the enemy" '. However, it does acknowledge that power differentials between women and men remain potent. It recognizes, for example, that women continue to be underrepresented in powerful roles in government and industry and seeks to address this. The acknowledgement of this situation, and the desire to change it, means being unafraid of utilizing the language and politics of feminism. As bell hooks (cited in Beasley 1999: 31) has stated:

> I think we have to fight the idea that somehow we have to re-fashion feminism so that it appears not to be revolutionary – so that it appears not to be about struggle . . . if our real agenda is altering patriarchy and sexist oppression, we are talking about a . . . revolutionary movement.

Radical feminism
This adds up to the idea that feminist research should be a force for change. I have already stated that there are two key sociological influences on this book, the first relating to the sociology of the body and the second to the ideas of the radical feminist movement. Neither of these sets of ideas is straightforward, and in some respects they sit uncomfortably with one another. From a personal perspective, I suggest that the roots of patriarchy are inextricably linked with women's reproductive status, and with the female body. In this sense, my views can be fairly closely aligned with the ideas put forward by radical feminists who were writing in the late 1970s and early 1980s – for example, Firestone (1970), Oakley (1981), Rich (1977) and O'Brien (1981). The 'radical' view of feminism regards society as inherently patriarchal and organized around male needs: 'men as a group dominate women as a group and are the main beneficiaries of the subordination of women' (Walby 1990: 3). I include a short discussion of radical feminist politics here because this is relevant to the beliefs underpinning this research, though I provide a broader explanation of radical feminism in Chapter 2.

Radical feminists believe that 'it is gender relations rather than class relations that generate fundamental inequalities in the social world' (Porter 1998: 186). They regard 'women's oppression [as] the oldest, most widespread, most obdurate and most extreme form of oppression that exists between humans' (Porter 1998: 186). Radical feminists regard the liberal feminist approach, which seeks to enhance women's rights through incremental social change, to be insufficiently challenging to social traditions which place men at the centre of society and social policy. Radical feminists thus 'give a positive value to womanhood rather than supporting a notion of assimilating women into areas of activity associated with men' (Beasley 1999: 54). Radical feminists focus on 'women's similarities and the pleasures of forming . . . bonds between women in a world where such bonds are marginalised or dismissed' (Beasley 1999: 54). Thus, special groups of women, such as lesbians and mothers, are celebrated by radical feminists on the basis that they have unique characteristics associated with womanhood that men cannot share.

The limitations of radical feminism
There are acknowledged problems with the politics of radical feminism, and these difficulties explain why the influence on this book of radical feminism is important, but limited. The first issue relates to the sense that the radical feminism of the 1980s tended to consider 'women' as if they were a homogenous group, and was regarded by some writers as a predominantly middle-class movement (Jackson and Jones 1998: 21). Thus (as noted in Gatrell and Swan 2008), the all-embracing approach of radical feminism may privilege the voices of some women at the expense of other groups, for example black and minority ethnic, and disabled, women. On this basis, Skeggs (1995) has observed how black women have needed to find alternative ways of being heard, challenging the (nevertheless constrained) institutional privileges of white women. Annecka Marshall (1994) has also criticized 'mainstream' approaches such as radical feminism, arguing that this 'does not sufficiently examine the experiences of black women' (1994: 106), who are often 'excluded from the creation of sociological and feminist thought' (1994: 108).

Similar arguments have been made in relation to feminism and class. Valerie Bryson (1999) points out how early and mid-twentieth-century white feminist challenges to notions of women being the 'weaker' sex, and consequently unsuited to the pressures of employment, were irrelevant to both black women and working-class white women in the UK and USA. This was because, while middle-class women were confined to the home, many black and working-class white women undertook hard manual labour in factories and agricultural settings as a matter of course – though they were excluded from senior positions and were paid considerably less than men in those jobs which they were permitted to undertake (Rowbotham 1997). At the end of the 1970s, hooks (1981) wrote of her feelings that black women had been ignored by the feminist movement of the time. As a result, she has argued for a black feminist political agenda since the beginning of the 1980s (hooks 1981). Significantly, however, although she cites the need for a feminist 'politics of difference', hooks nevertheless remains concerned at the prospect that women's differences make feminist unity impossible. While resisting universalist ideas of a feminist 'sisterhood' as unworkable, hooks (1991: 29–31) nevertheless asserts that

> abandoning . . . political solidarity diminishes [feminism] . . . There can be no mass-based feminist movement to end sexist oppression without a united front . . . Women are enriched when we bond with one another . . . We can bond on the basis of our political commitment to a feminist movement.

hooks's observation suggests the need to respect and acknowledge varying needs of different groups, at the same time as holding on to the idea that feminist writers and researchers should retain some sense of unity in their approach. This is not an easy task, but Lorraine Code (1991) offers possibilities for compromise in her development of the concept of positionality. She argued in favour of taking up a feminist 'position', a notion which has been helpful to me in seeking to understand the complex relationships between women's bodies and women's work, and reproductive and productive labour, while acknowledging differences of privilege and politics between women. Code (1991: 317) suggests that positionality enables the feminist writer/researcher to assume accountability for the position she occupies (enabling her to resist the male or institutional occupants of other positions) without assuming the ability to speak on behalf of all women. Code defines positionality as designating 'positions that are . . . sufficiently stable to permit active political involvement. . . . It creates a political space for reinterpreting and engaging critically with the forms of authority and expertise that circumscribe women's control over their lives' (Code 1991: 180).

Code cites the example of a feminist researcher campaigning for better childcare facilities, and suggests that positionality would assist this woman in her active political involvement while at the same time 'allowing for social and political critique, remapping, renegotiation' (Code 1991: 180). Positionality thus appears to offer the possibility of being political through research, without the presumption that other women will necessarily agree with the account of the social world which the research produces. In this book and elsewhere (Gatrell 2006b), therefore, I have attempted to adopt a feminist political position. This is based on the idea that politics, feminism and the female body are inseparable, while acknowledging that knowledge is situated and subjective and that I might relate other women's experiences and accounts without claiming that my individual construction of meaning would be interpreted in the same way by others. I hope that this enables me to retain the perspective that feminist theory (and research) may legitimately be related to policy, while acknowledging that it is neither possible nor desirable to generalize the circumstances of all women.

In the context of taking a feminist 'position', therefore, I do attempt to make some political points in this book. First, I argue that women's experiences in the labour market and in the birthing room remain closely related, and that in both instances women may be oppressed by institutionalized patriarchy. Thus, although legislation and policy may purport to treat women and men equally, the majority of paid positions of power and influence are 'reserved' for and held by men (Puwar 2004). In this respect, radical feminist debates about the body remain profoundly influential. I observe how, although it is over 30 years since Rich (1977) confronted the social disempowerment of women through their reproductive functions, women's bodily comportment continues to be constrained in relation to motherhood, in the birthing room and in the workplace (Young 2005; Kitzinger 2005). Whether they are performing the role of non-mother, mother and/or employee, notions of 'choice', for women, are more limited than they are for many men. In relation to paid work, while some discriminatory, embodying practices have changed their appearance, others are denied or hidden – but they have not gone away. For example, women may officially be entitled to extended paid maternity leave, but many feel pressured to relinquish this, to work from home while on leave, and/or to conceal their pregnancy altogether (Gatrell 2007a; Bacik *et al.* 2003). Such pressures are not exclusive to women in managerial roles, but may apply even more harshly to those in poorly paid unskilled occupations.

In Chapters 3–9, I take a feminist position and attempt to analyse women's embodied labour from a range of perspectives, some of which are contemporary and some of which date back as far as the nineteenth century. I begin the next chapter with a review of the positioning of women's bodies within sociology and biomedicine. This gives context to the literature from which I draw in the rest of the book, and will I hope assist in locating the debates in Chapters 3–9 in the context of this discussion.

2 Positioning women's bodies: Sociological and biomedical approaches

In this chapter I provide an overview of the literature on women's embodiment and women's work from two perspectives: the sociological and biomedical views of women's bodies. This overview is not exhaustive, but it offers background and context to the arguments and sources upon which I draw in forthcoming chapters. Here, therefore, I examine how far and in which direction the study of women's embodied labour has developed with regard to the consideration of women's productive and reproductive labour.

Sociologies of the body and work

As David Morgan (2005) has observed, the study of embodied labour, in relation to the concept of work, has been a focus for sociologists since the earliest days of the discipline. While explicit discussions about the body were not foregrounded in early sociologies of work, the rereading of texts by 'classical' sociologists such as Marx, Weber and Durkheim suggests that powerful concepts and images of the embodied worker were present, by implication, in the context of references to bodily actions and control, emotions and emotion work, physical appearances and family practices (Morgan 2005). The same could be said of studies of management science, such as Taylorism (described in Chapter 1), which measured individual physical activity in relation to set goals and targets (Morgan 1986).

I have already noted, in Chapter 1, how Taylorist studies of work in the early twentieth century were designed around men's paid labour. Similarly, David Morgan (2005: 19) suggests that 'a close rereading [of texts about work] may indicate significant silences and omissions', particularly in relation to the gendered body. Morgan's observation is interesting in the context of early sociological writings about work in which (as Morgan himself remarks) the class system and issues of social exclusion were challenged, but usually only in the context of the male body, with the labours of the female body barely acknowledged.

Thus, early- to mid-twentieth-century discussions about production and inequalities centred almost exclusively upon the employed bodies of *men*. The male body was treated as 'universal' (Grint 1998: 192) and the female body as other. As Anleu (2006: 357) points out, 'bodies are subject to considerable normative evaluation and regulation. Many of these norms are deeply gendered and construct inequalities between men and women'. The assumption that the male body 'counted' in relation to paid work, while the female body was not considered, and the gendered division of labour in which men were employed while women's principal responsibilities were in the home, went unchallenged by all but a select group of pioneering feminists. Before the second-wave feminist movement, 'the concentration upon men within sociology [was] so common that it was seldom perceived to require an explanation' (Grint 1998: 192). Classical sociological writings about work reflected dominant social practices and were thus based upon the assumption that women's bodies existed principally to provide reproductive labour and also (especially if they were working-class) a reserve army of cheap paid labour when men's embodied labour was insufficient or unavailable – for example, in times of economic growth or war.

Where the social role of 'woman' in Western society was considered within sociology, this was usually in relation to heterosexuality, wifehood, motherhood and domestic labour. In the post-war years, an image of 'ideal' womanhood was constructed by Talcott Parsons (Parsons and Bales 1956), an American sociologist whose descriptions of social life were influential in both Britian and the USA. Parson's portrayal of 'family life' was seized upon by policy-makers in both countries, because it offered governments and industry what appeared (to them) to be an appealing picture of 'family', in which women and men would be heterosexual and monogamous and would thus marry, produce children, and divide labour along gendered lines. This image fitted in perfectly with British and American models of social and economic policy in the post-war years (Morris 1990). In the Anglo-American post-war economies of the 1950s onwards, husbands were expected to take responsibility for productive labour and wage earning and wives were supposed to accept the reproductive role of child-bearer, spending the 'housekeeping' allowed them by their husbands on food and household products, thus providing the next generation while contributing to gross national product. Parsons and Bales (1956: 14–15) stated: 'the adult feminine role is anchored . . . in the internal affairs of the family as wife, mother and manager in the household, while the role of the adult male is . . . anchored in the occupational world, in his job'.

While Parsons and Bales were writing sociologies of the family – and did not explicitly concern themselves with bodies – their research located the (heterosexual) female body firmly within the private world of the household.

It is well known how the women's rights movement, during the 1960s and 1970s, resisted the Parsonian notion that having a female body should automatically restrict 'women's work' to the context of motherhood and unpaid domestic labour. As I explain below, writers such as Adrienne Rich and Ann Oakley celebrated women's 'powers of reproduction' (Rich 1977: 50), but nevertheless contested the notion that women should be excluded from opportunities within the labour market.

Nevertheless, despite both feminist protests and the fact that Parsons' picture of family life represented only a narrow – by implication, white middle-class – sector of the USA (Bernandes 1997; Gatrell and Cooper 2007), the Parsonian description of the heterosexual, female, reproductive body provided an authoritative and enduring blueprint for what the social role of the maternal body 'ought' to be (Parsons and Bales 1956; Parsons 1971). The white middle-class Parsonian image of 'mother in the home' predominated in popular culture from the 1950s onwards and the prevalent social concept of 'women's work' during the 1960s and early 1970s continued to confine women to the domestic setting for the purpose of bearing and nurturing children. For example, in the popular Ladybird children's reading series produced in 1960s Britain, the mother is the central figure within the home. She is shown to be the main carer for her husband and children and their three pets. In the colour illustrations which enhance the childish texts, the figure of Mummy is shown going about her business in the home, preparing and clearing away food, polishing and dusting furniture, hoovering, making beds, doing laundry and feeding pets. In each picture, she is well dressed and coiffured, wearing a frilly apron and surrounded by (or sometimes shown to be using) consumer products such as furniture polish, soap powder, washing-up liquid, crockery and glassware, kitchen implements and foodstuffs (Gagg 1961; Murray 1964). The Mummy of the Ladybird reading series is, by implication, fulfilling the gendered role of heterosexual womanhood by appearing to look 'feminine' and by consuming and utilizing products and foodstuffs which will enhance the appearance of the home and feed and clothe her family. Similarly, in the USA, the popular television series *Bewitched* portrayed an elegant white woman whose main purpose in life was to look after her small daughter and to maintain an immaculate home, a process which she achieved through witchcraft (this notion, arguably, serving to perpetuate the discounting of women's unpaid work in the home, which, as I discuss in Chapter 8, is seen as 'natural').

Murray (1964: 2) describes the Ladybird reading scheme as 'embrac[ing] not only the latest findings in word frequency but also the *natural interests and activities of happy children*' (emphasis added). Arguably, in 1964, the concept of 'happy children' was integrally bound up with the image of a stay-at-home mother whose main purpose in life was caring for her home and family, with the help of the products she consumed to assist her in this objective. In this context, in the UK, as recently as 1980, in the *St Michael* (Marks and Spencer)

Complete Book of Babycare, employed women were urged to relinquish paid work on childbirth, on the basis that (presumably married heterosexual) mothers should be at home full-time 'performing the most worthwhile job that life has to offer' (Nash 1980: 161).

Although it is fifty years since Parsons wrote about the embodied and familial role of motherhood, the Parsonian discourse which located the maternal body firmly within the context of heterosexuality, marriage and 'the home' remains a powerful influence on perceptions about the social roles which women 'ought' to play (Gatrell and Coper 2007). Arguably this has had two consequences, the first of which has been to contribute to the effective exclusion of black and minority ethnic women, and working-class white women, not only from particular types of paid work (Puwar 2004) but also from a range of popular and literary images of affluent family life in the UK and America, for almost half a century. The second consequence of the Parsonian approach is that it has perpetuated the association of the bodies of mid- to late twentieth-century white middle-class women with the home, but not with employment and career.

While ideas and assumptions about embodiment were present, either by implication or by omission, in sociologies of labour before the 1960s and 1970s, including Parsons's influential work, the explicit study of the body (and particularly of the body and work), in a sociological context is a more recent phenomenon. The text which has probably been regarded as most instrumental in foregrounding the social study of the body within mainstream sociology is Bryan Turner's (1984) *The Body and Society*. In the second edition of this book Turner (1996: 1) himself argues:

> When *The Body and Society* was first published in 1984, there was little interest in mainstream social sciences in the sociology of the body . . . in the intervening decade there has been a flood of publications concerned with the relationship between the body and society.

In relation to sociologies of the body, as Turner himself recognizes, there are two important things to consider. Turner acknowledges firstly the role of feminist scholarship with regard to the sociology of the body and, secondly, the continued privileging of male bodies in some texts regarding embodiment and work. I deal with the first issue below, and consider the second on page 32.

Feminism and the female body

As Turner (1984) observes, the female body (particularly in the context of the labour of childbirth, women's health, and women's relationship with reproduction and employment) had been the focus of feminist research for many years. However, feminist studies on the body were treated as marginal to 'mainstream' sociological research, because their focus was the female, and not the male, body. (This has also been the case in research on family practices, which was accorded majority status only when 'malestream' sociologists Beck and Giddens began to publish in the area (Smart and Neale 1999: 4–5).)

While it may not have been acknowledged by 'malestream' sociological writers, feminist writing on the relationship between women's bodies and women's work became available at the end of the eighteenth century. As early as 1792, Mary Wollstonecraft published *A Vindication of the Rights of Woman*, in which she challenged the cultural and social preparations of the bodies of young (middle-class) women for marriage, which implied a lifetime of bodily and sexual obedience to husbands (Wollstonecraft 2004). In 1903, Charlotte Perkins Gilman protested against the bodily confinement of (by implication, affluent), married women within the home, especially once they became mothers (Gilman 2002). In her 1899 novel *The Yellow Wallpaper*, Gilman wrote a semi-autobiographical account of the depression suffered by a woman undergoing enforced, and embodied, 'rest' following the birth of her first baby. More recently, in 1963, Betty Friedan's landmark feminist text *The Feminine Mystique* challenged the social and embodying convention that 'a woman's place is in the home' and refuted social assumptions that 'Anatomy [and childbirth] was her destiny' (Friedan 1965: 71).

In the early 1970s, the Boston Women's Health Book Collective promoted their belief that women could, and should, have greater control of their own bodies through improved personal knowledge. The American publication of *Our Bodies, Ourselves* (Boston Women's Health Book Collective 1973) enabled thousands of women to access previously closed information on the maternal body, on pregnancy, contraception and 'choice'. The notion of 'choice' was related to sexual autonomy, and also to ideas that women should be able, legally, to terminate pregnancies by qualified staff in health service settings which were clean and safe. *Our Bodies, Ourselves* was joined by a series of influential and widely disseminated feminist texts on both sides of the Atlantic, which considered the relationship between women's employment and the reproductive body. In 1970, Germaine Greer published *The Female Eunuch*, which asserted that the objectification of women's bodies by men was at the source of men's oppression of women (Greer 2006). Greer's book urged women to seek better information about their own bodies and argued for sexual rights and freedoms for women. In 1970, Shulamit Firestone explicitly constructed women's reproductive capacity as the instrument of women's oppression, and linked women's potential for reproduction to women's exclusion from paid work. Firestone regarded reproductive technologies as potentially transforming women's embodied status, imagining a future where childbearing and child-rearing would be shared throughout society. She saw this as potentially enabling women to challenge male privilege and to escape the 'power hierarchies' embedded in family practices (Firestone 1970: 73) and thus allowing women to become the economic and intellectual equals of men.

Firestone is regarded as one of the early proponents of the radical school of feminist thought. Firestone's scholarship was both built upon and critiqued in the 1970s and 1980s; by the work of Ann Oakley (1981), Adrienne Rich (1977) and Mary O'Brien (1981), all of whom embraced the politics of radical feminism through research on women's reproductive and domestic labour. They celebrated womanhood and motherhood, and challenged patriarchy as they sought to

> pursue revolutionary practice . . . with an emphasis on small group organisation . . . stress[ing] practical political strategies and . . . focus-[ing] on *the politics of the 'private' sphere*, in particular sexuality, motherhood and bodies.
>
> Beasley (1999: 56–7; emphasis in original)

Writers such as Oakley (1981, 1984) and Rich (1977) examined the productive labour of unpaid domestic work from the perspective of women's oppression. They further considered the labour of childbirth in the context of the medicalization of women's bodies. In their exploration of these ideas, many radical feminist writers investigated closely the everyday experiences of women, researching in detail the specifics of how women managed the embodied labour of mothering and of housework. Oakley (1981, 1984), Rich (1977) and Firestone (1970) challenged the heteronormative traditions of the 'institution of motherhood' which was seen to impose patriarchal and constraining social expectations upon women. Oakley, in particular, railed against the idea of women as 'angels in the house' whose role it was to undertake domestic and caring labour for little reward – an issue which is discussed further in Chapters 6–8. These radical feminist notions remain highly pertinent to this book, given its quest to reconceptualize the material labour of reproduction as 'work', and to surface aspects of women's work which are hidden behind discourses of 'natural' motherhood.

While some radical feminist writers such as Firestone (1970) and Valeska (1984) argued that women should be enabled to devolve to others the responsibility for bearing and rearing children, other writers did not accept the notion that women might give up their potential for maternity. O'Brien (1981), in particular, argued that for some women who wanted children, mothering may be just as important as intellectual fulfilment. O'Brien (1981) thus resisted Firestone's exhortations that women's bodies should be freed from the biomedical constraints of reproduction, putting forward the counter-argument that an inclusive feminist agenda could not support the 'devaluation of the intimate . . . and proud relations of women and children' (1981: 91).

Nevertheless, the arguments of 'maternalist' radical feminists supported those of Firestone in terms of their belief that society was utilizing women's potential for maternity as an excuse for excluding women from opportunities relating to education, career and personal development. Writers such as Oakley and Rich campaigned for the rights of women with children to combine mothering with interesting and fairly remunerated paid work and Oakley (1981: 3) contested the idea that women could not, or should not, 'have professional jobs and babies at the same time – only one or the other'.

Radical feminists also held very influential views on pregnancy and birth. Both Oakley (1981) and Rich (1977) regarded the experience of giving birth, and the medicalization of childbirth, as symbolic of the way that women were regarded, and treated by, society. Medicalization and technicalization, and the obstetric control of women's birthing bodies during the 1970s and 1980s, were seen as a metaphor for men's oppression of women within a patriarchal society and as instrumental in maintaining the gendered and unequal division of labour.

> As long as birth – metaphorically or literally – remains an experience of passively handing over our minds and our bodies to male authority and technology, other kinds of social change can change our relationship to ourselves, to power and to the world outside our bodies.
>
> (Rich, 1977: 185)

The idea of conceptualizing male control over women in late modern society through the experience of childbirth remains powerfully symbolic. Writing over 15 years after Rich, Cosslett (1994: 47) observed that 'Adrienne Rich is not alone in seeing the way birthing women are treated by the medical institution as emblematic of their oppression in society at large', and this is an argument that will be pursued further below.

While radical feminist ideas are less prominent now within mainstream feminist scholarship than they were during the 1970s and 1980s, they have remained central, throughout, to debates on the management of childbirth and infant feeding. Thus, campaigning organizations seeking to empower 'lay' women through information and advocacy, such as the UK's National Childbirth Trust, could be regarded as drawing heavily on radical feminist ideas about male domination and the need for women to 'reclaim childbirth' (Kitzinger 2005: 54). So, too, could influential writers on birth politics and women's health such as Sheila Kitzinger, whose work is drawn upon in Chapters 4 and 5, and who claims, for example, that:

> shame and disgust about breastfeeding are closely connected to the view of a woman's body as male property. It is a concept that can only be understood in the context of a social analysis of gender relations. It

turns out that men are the ultimate arbiters about what we do with our [bodies].

(Kitzinger 2005: 42)

In addition, radical feminist challenges to discourses of 'natural' motherhood are still the focus of work by feminist scholars on motherhood – in particular, Miller (2005), Mullin (2005) and Gatrell (2005). Furthermore, the radical assumption that women are oppressed by men and that society should ascribe a positive worth to womanhood still accords with the views of more contemporary scholars. For example, Höpfl and Hornby Atkinson (2000) do not hold with the idea that women should be obliged to 'fit in' with masculine traditions and conventions, but seek a political situation where women are valued in their own right as equal to, but different from, men.

While radical feminist politics may now be regarded as in some ways problematic (as described in Chapter 1), it remains that case that, during the 1980s and through to the present day, feminist writers on women's embodied experiences have continued to explore the concept of the female body as a site of oppression. Contemporary feminist research of women's bodies includes a wide range of different political and philosophical perspectives which now include the othering and marginalizing of the racialized, the disabled and the working-class woman's body. For example, Elisabeth Grosz, Sheila Kitzinger, Emily Martin, Amy Mullin, Nirmal Puwar, Margaret Shildrick, Imogen Tyler, Elaine Swan and Iris Marion Young variously consider issues such as abjection, exclusion, and the othering of women from the perspective of the lived female body. In particular, the problem of women's social exclusion – both from public spaces and from what Martin (1989) describes as 'success in the public realm' – is seen to be related to women's potentially reproductive or 'maternal' body', an issue which is a central theme of this book.

The social construction of the body

Since the 1990s, many sociological and philosophical feminist scholars, writing explicitly about women's bodies, have held the view that 'the body' is itself socially constructed, and that bodies are subject to what Mary Evans (2002: 4) describes as 'external, created fantasies and perceptions'. Evans (2002: 2) argues that 'present renegotiations of the body do not start from a "natural" state of the body, but from a body, and a set of expectations about the body, which are already deeply socialised'.

Some scholars thus argue that the body is a culturally determined entity, rather than something which may be biomedically defined. The body is regarded as a social construction, and womanhood understood in relation to social expectations about what women's bodies and women's work 'ought' to be and do. Understandings about women's bodies are related to social conventions, and reinforced through language, behaviour and tradition. For example, as Gatrell and Swan (2008) suggest – and as Baigent (2007) points out in relation to the fire service – masculine values and ideas about men as physically and emotionally stronger than women, may relate more to social behaviour than to the bodies of individual women and men.

Among researchers who view the body as socially and culturally controlled, there is often a tension between the desire to acknowledge what Evans (2002) describes as 'the created body of particular societies', which may be contested and negotiated in the abstract, and what Carol Thomas (2002: 76) describes as the 'real materiality of bodies'. In her consideration of social perceptions about gender and the body, Mary Evans highlights these tensions between what she describes as the 'real' body, and a more abstract understanding of the body. The notion of a body which is socially constructed but which is material and 'lived' (Young 2005: 9) is central to this book, which considers the everyday experiences of being a maternal body. The scholars and texts described in Chapter 1 under the heading of 'understanding women's bodies' are thus a principal source for this book. I am drawn to the work of those feminist scholars who, in writing about women's bodies, concentrate on the physical experiences associated with being a woman in a 'leaky' maternal body in the literal, as well as the metaphorical, sense: a body which menstruates, which has the potential to become pregnant and to produce another body as well as fluid and breast milk; a body which will, in late middle age, be menopausal (Martin 1989; Shildrick 1997; Kitzinger 2005).

As Howson (2005) and Evans (2002) have observed, some philosophical feminist writers, who also regard the body as culturally and socially defined, have tended to move away from such detailed materialist analyses. Mary Evans expresses concern that what she describes as the 'real' body, which may be unwell, tired and difficult to manage, may be lost in discussions which focus too specifically on the body as a socially constructed entity. More abstract analyses of women's bodies can be very helpful, however, in avoiding concepts that might reinforce an essentialist view of gender (Howson 2005). One of the most influential scholars to adopt a philosophical and more abstract view of the body is Judith Butler (1993), whose work on the gendered body I now briefly consider, partly because of its significance in feminist scholarship and partly because I refer to it later on in this text. Butler's work has been criticized (for example, by Howson 2005) for its abstract nature. However, as Howson does acknowledge, Butler's work is important because it challenges biomedical understandings about gender through highlighting and critiquing conventional, and constraining, notions about women's work, and women's bodily comportment, including the repetitive, everyday work of being a woman in late modern society. This is because Butler challenges the social norms associated with heterosexuality, gender, and gendered practices. She argues that the concepts of sex and gender are social, rather than biomedical, constructions. Drawing upon the concept of 'performativity' to explain her beliefs, Butler suggests that 'gender' is not an inherent characteristic which men and women are born with, but something that men and women are socially proscribed to 'perform', the repeated and repetitive performing of gender being underpinned by the social foregrounding of heterosexuality as the 'norm'. Performativity provides an explanation for why social notions of what male and female embodied behaviour 'ought' to be, remain powerfully resistant to change. Butler's ideas are important, because they contest long-standing and traditional notions about the gender and biology of women's bodies, by defining the body (as well as gender and sex) as a negotiable site which is produced and reproduced in the context of social and cultural conventions.

The body as biology

Challenges to the concept of the 'biomedical body', as outlined above, whether these are material or more abstract in nature, are important in a study of women's embodied labour. This is because ideas about women's 'biology' are often used as justification for assigning women a restricted social space. In contrast to the sociological view of the body, the biomedical view regards the body as 'real' and definable. The biomedical model of the body offers limited room for manoeuvre or change, because this approach regards bodies as stable and immutable in the sense that (with a small number of exceptions) all bodies are sexed, and gendered, and characterized by specific gendered functions.

Biomedical understandings of the body are closely embedded in the development of medical science, and date back over centuries. Historically, medicine has constructed the healthy masculine body as ideal, and the female body as an inferior version of male embodiment (Nettleton 2006). As modern medicine developed, the motivation for health professionals was to make the unhealthy body better and in this context to bring bodies, and bodily functions, under medical (and by implication male) control. As Rich (1977), Oakley (1981) and Kitzinger (2003) have argued, this has applied in particular to the female reproductive body. Nettleton (2006) has noted that medical texts often use the metaphor of a machine, or an organization, to describe women's bodies. She observes how the maternal body is usually reduced to its reproductive status and is seen as unreliable and prone to breakdown and failure. Menstruation, for example, is described as 'failure' to produce a baby and the end of menstruation as symbolic of the end of woman's useful and productive reproductive life (Nettleton 2006).

The relationship between the body, medicine and masculinity is important and, arguably, problematic. This is because the influence of the biomedical model of the body, and the notion of the male body as 'ideal' or 'normal', extends beyond the field of medicine, pervading all aspects of social life, including the workplace. Martin's (1989) description of medical definitions of women's bodies as fragile, unreliable and prone to breakdown and failure accords with Nettleton's (2006) approach. Martin notes how women's reproductive capacity is linked, socially, both with their ability to perform, and with their social and economic value, within the workplace.

In keeping with Martin (1989), the feminist scholar Bernice Hausman (2004: 276) has observed how the workplace may be seen as primarily a male space in which the heterosexual male worker represents the 'ideal' and women are obliged to fit in with 'norms of male embodiment at work'. As Hausman (2004), Puwar (2004), Martin (1989), Höpfl and Hornby Atkinson (2000) and Gatrell (2007a, 2007b) have all observed, in order to comply with late modern notions of employment and healthy masculinity, women are expected to conceal from colleagues all manifestations of the maternal body (menstruation, pregnancy, maternity and menopausal symptoms). Women's bodies in the workplace will be tolerated only if they maintain embodied boundaries which do not too obviously differentiate them from the male norm.

A further problem with the biomedical model of the body is that it is often presented by its proponents as superior to, and more relevant than, any other philosophical, sociological or feminist approach. Biomedical views on embodied needs and practices are often presented as 'fact', 'rational', 'proven' and clinical'. The medical model of the body is therefore seen to preclude any argument. In this context it is worth pointing out that many biomedical 'facts' have been disproved over time. For example, the view that women's reproductive organs were the same as men's (only turned inside out) has long been disproved (Nettleton 2006). And views of teenage pregnancy (as desirable in medieval times, but as a public health issue in the twenty-first century) have changed in keeping with longer life expectancy and greater affluence.

It is interesting to observe how biomedical research findings are mobilized as 'evidence' for maintaining the privileged positions of particular groups. In such contexts, biomedical theories of the body are 'wheeled out' by those in dominant positions in order to shore up outdated ideas of masculine domination. Biomedical explanations are thus used to justify social inequities, such as the small percentage of employed women who are appointed at senior levels in comparison to men. For example, in 2005, Professor Lawrence Summers (then President of Harvard) inferred that women have a lower IQ than their male counterparts, and that this consequently justified unequal employment opportunities. Summers's viewpoint underplays the social, historical and economic factors which might influence both the nature of IQ levels and IQ tests, and it fails to challenge the quality and/or the origins of the research which made the claims. Thus, the gendered and discriminatory nature of the statement is hidden because it is presented as biomedical 'fact'. Coming from the influential head of Harvard Business School, the above statement seemed calculated to ensure continuance of existing gendered inequalities in higher education in the USA and in the West more generally. Although Summers's position became increasingly difficult to maintain, he nevertheless continued to claim that he was discriminating against female academics not on social grounds but on scientific grounds. He was merely reporting the 'unfortunate truth' of women's inferior biology, which does not fit them for senior office in quite the same way that it does men, and induces young girls to play mummies and babies, even when their only toys are trucks (Summers 2005). This, he implied, alleviated Harvard University's responsibility for examining their appointments procedures because, presumably, women's lack of career progress could be blamed on their inferior brains!

Another difficulty with biomedical approaches to the body is that this understanding of the body is underpinned by a narrow view of what is 'normal', meaning that anyone who does not fit the mould of being able bodied and well is seen as defective and socially problematic. As Kitzinger (2003), Thomas (1999) and Mullin (2005) all observe, if women's bodies are seen to be 'other' (because they are pregnant or disabled, or both) they may be regarded as incompetent and socially inconvenient, because they may require 'special' facilities or arrangements. Thomas (1999) and Mullin (2005), in their respective research on disabled (Thomas) and pregnant and/or disabled bodies (Mullin), note how the 'impaired' female body is often treated in terms of its biomedical presentation – as lacking, or less than, an able body. Social responses based on what Thomas (2007) describes as the 'deviance perspective' mean that women whose bodies fail to comply within the narrow range of what is 'normal' may 'be treated as vulnerable and less capable than others to perform a wide range of tasks' (Mullin 2005: 64). Mullin (2005) asserts that that the notion of impairment, linked to pregnancy and disability, is a socially constructed concept formed on the basis of a narrow social viewpoint about what is 'normal', and about how particular social and organizational tasks should be performed.

The concept of women's bodies failing to meet the required standards associated with the 'normal' body suggests that ideas about healthy embodiment are gendered. This brings us back to Nettleton's (2006) argument that biomedical definitions of 'normality' derive from the medical definition of the 'ideal' healthy body as male. The relationship between male hegemony, and the oppression of the female body through traditional biomedical ideas about essentialist differences between men and women, is a concept which often went unchallenged prior to feminist critiques of modern reproductive medicine. The privileging of the male body within medicine, and the idea of women's reproductive bodies as flawed, which has since been contested by, for example, Rothman (1982), Kitzinger (2005), Mullin (2005) and Nettleton (2006), was largely taken for granted.

The male body as 'norm'

Medicine is not the only arena where influential research on bodies and embodiment has tended to privilege the male body, which is often, by implication, white, and able bodied. As I observed at the start of Chapter 2, early sociologies of work tended to universalize the bodies of men, and similar criticisms have been directed at philosophers who write about 'the body' but who, by implication, appear to be writing about men, not women. Tyler (2000) expresses her frustrations with philosophical studies of the body by suggesting that female (especially pregnant) bodies are excluded from philosophical 'space' both in the literal sense and textually. A heavily pregnant Tyler describes how she felt unwelcome and out of place when she attended a lecture within her discipline, but she also refers to the lack of consideration of the pregnant body in philosophical space. Tyler observes how philosophers have for centuries considered the relationship between the body and the mind, without specifying whose body is the focus of the discussion, this leading Tyler to believe that the supposedly 'ungendered body' is male. Similarly, Kristeva, in her analysis of mothers as writers, asserts that in order to succeed as an academic, a woman must deny the materiality of her maternity, and write as though her children do not exist, if she is to be allowed into the predominantly male world of philosophical academia (Höpfl 2000).

For example, while feminist scholars may draw upon the work of Pierre Bourdieu in the quest to understand how power operates through the body and social capital, it is seen as 'curious that he overlooks gender as a crucial element in the constitution of [social] capital' (Pringle 1998: 98). Likewise, the work of the philosopher Merleau-Ponty, who argues that mind and body are not separate entities, but 'fit together and interact within the context of the whole person' (Crossley 2005: 12), has been criticized by feminist scholars who 'object to his tendency to assume that his descriptions of bodily experience are gender neutral' (Crossley 2005: 22). Crossley himself does acknowledge that women's 'manner of being in the world' may be different from men's. Drawing upon Young's 1980 essay 'Throwing like a Girl' (see Young 2005), Crossley recognizes that women often do not enjoy the same bodily 'freedoms' as able-bodied men, because their bodies are objectified in a patriarchal culture, and the experience of being observed (in a way which does not apply to men) reduces women's ability to be comfortable within their own bodies. Interestingly, though, in his consideration of *The Social Body*, and in particular of mind and body dualisms, Crossley (2001) does not refer to the maternal body, or to pregnant embodiment. This is significant, since it is difficult to imagine how ideas of mind–body dualism might apply to the pregnant, female body (possibly containing more than one fetus).

Just as some texts on bodies and embodiment may appear to be 'gender neutral' (by which I am suggesting that they are privileging the male body without acknowledging this), so these texts may also exclude considerations of the bodies of women who are racialized minorities, lesbian or disabled. Nirmal Puwar (2004) considers the position of the female and racialized body in society and presents a view of women as 'other' – an inferior and deviant version of the male somatic 'norm'. Puwar (whose work I discuss further in Chapter 7) considers the position of women in relation to social and organizational spaces such as academia, law and politics which were, until the last quarter of the twentieth century, almost exclusively the preserve of white males. Puwar argues that contemporary women are allowed entry to male organizational spaces only under certain conditions. In most situations, open discussion of the female body and health, or of any health issue pertaining to female reproduction, will invite opprobrium or derision. Women are expected to conceal (and not to discuss) evidence of female bodily fluids, especially if these are connected with reproductive functions (such as menstruation or breastfeeding) because 'somatic masculine speech finds it difficult to deal with women's bodies from a perspective that does not exoticise, fetishise or ridicule them' (Puwar 2004: 88). Open transgression of these social niceties may lead to exclusion from public and/or organizational spaces which have traditionally been the province of men. Puwar observes that the justification for the requirement for women to regulate their bodies in this way is often presented as 'rational' and part of the rules which apply to all – as if it is 'gender neutral'. For example, in 2000, British MP Julia Drown was observed breastfeeding her baby in the House of Commons and was prevented from continuing the baby's feed – as was Kirstie Marshall in Australia (Shaw 2004). The reason given for Drown's exclusion from the Chamber by the then speaker Betty Boothroyd was not related to the act of infant feeding but was justified on the basis that 'beverages were not allowed in committees,' (Puwar 2004: 88). Thus, Puwar (2004: 88) suggests,

> the most archaic of rules and ritual, wrapped up in an apparent language of gender neutrality, can be utilised to differentiate the prescribed from the proscribed . . . so we see how rituals, working practices and performative genders coalesce in the accomplishment of specific institutional scripts that take specific [i.e. white male] types of bodies as the norm.

Thus, gendered, embodied and arguably discriminatory practices are accepted because they are cloaked in a 'gender neutral' disguise. The connotation of Puwar's work is that 'ideal' bodies must be male, and healthy. The overtly maternal body, with its propensity to leak, to grow other bodies and, in middle age, to undergo physical changes, is thus seen as 'out of place' in the corridors of power which have so long been reserved for white, able-bodied males.

Sociological and biomedical ideas of the maternal body, of social definitions of maternal success and failure (Nettleton 2006), of the embodying social expectations which confine and constrain women's choice, including the very issue of whether or not to have children, are central to understandings of women's work. In what follows I draw upon a range of these perspectives and begin, in Chapter 3, by considering the particular perspective of non-mothers, and the 'choices' and constraints imposed upon this group, both socially and in the workplace.

3   'Think again old girl': Reproduction and the 'right' body

Introduction

In this chapter, I examine the boundaries which define women's choice about whether, and when, to have children. I suggest that the social value ascribed to women's reproductive labour differs depending on their social and economic circumstances, including age, ethnicity, education and the number of children they already have. Women who are considered too young, too old, or as second-class citizens either metaphorically or literally, as in the case of asylum seekers, are subject to criticism and their reproductive labour is often excluded from narratives about social contributions

I begin by observing the pressures on some groups of women to bear children and note how women who are in paid work with 'prospects' (and who are therefore also likely to fulfil contemporary cultural notions of 'ideal' bodies for reproduction) are still expected to make a 'choice' between motherhood and career.

I then consider how, for women with no children, the available 'choices' within the contexts both of paid and unpaid work are limited by discourses about the 'natural' nurturing qualities which all women are assumed to possess and which are seen to be underutilized in the case of non-mothers. On this basis, women with no children may be expected to play a 'pastoral' role in the workplace and may be expected to care for elderly parents on behalf of siblings. Drawing upon the views of Ramsay and Letherby (2006), I raise the possibility that, while mothers are undervalued in many circumstances, women who have no children are afforded less respect by employers and associates than if they were mothers.

Finally, I turn to women whose bodies are seen to be inappropriate for child-bearing, considering, in particular, the case of older mothers who are seen to be variously selfish, irresponsible and immoral.

Confinement and care

Although, as noted in the previous chapter, the labour of reproduction is rarely made explicit in sociologies of 'work', it had been assumed that, at the point when labour became industrialized within capitalist societies, men 'went out' to work and women's primary form of labour became child-bearing. Middle-class women were confined to the home and were expected to produce the next generation of heirs, bureaucrats or businessmen – as well as the next generation of mothers. Working-class women were expected to give birth to the next proletariat – the working classes who would provide new generations of industrial labour. Working-class women might also have been required to undertake manual, paid work, and to contribute to family income. However, as a 'unit of production' the economic value of the female body was considerably less that of the male body. Thus, for hundreds of years, employed women were paid a good deal less then their male counterparts and, as Morris (1990) and Bruley (1999) observe (and as I consider at greater length in Chapter 6), often had little or no support from trades unions.

The gender pay gap provided working-class women with insufficient social incentive to make paid work their chief form of production. Thus, in early industrial societies, having babies and taking responsibility for, and within, the household was women's principle form of labour. As long ago as 1903, the writer Charlotte Perkins Gilman distinguished between the embodied labour provided by (middle-class) women within the home and what she saw as more fulfilling paid labour, external to the home, from which women were excluded but which was available to men, who were employed to perform 'the service of other people in some specialised industry [doing] good service in the world' (Gilman 2002: 264).

Social attitudes towards non-mothers

Arguably, although women's labour market participation has greatly increased and the gender pay gap narrowed since Gilman's (1903) observations, the labour of reproduction – of becoming pregnant, giving birth and raising children – is still seen to be one of women's principle roles in late modern society. Western women – particularly those who are educated and in high-status paid work – are seen to be failing both in their social duty and in their performance of femininity if they do not use their fertile bodies, during their fertile years, to produce children. Governments in Europe and America are worried about falling birth rates, especially among well-educated, employed women, the group among whom birth rates are at their lowest (Williams 2008). In 1998, 19% of American women were childless at age 40–44. However, the numbers of childless women are seen to be increasing in relation to levels of salary and education. A survey undertaken in America in 2001, which applied to women earning over $30,000, showed that 33% were childless, this figure rising to 42% for women working at senior level in corporate America (Hewlett 2002).

Child-bearing continues, nevertheless, to be regarded as the social 'norm', and mothers in heterosexual partnerships and with an income are expected to give birth. In some countries, such as France and Germany, where birth rates have fallen well below government ideals, cash incentives are offered to working women who produce a third child (Powell 2005: 14). Women with no children may be seen as 'selfish' or 'odd' because they have failed to make their reproductive contribution to society (Davidson and Cooper 1992).

Non-motherhood through lack of opportunity

Women who apparently lack the opportunity to have children either through circumstance or due to infertility are singled out for negative attention as a source of both pity and opprobrium. This group of non-mothers may be charged with being too highly educated and/or with investing too much time in their careers, at the expense of their fertility, especially if they are over 35. On the part of sociologists and medics, the responses to childless, professionally employed women range from the sympathetic (Hewlett 2002) through to the cautionary (Bewley *et al.* 2005) to the disparaging (Tooley 2002). Whatever the sentiments of others towards their non-motherhood (supportive or otherwise), women over 35 who are infertile are labelled as poor planners, who have 'failed' to give birth because 'the brutal demands of ambitious careers, the assymetries of male/female relationships, and the difficulties of late-in-life childbearing conspire to crowd out the possibility of having children' (Hewlett 2002: 29).

Infertile women in their mid-thirties and early forties are often unfairly or inaccurately accused of having left it 'too late' (Bewley *et al.* 2005). Hewlett (2002), who acknowledges the unfairness of the continuing pressure on contemporary women to make a choice between motherhood and career, nevertheless warns of the dangers of 'baby hunger', a syndrome which she believes is likely to affect the majority of non-mothers when they reach their thirties and forties. Hewlett outlines the problems involved both in conceiving a child after age 35 and in finding a male partner after the age of 24. Emphasizing the importance of child-bearing and child-rearing within a heterosexual relationship, in relation to the fulfilment of adult womanhood, Hewlett (2002: 261) urges women to 'give urgent priority to finding a partner'. Hewlett underlines how:

> This project is extremely time-sensitive and deserves special attention in your twenties. Understand that forging a loving, lasting marriage will enhance your life and make it much more likely that you will

have children . . . [and] have your first child before 35 . . . do not wait until your late thirties or early forties before trying to have that first child. As we now understand, late-in-life childbearing is fraught with risk and failure.

Writers such as Tooley (2002) proffer the same advice as Hewlett, albeit in a less sympathetic light. Tooley claims that, in heterosexual relationships, child-bearing is essential to women's happiness. Using as the basis of his argument the fictional character Bridget Jones, he suggests that highly educated career women may be unattractive to men, especially if they are over 30 and earning high incomes. The reason he gives for this view is his hypothesis that women's material success is a threat to men's sexual and masculine identity. According to Tooley, the better the woman's salary, the greater the likelihood that she will price herself out of opportunities for marriage (and thereby motherhood). This, he argues, is because women who are economically successful are satisfied only by men in higher-status jobs than their own – and such men do not wish to marry career women, preferring, instead, to target partners who are prepared to leave the labour market in order to produce children and provide unpaid domestic labour. Drawing on the imaginary account of Bridget Jones's life to substantiate his hypothesis, Tooley advocates, patronizingly, the need for women to relinquish material achievements because these may be acquired at the expense of child-bearing, which he believes will make women happier than a career. Giving as his example Milton Friedman – whose talented wife Rose, 'when she married, gave up work *as was expected* and concentrated on full-time motherhood when it quickly arrived' (Tooley 2002: 111; emphasis added) – he argues that Rose's relinquishment of career was a sensible strategy for a woman because 'someone in [Friedman's] position would have grown tired of making sacrifices to further *her* career and would instead have gone looking for . . . a devoted full-time wife'.

Like Hewlett, Tooley goes on to explain the need for women to marry young, before they have established careers since, in his view, men require partners who will become pregnant quickly and will then take responsibility for childcare and domestic labour: 'It is a well-known phenomenon that male sexual preference is for young women [however] . . . what men desire is not youth per se, what they look for are features of women with fertility' (Tooley 2002: 168).

Dismissing women's ambition, Tooley also gives scant attention to the notion of lesbian or single motherhood, or to the possibility that women who relinquish careers at the prospect of heterosexual marriage might need to earn money within marriage or might later be divorced – due, presumably to his inferred view that divorce is caused by women's employment, and that in marriages where women are confined to the home, divorce is less likely to occur.

If social attitudes towards women are as entrenched as Tooley, Hewlett, and Ramsay and Letherby claim, this suggests that women – despite their increased participation in the labour market – are 'measured' on a very different basis than men. The social diktat that women under 35 should have children suggests that women who are non-mothers beyond that age may be regarded as 'unsuccessful' in late modern society, regardless of what they may achieve personally. As Bates Gaston (1991: 69) has observed, 'a woman's career and her childbearing years run in parallel'. Yet despite thirty years of equal opportunities, it appears that women are still expected to make compromises and sacrifices in the context of their employment, if they want children. In respect of the advice offered by Hewlett and Tooley, very limited progress seems to have been made with regard to the objective, outlined by the radical feminist movement, that society should accommodate child-bearing so that women are no longer required to 'choose' between motherhood and career but are entitled to both. Furthermore, in relation to ideas about the 'articulation of work activities' (Glucksmann 2005: 19), it would seem that women's work continues to be measured, in a Taylorist manner, less in relation to their productive paid employment, than in relation to reproduction and whether or not women have borne children. In respect of this particular and embodied form of measurement, expectations that adult womanhood ought to encompass child-bearing extend to the number of children produced. While women from impoverished backgrounds with large families are likely to experience social disapproval, middle-class women who have only one child are regarded either as unfortunate or as unsuccessful, especially if they are in their late thirties or early forties (Hewlett 2002).

Thus (while, ironically, the work involved in child-bearing is often discounted, as I argue in Chapters 4 and 5), the value of women's contribution within the formal labour market is questioned. Women's investment in their career or other aspects of their personal life is seen, by employers and colleagues and by some sociologists, to be of insignificant value if this produces economic results, but concurrently compromises women's ability to produce children.

Women who choose not to have children

Women who enter the menopause without children due to circumstance or infertility may be seen as poor planners or as objects of pity (Hewlett 2002). However, women who declare in public an intention not to have children are a particular target for criticism. Purdy (1997) argues that young women are expected to retain notions of child-bearing as central to their identity, despite increased opportunities for employment and the likelihood that they will need to be economically active. Hughes (2002: 68) further observes how 'the centrality of motherhood to womanhood means that it is almost impossible to hear positive discourses related to voluntary childlessness'. Those women who make an active decision against giving birth are blamed not only for their 'selfish' attitudes in general but also with regard to specific social problems, to which they are seen to be contributing, for example predicted pension short-falls (Mollen 2006). The journalist Suzanne Moore (2006), who writes in defence of women's choice to remain 'childfree', observes nevertheless that: 'A Baby Gap is upon us and it's not a cute clothes shop, it means women have gone on baby strike so there will not be enough youngsters to pay taxes and to look after the oldsters'.

Thus, individual women without children may be subject to 'endless questioning' about their childless status and accused of failing to 'fulfil their moral duty' and of being 'self-centred', due to their childless status (Defago 2005: 25, 23, 37). The psychologists Marilyn Davidson and Cary Cooper (1992) and journalist Nicky Defago (2005) have observed how some women decide against having children because they fear that motherhood will dam-age their career prospects. Such women often find themselves the subject of censorious behaviour and conversation among family and colleagues. Defago (2005: 39) observes how 'It's often implied, though never with compassion, that childfree people opt out of parenthood because they are psychologically (if not physically) flawed'. Defago recalls being told that 'it's abnormal for women not to want babies' (2005: 38) and makes the point that 'Everyone asks "why *don't* you have children?" Nobody asks parents "Why *do* you have children?" which is an equally good question' (2005: 52; emphasis added).

University academics Ramsay and Letherby (2006) observe how assump-tions are made that non-mothers 'ought' to have a strong career orientation, as if this represents compensation for their lack of children. A powerful work orientation on its own is not enough, however, and devotion to paid work must apparently be combined with material success if women without chil-dren are to be accepted by colleagues and relatives. Marcel D'Argy Smith (quoted in Defago 2005) recalls how her own mother found it hard to come to terms with Marcel's chosen childless status, only managing to accept this once her daughter had achieved high status in the magazine world as editor of *Cosmopolitan*.

Maternal bodies without children

It might be assumed that the labour market position of contemporary women who do not have dependent children is easier than it is for women with babies and school-age sons and daughters. However, while the problems faced by women with no children may be *different* from the difficulties experienced by mothers at work, these do not disappear. Ramsay and Letherby (2006) have undertaken research on non-mothers and employment, focusing on women who, like themselves, work as university academics. Ramsay and Letherby argue that all women are defined through their reproductive status. They acknowledge that the effect of being identified through the womb may be different, depending upon the status of the woman concerned (including her age, ethnicity, class and whether she is a mother or a non-mother). However, they make the observation that 'both mothers and non-mothers are affected by the dominant discourse and the ideology of motherhood that pervades our society' (2006: 28).

Ramsay and Letherby argue that women without children are given a subject position, at work, in relation to their non-maternity – just as those who have given birth are categorized as mothers. In a general context, the writers contend that non-mothers should be identified as a group with legitimate needs which are different from, but just as important as, the needs of mothers. They consider non-motherhood from the perspective of both women who are 'voluntarily' childless and those who are non-mothers 'involuntarily', recognizing that the boundaries between these two groups may sometimes be blurred.

In the context of paid work, while they acknowledge the pressures on employed mothers, Ramsay and Letherby suggest that non-mothers are disadvantaged because their childless status saddles them with a double burden. Firstly, the discourse of 'natural' motherhood (Miller 2005) may be applied to non-mothers as well as mothers – especially if this relates to a task which employers wish them to undertake. According to Ramsay and Letherby, it is assumed by employers that non-mothers must have a 'natural' ability to nurture which, if not expended on children, ought to be channelled into pastoral work. This presumption is combined with an expectation that their lack of childcare responsibilities leaves non-mothers with ample 'spare' time to offer: 'you are a childless woman, [therefore] you must have lots of time' (Ramsay and Letherby 2006: 39).

Consequently, Ramsay and Letherby suggest, non-mothers are expected to undertake high levels of pastoral care, on the presumption that childless women ought to provide care for students, since this will offer them the chance not only to put to good use their 'spare' time, but will also compensate their supposedly underutilized womanly caring qualities. They are also given heavy workloads and asked to make themselves available to their employers in a manner which is not required of mothers, or of men. Writing in the context of higher education, Ramsay and Letherby observe workplace expectations that non-mothers should be:

> available to work 24 hours a day . . . we are at times expected to place the organization at the centre of our emotional lives and extend our mothering capacity to our students, colleagues and to the greedy institution. Indeed at times, women 'without' children may be viewed as having no responsibilities outside the organisation and therefore able to give their all to work.
>
> (Ramsay and Letherby 2006: 34)

Non-motherhood therefore becomes an extra 'organizational resource' (2006: 39) which employers regard as a legitimate reserve to be drawn upon as required for tasks which are over and above ordinary workloads and which involve some element of care work. Non-mothers are thus required to fulfil pastoral roles as a substitute (or even a penance) for their lack of children. By contrast, Ramsay and Letherby suggest, mothers may be excused some of the caring duties which are imposed on women with no children, because they are seen both to be short of time and to have fulfilled their feminine duty by bearing children. At the same time, the desire on the part of some male academics to privilege research over teaching is accommodated and male academics are also, therefore, often excused from pastoral duties. For non-mothers, however, the demands are perceived to be different, as explained by Rachel, one of Ramsay and Letherby's research respondents:

> During the student holidays [non-mothers] are the ones who always get pulled in to sort out problems . . . When I first [arrived] my manager said '[we] need you . . . because [we] need someone who will look after the students'. What he meant was, 'you can do all the running around while the men get on with their research and build up their careers'.
>
> (Ramsay and Letherby 2006: 38)

Acknowledging that not all male academics privilege research over student needs, and recognizing that some men may be very 'responsive to students', Letherby and Shiles (2001: 128) have nevertheless argued, in the same vein, that pastoral work when undertaken by men 'is often seen as additional to [men's] responsibilities and as more of a gift, where when women provide [care] it is seen as a natural aspect of their femininity and part of their job'.

Given these circumstances, it seems both ironic and unfair that the ability of non-mothers to provide appropriate pastoral care for students is concurrently questioned. However, it appears that this does occur due to the limited and stereotypical view that, while non-mothers 'ought' to be utilizing their 'natural' maternal qualities and their spare time on pastoral work, they will be unlikely to do this as effectively either as mothers or as gifted men (Ramsay and Letherby 2006).

Ramsay and Letherby's account suggests that non-mothers are regarded as a resource for maternal labour in the workplace. The same discourses relating to women's supposedly 'natural' maternal qualities, which serve to obscure the labour of reproduction and maternal labour, seem to be applied to the pastoral work undertaken by employed non-mothers. As such, this work is not articulated as 'work', or valued in the same manner as when it is performed by mothers or male colleagues. Recalling Glucksmann's (2005: 21) concern with the 'shifting and permeable nature of boundaries', referred to in Chapter 1, it appears that some non-mothers may be given less opportunity to set either their temporal or emotional boundaries than mothers or men. According to Ramsey and Letherby, non-mothers are afforded less autonomy with regard to their time management than other groups, and their effectiveness at providing pastoral care is measured on a different basis than for men (who are able to choose whether on not to undertake this work) and mothers (who are under less scrutiny than non-mothers, since is it assumed that mothers will be 'naturally' good at it).

Ramsay and Letherby conclude that non-mothers are often treated disrespectfully by employers and others. They note how, in the workplace, the bodies of younger, childless women are under scrutiny as colleagues anticipate potential pregnancies. However, in their account, this appears as a minor problem compared to the opprobrium which they believe to be directed towards women who are seen as non-mothers and unlikely to have children. This is so strong that such women claim to feel almost 'dehumanized' in the eyes of men, and of women with children. One respondent quoted by Ramsay and Letherby (2006: 35) reports feeling that others are unable to 'locate [her] as a person' due to her childless status. Another interviewee recounts how her female friends with children 'make me feel less than an adult, less feminine [than they are] and I really resent that' (2006: 30). Ramsay and Letherby's findings support earlier research by Cooper and Davidson (1982) and Davidson and Cooper (1992) on women managers, in which is it observed that women managers without children may be openly criticized for failing to perform 'womanhood' in accordance with social expectations. Women leaders are often accused of (and censured for) adopting male behaviours, and childless women without male partners may be labelled as being 'not quite normal' (Davidson and Cooper 1992: 134).

The expectation that non-mothers should have available spare time and underutilized nurturing capacities extends beyond the workplace and into the context of family labour. Charlotte Perkins Gilman observed how, in 1903, women's capacity for reproduction excluded them from career opportunities but compounded social expectations that they would personally provide bodily care not only for their own children, but for needy and infirm parents. This was for both social and economic reasons relating not just to opportunities in education and the job market, but also to embodying expectations about the gendered nature of 'duty' – which, for women, involved the provision of hands-on care for family members who needed it, for as long as it was required. Gilman contends that:

> Whatever of filial gratitude, love and service is owed to the parent is equally owed by boy and girl. [But] what is the accepted duty of the boy to the parents when they are old, feeble, sick or poor? First, to

provide for them [financially] ... then to procure for them service and nursing. ... What is the accepted duty of the girl to the parents in like case? She is required to stay at home and wait upon them with her own hands, serve them personally, nurse them personally. ... Why does she have to be herself the nurse and servant? Because she has always been kept at home and denied the opportunity to take up some trade or profession.

(Gilman 2002: 264–5)

The theme of women's confinement to the home, due to expectations that daughters should perform physical labour to support the embodied needs of older relatives, is important. So is the recognition that embodied and gendered forms of labour within the home were rarely 'articulated' as 'work' or valued on the same basis as men's paid work. It is a theme that runs through this book, and the assumption that things have changed, with women now more able to occupy public spaces previously the preserve of men, continues to be challenged by, for example, Longhurst (2001), Gatrell (2005) and Hausman (2004). In relation to employment and elder care, the social view of women with no children is closely related to their reproductive and embodied status. Even in late modernity, this may still involve assumptions that women should personally provide physical and emotional familial care, because expectations that it is the 'accepted duty' of women to care for elderly parents have not disappeared (Finch and Mason 1993). Finch and Mason (1993: 76) have observed how questions regarding the provision of elder care may not even be raised among families (unless women protest) since it is seen as automatic and inevitable that women should 'take responsibility ... for providing assistance'.

In this respect, women with no children may be viewed by relatives as 'the obvious family carer' (Finch and Mason 1993: 78). Thus, expectations of mature non-mothers may be higher than for women with dependent children, who are thought of as already busy and nurturing. Even if she is in full-time paid work, it may be expected that a women with no children will 'obviously' undertake elder care for relatives. This was the case for one participant in my own research on part-time study. Gina, who was studying part-time while also in full-time employment, was expected by all her family to care for her widowed mother. Gina recalled:

I was happy to spend time with mum and give her my support but she became very dependent. And I felt [resentful] when I realized my [sisters] were just assuming that this was 'my' job and that they were let out of it because they had kids. They really did little to help.

(Gatrell 2006a: 57)

It thus appears that assumptions about women with maternal bodies, but with no children, as 'obviously' having the 'spare' capacity, the 'natural' ability and the desire to undertake caring work extend beyond the home and into the workplace.

Reproduction and the 'wrong' body

While middle-class women such as Nicky Defago may be expected, and even pressurized, to have children, society's view of acceptable motherhood is strongly related to ethnicity, age and class. Teenage women, disabled women, ethnic minority women (especially those who are impoverished and/or who do not speak the language of their host country) and women over 35 are all among those who may be excluded from narratives of ideal mothering. Reproductive labour on the part of this 'excluded' group is discounted and is regarded as of low value, or of no value at all, by those with high social influence such as wealthy political parties and the press.

Thus, disabled women who are mothers may be afforded less social value than able-bodied women. This is especially likely if they require assistance to care for their children, in which case they are treated both as a cost to society and as failing to meet idealistic visions about the ability of mothers to personally manage the emotional and physical care of their children (Mullin 2005). Similarly, Brown and Ferree (2005) have observed how ethnic minority women may be accorded a lack of respect and understanding in relation to their child-bearing choices and decisions. For example, they note how rational reproductive choices to have more than two children, on the part of ethnic minority women, may be reframed by others as negligent or foolish. In a report produced by the UK's Maternity Alliance (2004) it was further observed how some ethnic minority mothers, giving birth in UK hospital maternity wards, feel they are treated insensitively in comparison with local women.

There are some ethnic minority women who are made by governments and policy-makers to feel completely worthless in respect of the labour of maternity and who are treated as second-class citizens in the most literal sense. According to Tyler (2006), pregnant asylum seekers (who may have become pregnant as a consequence of rape) and new mothers in asylum are singled out for particularly harsh treatment and criticism. Hidden from the public sphere in detention centres, in cramped conditions and for indefinite periods, Tyler quotes one woman's horror at the prospect of giving birth in a detention centre:

> Having a baby in here would be like asking a person to commit suicide. Having a baby in here, that is the most inhuman thing that

you can do to another person. We are crammed in here, we are fenced in. I find it hard to breathe . . . I am very depressed.

(Tyler 2006: 187)

Tyler (2006: 187) observes how pregnant asylum seekers are unrecognized and unprotected by Western legal systems, treated as social outcasts, leading 'an unliveable life in a legal and social desert at the very borders of visibility' (Tyler 2006: 187). Tyler observes how the process of abjection faced by these women may cause them to lose all sense of their human and social status to the point that they feel stripped of their identity as human beings. As another women described: 'The situation I am in makes me believe that I don't have any value and I'm nothing for ever . . . Who am I? What can I say? Nothing, What can I do? Nothing' (Tyler 2006: 187).

While pregnant asylum seekers are treated as if their reproductive and maternal labour is of very low value due to their ethnic minority and non-citizen status, other women are the subject of opprobrium due to their maternal age at pregnancy and birth. For some women, childbirth is seen to be inappropriate because they are still in their teens. In respect of teenage mothers, it is important to explain that I do not wish to underestimate the complexity, or seriousness, of issues around the health and social impact of pregnancy on teenage girls and women (outlined by Berrington *et al.* 2005). However, according to Hirst *et al.* (2006), it would seem that the difficulties of being a teenage mother are compounded by negative government and media discourses around young mothers. For teenage mothers, narratives around risk and inadequate mothering during pregnancy and afterwards are much more prominent than are any positive constructions of teenage birth (Hirst *et al.* 2006). It has been argued that 'choices' for teenage women may be more constrained than for other women during pregnancy and that, following birth, teenage mothers are required to demonstrate convincing public performances of competent motherhood (especially when in the company of health professionals), in a manner which does not apply to other women. The sense of being stigmatized can leave women who give birth during their teenage years with feelings of guilt and low self-esteem, which continue throughout their lives (Hirst *et al.* 2006).

Deferring pregnancy: defying 'nature'?

While teenage mothers may be criticized for giving birth at too young an age, women who delay childbearing beyond the age of 35 are, conversely, considered irresponsible (or at least misguided) because they are leaving it 'too late.' Obstetrician Susan Bewley and colleagues warn: 'Women want to "have it all" but biology is unchanged. Deferring (pregnancy) defies nature' (Bewley *et al.* 2005: 588) Mothers who give birth during or after their menopausal years are regarded as having overstepped the socially defined boundaries about who may give birth (and at what age) to an intolerable degree. Their bodies are considered to be of the 'wrong' type for reproduction, and they are singled out for harsh treatment and social opprobrium.

Late pregnancies are seen as expensive in both medical and personal terms. 'Older' mothers are classified as those aged over 35 years (Bewley *et al.* 2005), and since 2000 there has been a focus on 'older' women in biomedical research on pregnancy, which investigates costly medical interventions and procedures (such as rising rates of Caesarean section and fertility treatment) and relates these issues to maternal age (WebMD 2000; Bewley *et al.* 2005). As with the debate about teenage motherhood, it is difficult to make a distinction between accounts which make 'older' mothers the subject of social disapproval, and biomedical research which claims to 'prove' health and social problems associated with mothering, and attempts to mother, after age 35. For example, the rates of Caesarean section are higher among US women over 35 than among younger women, but research has not yet explained why this should be the case. Yet although the correlation between rising rates of Caesarean and maternal age could be caused by age-related health problems, research in 2007 also suggests that this may be due also to social pressures, for example fear of litigation on the part of doctors, should complications arise during a vaginal birth (US Department of Health and Human Services 2007).

Women over 35 are 'cautioned' by 'experts' that 'they are at a serious disadvantage compared with younger women . . . [Older motherhood] is a dangerous trend and women quite often have unrealistic expectations about fertility' (WebMD 2000). Older mothers are blamed for perceived rises in infertility rates, and the concept of the 'biological clock' has become 'stereotypically identified with a cohort of largely Caucasian, educated, upper-middle class women . . . who choose to have children in their mid to late thirties' (Friese *et al.* 2006: 1551). Friese *et al.* observe that notions of increased, age-related infertility are difficult to substantiate because historical infertility statistics are difficult to obtain, but acknowledge that there is a 'predominant *belief* that infertility is a greater problem now than previously'. This, they argue, has led some women to see the 'biological clock as a kind of deadline as they made decisions about childbearing, a notion through which women have been implicitly blamed for their infertility' (Friese *et al.* 2006: 1551).

It is acknowledged, here, that inability to conceive may cause extreme unhappiness among women who want children. It is also recognized that the chances of a live birth after a cycle of in vitro fertilization (IVF) are calculated to fall from 1 in 3 for women under 35, to 1 in 10 for women over 40, and to less than 1 in 20 for women over 42 (Friese *et al.* 2006). Nevertheless, it seems ironic that the narrative of being 'too old' to mother affects a growing number of women in Australia, North America, Canada and Europe, where the percentage of births among women aged 35 and over has grown rapidly over the past decade. For example, in Australia in 2005, women aged 35–39 had 60.6 babies per thousand women, and the number of Australian women aged 40–44 giving birth accounted for 10.6 per 1000 births, up from 6.7 in 1994 and 4.3 in 1984 (Mothers 35 Plus 2007). In England and Wales in 1994, there were 63,061 live births to women aged 35–39, a figure which rose to 102,228 in 2004. The number of live births among women aged 40–44 almost doubled over the same ten-year period. Nevertheless, despite the growing number of women who give birth during their late thirties and early forties, women over 35 are commonly described as 'older mothers' and are seen unfairly as a drain on health and social resources. In Australia, Professor Michael Chapman, head of women's and children's health at the University of New South Wales, expressed concerns about statistics showing that one-eighth of Australian women now have their first child at age 35 or over. Referring to Australian publicity campaigns warning women that 'putting off childbirth' results in 'an increase in infertility, miscarriage and foetal abnormalities', Professor Chapman has called for more funding for education campaigns aimed at persuading women to have babies before age 35 (Bunce 2006).

Young mothers versus 'old girls'

Although it has been demonstrated that increased maternal age reduces the chances of successful IVF treatment, there are some women who succeed in having children beyond their 'natural' reproductive years via reproductive technologies. These women are the focus of extensive public scrutiny and have been accused, variously, of 'selfish', irresponsible and immoral behaviour, one woman's decision to have a child after menopause having been described in a newspaper as 'an affront to God' (Rogers 2006). Irrespective of their social background, level of education and ability to provide financial support for their children, mothers who have children in their sixties are international news and attract criticism.

Thus, even women with the social characteristics which would mean that they met the social criteria for idealized mothering norms when aged 25–35, are excluded from narratives of ideal motherhood if they give birth during, or after, their menopausal years. Fertility treatments in Europe and America are highly regulated, and many fertility clinics refuse to admit women over 45 for treatment – despite the fact that babies may be conceived 'naturally' beyond the age of 50 (Biggs 2002). Gynaecologists who seek to offer assisted conception (e.g. through egg donation) to women over 50 are thus obliged to open practices in countries such as Russia, where Adriana Iliescu, a highly educated, retired Romanian professor, who would have fulfilled social criteria for mothering 'norms' at an earlier stage in her life, became pregnant aged 65 (Barton 2005). In the UK, 63-year-old Patricia Rashbrook, who had 'craved another baby since giving birth to her third child at the age of 45', became pregnant using donor eggs and her husband's own sperm (Rogers 2006). Rashbrook was both mocked and derided in the UK press as foolish and selfish, India Knight (2006) suggesting in the *Sunday Times* that she should 'think again, old girl'.

While there are no 'official' policies dictating which women should bear children, or when (other than the formal guidelines imposed upon fertility clinics), there appear to be in place social conventions which make it evident when women are accused of having crossed the boundary between what is accepted social practice and what is frowned upon. Patricia Rashbrook, for example, can be in no doubt that some social commentators disapprove of her decision to bear a post-menopausal baby.

Conclusions

In conclusion, therefore, I suggest that the boundaries which define the desirability, or otherwise, of women having children are socially determined. Women's reproductive labour is valued only in certain circumstances, and the notion of 'value' is measured in relation to a woman's age, ethnicity, relative affluence and the number of children she already has. As in so many other instances, women's 'choice' about whether and when to have children is highly circumscribed. Thus, while reproduction is often discounted as a form of 'work', because of social tendencies to obscure the labour of child-bearing behind narratives of 'natural' motherhood, women who have no children may, nevertheless, be afforded less respect than mothers. This may be due to the Parsonian articulation of the gendered nature of 'work' (discussed in the previous chapter) which defines women's contribution to society as heteronormative and based principally on child-bearing. Furthermore, it appears that women who are in paid work with 'prospects' are still expected to make a 'choice' between motherhood and career along the lines described by radical feminist writers in the 1970s and 1980s. The views expressed by Hewlett (2002) and Tooley (2002) imply that the job market will do little to accommodate women's possible desire for children. Thus, it must be the woman herself who makes compromises in order to fulfil her supposed 'duty' to herself, her husband and society.

The idea of limited choice is not restricted to women who have children. While women who do have children are unlikely to find the labour market accommodating of their needs (as I show in Chapters 4 and 5), I have observed in this chapter how women who are non-mothers find that the social view of them as maternal bodies influences their position both within a social and an employment context. Thus, women with no children may be required within family settings to undertake caring duties which are not expected of kin who are mothers, or of men. A woman's non-motherhood may also be constrained by the discourse of the 'good' maternal body. This may define the manner in which she is expected to behave in the workplace, as well as the types of tasks she is required to undertake.

Conversely, women with children are faced with the double bind that child-bearing may be socially expected of them, and their abilities as 'good' mothers may be measured – but their pregnant bodies will not be valued, or accommodated in the workplace. This leads me on to the next chapter, in which I consider the labour of reproduction, both on its own terms and in the context of paid work.

4   Pregnancy: A non-work process?

Pregnancy is a unique period, since psychological changes and dramatic changes in physiology, appearance and body, and social status are all occurring simultaneously. . . . No other stage in a women's life is as replete with cultural stereotypes as pregnancy. Indeed, attitudes toward pregnancy have been one of the most prevalent sources of discrimination against women.

(Leifer 1980: 754)

Introduction

In the previous chapter, I considered how non-mothers find it difficult to negotiate their social position both within a social and an employment context. In this chapter, I move on to analyse the labour of reproduction, specifically in relation to pregnancy, both on its own terms and in relation to paid work. I began the chapter with a quote from Leifer's (1980) article 'Pregnancy' because it summarizes the manner in which, for many women, the social experience of pregnancy and birth may be confusing and fraught with tension. At the same time as undergoing rapid bodily changes and, gradually, experiencing the sense of two persons inside one body, women are expected to exercise extraordinary levels of personal behavioural and bodily control. While complying with the timetables and procedures required by health services (which, understandably, foreground pregnancy), employed pregnant women are probably also trying to meet the conflicting demands of the workplace, which entail the downplayment of pregnancy in favour of organizational goals and targets.

In this chapter, I conceptualize pregnancy as an embodied form of women's work which often goes unrecognized and unrewarded. Pregnancy work – in keeping with Truman's (1996) more general observations about the obfuscation of women's work – has conventionally been excluded from what Glucksmann (2005: 19) describes as 'the articulation of work activities'. This is because pregnancy is assumed to be a 'natural' part of the performance of 'good motherhood' (Miller 2005) and is therefore classified as a 'non-work process' (Glucksmann 2005: 19). In the first part of this chapter, I thus argue that the labour of pregnancy should be acknowledged as a form of work. I consider the idea that most pregnant women in 'technologically sophisticated Western societies' (Young 2005: 47) are required to comply with, and may even be expected to welcome, a level of medical and social surveillance more usually associated only with the very sick. As Young (2005) observes, 'Medicine's self-identification as the curing profession encourages others as well as the woman, to think of her pregnancy as a condition that deviates from normal health'. Medical surveillance of pregnancy, and requirements for women to regulate their own dietary and social behaviours are, I suggest, forms of labour which relate to the notion that pregnancy is a 'condition'. This notion entails pregnant women adopting medical, dietary and behavioural regimes for the benefit of the fetus – the pregnant woman's body is treated as a container for the growing fetus which must be 'contained and controlled', meaning that 'Pregnant women's rights to bodily autonomy are . . . questionable' (Longhurst 2001: 55). Pregnant women are thus expected to regulate their own embodied behaviour, measuring themselves (and being measured by others) in relation to complex and demanding standards and goals. This self-regulation is a taken for granted form of pregnancy work, and individual women's success or failure in meeting goals and targets is seen to be in the public interest. Thus, individual pregnant women are seen to be a legitimate subject for the 'public gaze' (Davidson 2001; Kitzinger 2003). As Longhurst (2001: 58) observes, the behaviour of the pregnant woman, and her compliance or otherwise with self-regulatory regimes, is

> frequently policed not just by health practitioners but also by employers, colleagues, neighbours, friends and loved ones. People frequently regard themselves as societal supervisors of pregnant women's behaviour and so it may make sense to touch a pregnant woman's stomach; to look after that property, that potential citizen in which there is a collective interest.

In contrast to the notion of the fetus as central to the public gaze, I focus, in the latter half of this chapter, on the challenge of being pregnant within the workplace. I observe the pressure placed upon employed pregnant women to perform pregnancy work in secret in the workplace, where they are expected to conform to 'embodied male norms' (Hausman 2004: 276). I observe how pregnant women are often, in relation to the workplace, under pressure to contain bodily fluids. In contrast to the social and medical interpretation of pregnancy as a 'condition', employed women are required to manage the pregnant body so that it does not disrupt employers' routines on the basis that pregnancy is 'not an illness'. Thus, satisfactory fulfilment of 'pregnancy work' to an appropriate standard within the workplace usually requires women to present their bodies as operating 'normally'. Women are thus expected to conceal, as far as possible, the physical and physiological changes brought about by pregnancy within workplace settings which are not designed to accommodate the changing requirements of the pregnant body. Interestingly, Young (2005), Tyler (2000) and Höpfl (2000) have all observed how the absence of reference to pregnancy in scholarly and philosophical discussions about the body (as discussed in Chapter 2) are mirrored in the social denial of pregnancy in the capacity of employment.

'Good' mothers and the hidden costs of pregnancy 'work'

I begin by analysing the hidden costs of pregnancy 'work' in the context of the social performance of 'good' motherhood as described by Miller (2005). In order to perform the labour of pregnancy to certain standards, as required in late modern cultures, women are expected to conform to a series of prescribed, highly medicalized and obstetrics-led procedures. The following of medical guidance often involves pregnant women in embodied pregnancy 'work' prior to conception and throughout pregnancy. It is important to recognize that many of the activities which constitute pregnancy 'work' are the result of years of medical research. I would, therefore, wish to acknowledge that the pregnancy 'work' undertaken by individual women, which has increased in response to obstetric and health research, is important and has contributed to improvements in maternal and infant health.

It is equally important, however, to articulate how compliance with late modern medical routines and procedures involves effort, meticulous organization, and often personal expense on the part of the pregnant woman. Even before conception, women are advised to adopt dietary and behaviour regimes requiring high levels of self-regulation. Women seeking to become pregnant are advised to begin lifestyle changes and to attend to their own health in order to maximize infant health prospects. The American web magazine KidsHealth advises:

> Ideally, prenatal care should start before you get pregnant. If you're planning a pregnancy, see your health provider for a complete checkup . . . If you're already being treated for a chronic condition . . . you may need to be even more vigilant about managing your condition. . . . This is also a good time to talk with your health care provider about other factors that can pose a risk to your baby, such as drinking alcohol or smoking. . . . It's especially important for women who are planning to become pregnant to take vitamins with folic acid

> beforehand, because [these help prevent] ... problems with the development of the spine and nervous system [which] happen in the first 28 days of pregnancy, often before a women knows she is pregnant.
>
> (Macones 2004)

The implication of failure to adhere to a pre-pregnancy plan, perhaps because a pregnancy was unplanned or because taking such measures was impractical over a long period of time, is that women may be regarded as having performed the labour of pregnancy work inadequately – even before the moment of conception. However, poor implementation of pre-pregnancy advice may be forgiven, so long as pregnancy regimes are followed to a high standard once pregnancy occurs. As Macones (2004) states:

> If you find out that you're pregnant before you do any of this, don't worry. It's not to late to get the care that will help to ensure your health and that of your baby.

Once pregnant, women are under immediate pressure to conform to a particular set of obstetric and health guidelines, which are presented as 'choices' but which are in practice hard to resist, and which require adherence to some fairly rigid, Taylorist-style standards of behaviour. However, the intensive nature of such pregnancy 'work' is not accounted for because it is hidden behind discourses of good mothering and maternal duty which obfuscate the notion that forms of compliance, involving intense, embodied self-regulation, are 'work'. Thus, from the early stages of pregnancy, women are defined by health professionals in relation to their pregnant bodies, and this definition shapes the new behavioural patterns which women are expected to adopt. As Miles (1992: 192) has observed,

> from the day a woman's pregnancy is announced until after delivery, what she eats and drinks and [everything she does] becomes the concern of health professionals. In the name of health, not only her own, but with even greater emphasis on that of the fetus, the activities of the pregnant woman are controlled and so is her labour and the delivery of her baby.

Once pregnancy is confirmed, women find themselves under surveillance. They are expected to attain (and are measured against) standards and targets which they cannot hope to achieve unless they successfully fulfil criteria relating to health appointments, screening, diet and lifestyle. Thus, 'choices' about what to eat and drink, and how best to cope with the work involved in managing pregnancy, are rarely left to the discretion of the pregnant woman herself and are in practice limited and limiting. Women who are accustomed to smoking and drinking alcohol are expected to give these up completely, and to cut down on the amount of coffee and tea they drink. Many health programmes for pregnant women make no distinction between an occasional glass of wine or cigarette and heavy smoking and drinking, but define all tobacco and alcohol consumption as unhealthy. Consequently, mothers who fail to eliminate cigarettes and alcohol from their lifestyles are seen as failing to perform adequately the work of pregnancy when measured against the exacting standards required of the 'good mother'. For example, the American government's advice on 'having a healthy pregnancy' (Centers for Disease Control and Prevention 2005) describes caffeine and alcohol as legal drugs. It is stated that the use of these legal drugs among pregnant women is risky, and it is noted specifically that there is no known 'safe' amount of alcohol a woman can drink while pregnant. The advice then goes on to discuss fetal alcohol syndrome, one extreme interpretation of this discussion being that there is a link between moderate alcohol consumption in pregnancy and fetal alcohol syndrome.

Hilary Graham (1993) has recognized that such health advice and associated pregnancy health programmes may be more difficult to follow for women on low incomes than for more affluent women. The following of Taylorist health regimes and the pressure to attain particular goals and standards may be especially difficult for women who are on welfare and/or benefits programmes, and who already have other small children to look after. While focusing on mothers with babies and pre-school children (she does not specifically mention pregnancy), Graham (1993: 182) suggests that mothers on the poverty line may smoke cigarettes not only to help 'maintain normal caring routines' but also to assist such women in 'fac[ing] demands they cannot meet . . . smoking a cigarette provides [accessible support] when mothers feel that their breaking point has been reached'. Graham acknowledges the irony of women's reliance on cigarette use in order to better manage mothering in difficult circumstances. She observes:

> Viewed in the context of mothers' daily lives, cigarette smoking appears to be a way of meeting rather than shirking responsibility. It provides a way of coping with the constant and unremitting demands of caring, enabling mothers to remain calm in a situation where resources are few and responsibilities are many . . . Such resources offer a very contradictory kind of support . . . [there are] conflicts that go with caring . . . in circumstances of hardship.
>
> (Graham 1993: 183)

One might suggest that the pregnancy work involved in following recommended food regimes over a nine-month period or longer (assuming women may begin such regimes before becoming pregnant, 'just in case') is also class-based, and presupposes mothers' ability to shop, and select from, a wide range of foodstuffs. Mothers are advised to 'steer clear of' foods which are most likely to carry food-borne illnesses such as listeriosis (in soft cheese) or *E. coli* (in undercooked meats). The UK National Health Service (NHS) list of foods to avoid during pregnancy is clearly designed to protect women and developing babies from the potentially serious risks posed by food poisoning. However, it involves women in adopting potential lifestyle changes (perhaps avoiding eating outside the home), assessing risk, and exercising extreme caution in what they eat. Below, I summarize in some detail the NHS advice on diet during pregnancy in order to demonstrate the extent and complexity of the advice offered, and consequently of the self-regulation expected of pregnant women. Advice proffered by mainstream health agencies in the USA is very similar.

NHS advice on pregnancy

In addition to advising pregnant women to avoid alcohol and cut down on caffeine, NHS Direct (2008) provides a list of foods which women must not eat in order to avoid food poisoning, and which are regarded as 'potentially dangerous to your unborn baby'. The guidance on what not to eat is lengthy and complicated and is related to the contracting of toxoplasmosis, salmonella and listeriosis which, although rare in the UK, can cause 'stillbirth, miscarriage, or severe illness in newborn babies'. Mothers are thus advised to avoid foods which could potentially contain high levels of listeria, and these are listed as including ready-prepared meals, reheated food, soft and blue-veined cheeses, pâté (including vegetable), and salads such as coleslaw and potato salad.

The NHS advice then goes on to focus on the problems which foods containing salmonella could cause to unborn babies. Mothers are advised that 'Salmonella is found in unpasteurised milk, raw eggs and raw egg products, raw poultry and raw meat . . . it is advisable to take precautions to avoid foods that may contain salmonella'. It recommends the following steps:

- Avoid food containing raw or partially cooked eggs, such as homemade mayonnaise, . . . mousses and sauces. . . . only eat eggs if they are cooked until both the white and the yolk are solid.
- Avoid unpasteurised dairy products.
- Cook all meat and poultry thoroughly, and take particular care with products made from minced meat, such as sausages and burgers. . . .
- Take particular care with meat at barbeques, parties and buffets. . . .
- Make sure that raw meat does not come into contact with other food (for example, in the fridge) . . .
- Always wash your hands after handling raw meat. (NHS Direct 2008)

Finally, mothers are told not to eat raw shellfish during pregnancy, as raw shellfish may also contain dangerous germs which might result in food poisoning.

The above basic advice offered by the NHS is supplemented by other advice offered, and discussed at length in pregnancy magazines and on pregnancy websites. Expectant women are thus also advised to avoid other foodstuffs commonly used to 'fill up' when a snack is needed, such as peanuts and peanut butter, which, if eaten during pregnancy, have been linked with subsequent allergies experienced by babies and young children. The *British Medical Journal* has stated: 'Maternal consumption of peanuts and peanut products seems to be associated with . . . increasing prevalence of allergy' (Kmietowicz 1998).

Pregnant women are further, and commonly, advised to eat only 'healthy' foods which will benefit the fetus and will also enable them to maintain control of their weight. Babyworld, for example, warns against eating salty and fattening convenience foods such as sweets and instant noodles and pregnant women are cautioned:

> Your pregnancy nausea is over, only to be replaced with the worst case of the munchies you have ever had! Beware becoming champion of the sweetie shop run – you'll put on more pounds than you walk off.
> (Kilby 2007)

While recognizing the value of medical advice and research on diet during pregnancy, and acknowledging the serious nature of infections such as salmonella, I also seek, here, to highlight the extent of the work involved for women who are trying to follow a 'suitable' diet during pregnancy. The following of recommended dietary regimes consists of more than the practical effort and expense involved in well-organized food shopping and cooking and the exercise of caution in restaurants, fast-food outlets and as guests in the homes of others. Adherence to dietary guidelines offered by health professionals during pregnancy also requires the exercise of complex personal judgement in the context of food advice which is often (to say the least) confusing, and which thus seems likely to induce anxiety among women attempting to perform pregnancy work in line with recommendations. Consider, for example, Macones's (2004) advice with regard to eating fish:

> You should avoid . . . eating shark, swordfish, king mackerel, or tilefish. Although fish and shellfish can be an extremely healthy part of your pregnancy diet (they contain beneficial omega-3 fatty acids and are high in protein and low in saturated fat), these types of fish may contain high levels of mercury, which can cause damage to the developing brain of a fetus.

The same might be said for the NHS advice on the same subject:

> Oily fish is good for your health but we need to limit the amount that we eat because it contains pollutants, such as dioxins and poly-chlorinated biphenyls. . . . If you're pregnant, you should eat no more than two portions of oily fish a week. Oily fish includes fresh tuna (not canned tuna, which doesn't count as oily fish), mackerel, sardines and trout.
>
> There are a few types of fish that you should avoid eating while pregnant, and some others that you should limit the amount you eat. Limit the amount of tuna you eat because it contains a high level of mercury which can have a damaging effect on your baby's developing nervous system.
>
> (NHS Direct 2008)

Advice to pregnant women regarding their intake of vitamin A seems equally confusing. Women are instructed that, although some vitamin A is required for a healthy diet, having too much of this could be harmful to the fetus. Women are advised against eating liver, or liver products such as pâté, as liver contains high levels of vitamin A. Pregnant women are also advised to check with their doctor before taking any high-dose multivitamin or cod liver oil supplements, as these may also contain vitamin A. Nevertheless, women are advised that they will need some vitamin A as part of a 'normal' diet (NHS Direct 2008).

Given the conflicting nature of pregnancy advice from the experts, it is apparent that behavioural and dietary regimes in pregnancy involve not only self-control and self-regulation, but also the negotiation, absorption and inter-pretation of complex information which may provide more questions than answers, and which may require expenditure in both personal and economic terms. Pregnant woman are treated, concurrently, as both patient and as a container with a precious cargo. 'Choices' about what to eat and how best to cope with the work involved in managing pregnancy are rarely left to the discretion of the pregnant women herself. Pregnant women are expected to attend regular antenatal appointments for screening and general health checks, during which advice on diet and lifestyle will be offered, questions will be asked relating to the consumption of cigarettes and alcohol, and maternal weight will be measured. It is acknowledged that these checks offer benefits to both the pregnant woman and her baby and may, for example, assist in clarify-ing some of the more confusing advice. However, such checks will also require pregnant women to travel to and from the clinic, where emphasis will be placed on the need for pregnancy work required to stop smoking, give up alcohol, reduce coffee and tea intake and follow a restricted diet. At the same time as acknowledging the benefits of 'healthy' diets, I am thus also suggesting that pregnant women are subject to embodied controls and standards, against which they are measured, which are all the more effective due to the strong element of self-regulation involved.

Pregnancy and the 'public gaze'

The surveillance of pregnant women, and the measurement of their performance against the conventional standards of 'good mothering', often extends beyond medical boundaries (Miles 1992). Davidson (2001) has argued that once women become pregnant, their rights to privacy and personal space are eroded because strangers, as well as friends and family members, appear to claim the 'right' to judge women's mothering abilities. Those who engage in this form of surveillance justify the notion that pregnant women should be subject to the public gaze on the basis that women's bodily adherence to pregnancy guidelines is in the public interest. The idea that pregnant women's bodies are, in a sense, public property is seen by writers such as Davidson (2001) as an invasion of women's private space. Davidson argues that other people deprive pregnant women of the right to determine their behaviour because

> it appears that pregnant women are somehow 'answerable' to public concerns about their appearance and behaviour. The female subject's usual sense of accountability is intensified as she is *reduced* to her role as expectant mother. This places added limitations upon her (already socially restricted) behaviour.
>
> (Davidson, 2001: 289; emphasis in original)

The tendency for strangers to 'police' the behaviour of pregnant women extends to an invasion of their personal space which, Davidson argues, has a profound impact on women's confidence and social identity. Davidson (2001: 290) quotes one of her research participants, who states that: 'I feel as though being pregnant automatically deprives me of my individual identity and personal space – I've become public property.' Davidson goes on to explain that:

> Visibly pregnant women forfeit . . . their right to privacy, to keep strangers at a respectful distance and their sense of independence diminishes at the hands of others, sometimes . . . literally. Pregnant women's 'condition' . . . confers rights on the public to take an active . . . interest in their bodies not only by looking but also by commenting on and even touching, behaviour that would not normally be sanctioned'.

Davidson's (2001) views on pregnancy are in keeping with those of Robyn Longhurst (2001: 55) who argues, similarly, that the fetus is often treated as if it were a public concern. Pregnant women's rights to bodily autonomy are considered to be questionable. Pregnant women are often treated as though they are little more than containers for unborn children [which] leads to pregnant women's bodies being subject to public gaze and often touch. Their 'bodily space' is frequently invaded.

Longhurst's viewpoint is shared by Rachel Cusk, who noted of her own pregnancy: 'It is the population of my privacy . . . that I find hard to endure . . . the baby's meaning for other people, the world's sense of ownership stating its claim' (Cusk 2001: 34–5).

Kitzinger (2003) also observes how pregnant women are subject to the public gaze when they eat and drink outside the home, and notes how complete strangers may openly criticize pregnant women who are considered to be transgressing what are seen to be appropriate dietary and behavioural regimes – one pregnant woman, for example, being verbally attacked for sipping a glass of wine while dining.

The question of whether it is acceptable for others to touch pregnant women, or to make uninvited comments on their behaviour, is considered by Family Education (2007) in the context of paid work. Employed women are counselled to deal with intrusive verbal and physical behaviours from co-workers in a conciliatory manner: 'sometimes you just have to accept things you can't change'. Pregnant women are advised: 'Many pregnant women experience having their tummies rubbed by strangers who do it because they are just unthinking . . . Try to understand the point of view or the motivation of the people . . . doing [this]'. Family Education also suggests that pregnant women should be accommodating in circumstances where others offer 'unsolicited advice', suggesting that women should avoid the temptation to 'snap back', especially in the workplace, providing, instead, diplomatic, responses to intrusive behaviour.

Pregnancy and medical screening

The 'work' involved in pregnancy is not limited to changes in diet and lifestyle. Pregnant women are expected to attend regular antenatal appointments for screening and general health checks. Contemporary pregnancy screening and health checks involve women in a range of activities which I seek to conceptualize as pregnancy 'work'.

The maternal effort involved in fulfilling the requirements for antenatal attendance is not to be underestimated – especially if women are attempting to combine this with paid work and the care of other children. Depending on their age, weight and general health, pregnant women will be advised to attend for various screening appointments throughout pregnancy. For example, all pregnant women in the UK will be expected to attend their first antenatal appointment between 8 and 12 weeks into pregnancy, after which antenatal checks will usually take place every four weeks until 28 weeks into pregnancy, when they increase to every fortnight. Antenatal appointments involve various 'routine' tests for infection, blood group and anaemia. Many such tests require women to give a sample of urine, and to have blood taken, by syringe, for testing. From 36 weeks onwards, women will usually be checked at least fortnightly, and sometimes weekly, until their baby is born (NHS Direct 2008). In addition to the expectation that they will proactively attend for general antenatal screening, pregnant women are also expected to be available for formal medical appointments involving technological (and some-times invasive) surveillance. The majority of pregnant women will be expected to attend for at least two, sometimes three, 'routine' ultrasound scans: at 10–13 weeks to date the age of the unborn baby, at 18–20 weeks to detect for physical abnormalities and sometimes at 36 weeks to detect the position of the placenta (Patient UK 2004). Women may be offered the possibility of a 'nuchal scan' which is carried out in conjunction with blood tests to detect the possibility of Down's syndrome, and which may necessitate travel to a centre of excellence. Women over 35, or with a family history of fetal 'abnormalities', will be 'offered' the possibility of invasive tests such as amnio-centesis (in which a needle is inserted in the uterus and amniotic fluid drawn out) or chorionic villus sampling (in which a needle is inserted into the vagina and a sample of tissue is taken from the developing placenta (Kitzinger 2003).

The purpose of these sophisticated and invasive screening techniques is to detect fetal 'abnormalities' in the womb. However, the advent of screening requires women to undertake the work of decision-making in highly complex and sensitive situations – for example, invasive pregnancy screening carries a 1–2% risk of miscarriage, and if problems are detected or suspected in fetal development, expectant women are confronted with extremely difficult and individualized 'choices' about what steps to take. Once again, it is important to acknowledge that technological advancements and the opportunity to be screened may in some circumstances be hugely beneficial to maternal and fetal health. Technological screening does make pregnancy more transparent, and may offer greater certainty in situations where, prior to the development of contemporary screening, 'answers' would have been difficult to come by. For example, early ultrasound scans can confirm pregnancy, and may also allow health professionals to identify miscarriage at an early stage. These technolo-gies are not, however, a panacea – if the baby on the scan picture has no heartbeat, this cannot be resolved through the technologies. Furthermore, the 'answers' provided by tests are not always conclusive, and may require decisions about further, and more complex, tests and/or possible termination of pregnancy.

For example, as Patient UK (2004: 3) explains, 'early' screening for Down's syndrome, which is likely to involve a combination of ultrasound scanning and blood tests, is not 'clear-cut':

- 'A "positive" test means that you *may* have a child with Down's syndrome. If you have a positive screening test, further tests are needed to confirm the diagnosis, In some positive tests the baby does not have Down's syndrome (a "false positive" result).
- A negative test does not completely rule out Down's syndrome. (That is, in some cases there is a "false negative" result.) Currently the [blood and scan] screening tests identify about 60–80 in 100 babies who have Down's syndrome.'

Thus, in addition to being under pressure to regulate their own social behaviour regarding diet, contemporary pregnant women are also involved, throughout pregnancy, in complex, and often obligatory, forms of surveillance which involve them in personal effort (women must arrange to be physically present at hospital or local clinics in order to be screened and tested). Technological surveillance also requires women to make decisions at all levels in situations where outcomes and options may be unclear. At each stage, pregnant women may have to try and form their own views about their preferred option in the context of considerable pressure from health professionals and/ or from partners and family members. Gatrell (2005: 104) records the experience of one pregnant woman who faced 'real hostility' from hospital staff when she refused an ultrasound scan. Pollock (1999) recounts the struggle of a woman whose pregnancy tests indicated fetal 'abnormalities', trying to consider the reasons for and against termination while under considerable duress from her partner.

Conceptualizing pregnancy as 'work'

Thus far, I have argued that the social expectation that women have a duty to perform pregnancy in accordance with contemporary health and obstetric guidelines involves them in a substantial amount of physical and emotional 'pregnancy work' – changing diet and lifestyle, attending appointments and so on. However, the social and medical labour of pregnancy is not generally 'counted' as work, even though, in practice, it involves a substantial investment of personal time and effort, especially if the woman concerned is managing her pregnancy alongside paid employment, caring for other children and accounting for the needs of partners and/or other household members.

Why should this be? One reason for the unrecognized nature of 'pregnancy work' is that the work of pregnancy is hidden within the idealized narrative of the 'good mother', which constructs motherhood as a 'natural' characteristic of womanhood (Miller 2005). Grosz (1994), Shildrick (1997) and Tyler (2000) all conceptualize the female body as a negotiated site, constrained more by social and gendered expectations about female bodily comportment than by essentialist biomedical definitions. Nevertheless, essentialist views remain a powerful influence in relation to social conventions about how the role of mother and expectant woman 'ought' to be performed. The image of the 'good mother' has for centuries been wrapped up in notions of 'natural' mothering which imply that 'good mothers' are supposed, automatically, to be endowed with 'nurturing' qualities, as opposed to learning mothering skills through repetition and practice (Marshall 1991). By implication, women who find these 'unrealistic expectations' completely 'baffling' (Miller 2005: 57) are seen as failing to meet the standard of 'good mother'.

Since the 1970s, feminist scholars have contested the concept of 'natural' motherhood. Rich (1977: 23), for example, challenged the notion that 'a "natural" mother is a person without further identity and [that] . . . maternal love is, and should be, completely selfless', and Ribbens (1994: 6) has observed how 'expert' views on what makes a 'good mother', combined with the social expectations about 'appropriate child-rearing can be a source of oppression to women'.

Despite such challenges to the ideology of 'good' mothering, however and despite rapid changes in family practices and in women's labour market participation, 'Ideologies around "good" mothering persist . . . change has been slow' (Miller 2005: 57). Romito (1997: 172) suggests that 'despite twenty five years of feminism, motherhood still retains its sacred aura. Mothers still do not dare to admit how burdensome the constraints and difficulties of their condition can be.'

If notions of 'natural' motherhood are still current, and if these do not allow for acknowledgements relating to the 'burdens' associated with mothering (and, by association, with pregnancy), then it becomes very difficult for women to reconceptualize the labour of pregnancy as a form of 'work'. Thus, while domestic labour – while still unpaid – is at least recognized as 'work' by government research bodies and within the media (Womack 2008), the work of pregnancy is not seen to 'count'. If pregnancy is encompassed within the narrative of 'good' motherhood, the implication for expectant women is that medical and social expectations about self-regulation, and compliance with screening regimes, are wrapped up in the role of 'good' and 'selfless' mother. Thus, the behavioural changes demanded of pregnant women are not recognized as 'work' but are socially discounted as 'natural'.

Having put forward this argument, I would like specifically to join the voices of Rich (1977), Oakley (1981), Marshall (1991), Ribbens (1994) and Miller (2005) in contesting the dominant [essentialist] ideologies that perpetuate the notion of the 'good', 'natural' mother. Specifically, as noted at the start of this chapter, I would like to add to the debate around 'good mothering' by conceptualizing the health and related social requirements of pregnancy as a form of work. In this context I seek to make transparent the labour involved in fulfilling the requirements expected of 'appropriate' pregnant behaviour in late modernity. In making this argument, I have thus focused on the labour of pregnancy work as defined by health professionals. In what follows, I shall consider a very different aspect of pregnancy 'work' which is fraught with tensions as contemporary women attempt to manage pregnancy, and their pregnant bodies, to the standards of appropriate embodied behaviour as defined within the workplace.

Pregnancy work and employment

Although this book is a research text, not a personal account, there are precedents among feminist scholars for including aspects of the self in writing. Imogen Tyler (2000) offers a vivid description of experiencing late pregnancy in the workplace, Tess Cosslett (1994) includes a description of her own labour in her anthology *Women Writing Childbirth*, and Longhurst (2001) describes her feelings of nausea in early pregnancy to illustrate her research on the pregnant body at work. I have clear memories of the tensions of trying to manage my own pregnant body within the workplace and, in keeping with the approach of the above writers, I include as an introduction to this section on 'pregnancy work and employment', two passages describing my own experiences of being pregnant in the workplace. I have incorporated these two particular accounts into this chapter to illustrate some of the issues I intend to consider below, namely the idea that pregnancy work within the workplace cuts across the requirements of pregnancy work in relation to health guidance and 'good motherhood'.

I argue firstly that pregnant employees (while they may concurrently be criticized if they are seen to be transgressing the rules of good mothering by, for example, eating snack foods), are, generally expected to distance themselves from pregnancy while in the workplace, presenting themselves primarily in the image of healthy, reliable and 'professional' workers. Secondly, I observe how expectations that pregnant women will, metaphorically, put to one side their pregnant status while at work, privileging the requirements of employers while performing the work of the 'good' pregnant mother in secret, affect employed women at all levels in the labour market. It appears that many pregnant women, whether in well-paid skilled or poorly paid unskilled employment, are required to accommodate the needs of employers by fulfilling health-related pregnancy work in secret, while simultaneously maintaining a 'sparky professional front' (Kilby 2007) if they are to be accepted in the workplace. I begin by describing my own experiences of being pregnant and employed.

The first recollection I propose to share is of being at a UK medical conference with 200 delegates and of engaging in a debate about community health services with a senior public health doctor, and a hospital manager (both were colleagues and both were male). I was around 24 weeks pregnant, neatly dressed in a long dress which effectively shrouded, but could not entirely conceal, the pregnancy. My two colleagues knew of the pregnancy, but neither of them mentioned it and, as usual, neither did I. I felt well, yet distracted. The conference room was busy and I felt present and part of what was happening, yet at the same time absent. I was trying to focus on what my colleagues were saying and to give sensible answers. At the same time I was finding it difficult to pay attention to what was being said because, all the while, the baby was wriggling around and kicking. In the words of Sheila Kitzinger (2003: 15), it felt as if I had a 'jumping bean inside me'. As the baby kicked and squirmed, the public health director asked me a question. Instead of providing a direct answer, I blurted out: 'I'm sorry, I can't concentrate on what you are saying because the baby is moving all the time, it's been wriggling all morning.' This proved a real conversation stopper. Both colleagues looked nonplussed and stared at me open-mouthed. The doctor let out a surprised 'Oh!' A few moments of silence elapsed, then he repeated his question. I answered it, and we all continued as if nothing had happened.

The second memory relates to a subsequent pregnancy, during which I was unwell for the first four months and returned to my university post part-time, feeling guilty about having taken time off sick. The event which I recall took place in 2001, when I was eight months pregnant and facilitating a group of 30 childcare experts who were attempting jointly to agree a set of values. At the time, I did not have a permanent academic post and was worried about my contract, which was due to expire. This meant a possible reduction in maternity pay, plus an uncertain future. On that particular day I was tired, having attended a works dinner the previous evening. The process of facilitating the childcare group involved annotating flip charts which were strung across along all four walls of a large training room, like wallpaper. As the facilitator, I chaired the discussions, negotiating the exact form of words to be used in the childcare values, and transcribing the text onto the flip charts. The atmosphere was tense as participants tried to accommodate one anothers' needs, while each cherishing their own. On this occasion, the day was warm and the large room airless, and I was exhausted. My pregnant body felt heavy and unwieldy and was concealed within a voluminous borrowed dress. My feet and ankles were so swollen I could barely walk. My experience was similar to that of the pregnant woman described in Young's (2005: 53) account, in which 'the most ordinary efforts of human existence, such as sitting, bending and walking, which I formerly took for granted, become apparent as the projects they themselves are. Getting up, for example, increasingly becomes a task that requires my attention'.

Under normal circumstances I would have stood throughout the exercise, moving around the room as required to invite dialogue, mediate between participants and write on the flip chart 'wallpaper' as forms of words were agreed. On this occasion, however, I was so weary that I could barely stand. I sat down whenever possible and as comments were offered by each delegate to the wider group, I heaved myself from my chair and struggled to the flip charts, where I then transcribed what had been said. I had worked with the group for 18 months, knew them well, and usually enjoyed the challenge of helping them reach agreement using this method. On that day, though, I was struggling.

Each attempt to haul myself out of my chair seemed more of an effort and I felt worried about the impression I was giving the participants (might they perceive that I was not capable of doing my job to the usual standard?). I also felt guilty about the impact that pushing myself might have upon the baby (was I overdoing things?). I could have asked if someone would take over my role, at least in terms of the physical labour of roaming around the room and writing on flip charts, enabling me to continue to mediate the session from my chair, but I did not do this. Nor did I refer at all, at any time, to my pregnant status. Equally, one of the delegates could have offered to do the writing up on my behalf, but nobody did. The conversation remained focused strictly on the matter in hand and my ungainly body, my state of utter exhaustion and the presence of an almost fully grown baby, ill concealed by the unfamiliar dress, were not alluded to. On that day, in the context of the task and as a worker, I was present. But as a pregnant subject I was totally absent.

I have given these two examples to help explain how the challenge of combining the labour of pregnancy alongside the labour of paid work can be an extraordinary experience of presence, absence and conflicting obligations. As Young (2005) notes, there is a wealth of health research on pregnancy, and this is complemented by important feminist research on the experience of being a pregnant subject within highly medicalized Western settings (Pollock 1999; Oakley 1981, 1984). However, there has been a tendency to consider the labour of pregnancy (reproductive labour) and the labour of employment (productive labour) as two separate entities. Kitzinger (2003), for example, describes in detail the bodily and psychological process of pregnancy work, but devotes only two of 448 pages to the issue of being employed while pregnant. Many feminist writers focus on the labour of giving birth and writers such as Della Pollock (1999) and Ann Oakley (1981) write movingly of the social and familial experiences of being pregnant. However, while it is acknowledged that the issue of employment *following* maternity leave has been considered in detail in research on motherhood, the body and work (Hausman 2004; Boswell-Penc and Boyer 2007; Gatrell 2007a, 2007b), and while research exists on pregnancy discrimination at work (Equal Opportunities Commission (EOC) 2005a; Gatrell 2005; Collinson 2000), with certain exceptions (Longhurst 2001 and 2008; Gatrell 2005 and 2006c; Miller 2005), research on the social experience of combining pregnancy and paid work remains limited.

This could be seen as surprising, given the efforts, on the part of government agencies, to promote inclusive policies aimed at protecting the rights of employed pregnant women (Tahmincioglu 2007; Department for Business Enterprise and Regulatory Reform 2007). In theory, especially in Britain and America, pregnant women should be able to maintain their position at work without censure, due to legislation requiring organizations 'not to discriminate against women due to pregnancy . . . women must be treated equally with their male counterparts in all employment decisions' (Kohl *et al.* 2005: 427) and 'regardless of [their] employment status' (Department for Business Enterprise and Regulatory Reform 2007).

Despite 30 years of anti-discrimination laws, however, incidences of unfair treatment of pregnant women remain high in both Britain and America. In the UK, for example, as noted in Chapter 6, the EOC calculates that up to 30,000 women experience pregnancy discrimination each year. The EOC argues that such discrimination occurs partly due to an inaccurate belief, on the part of employers, that mothers lose their job focus once they become pregnant, and that motherhood is in any case 'incompatible with paid employment' (EOC 2004: 2).

In spite of the existence of anti-discrimination laws, pregnancy discrimination – like pregnancy itself – is both absent and present in the context of paid work and policy. In the USA and the UK, although anti-discrimination laws emphasize the need to treat pregnant women 'equally', specific references about how the pregnant body might be accommodated in the workplace are limited. In the UK, some employers are obliged to allow time for antenatal appointments, and there are guidelines in the UK and the USA about safety and sick pay. However, the notion that employers might change everyday working practices in order to accommodate pregnancy is largely absent from policy and recognition of the bodily changes associated with pregnancy is lacking.

In what follows, I underline the chasm between the health-related pregnancy work expected of individual women, which requires them to change their lifestyles in order to accommodate pregnancy, and the approach to pregnancy of most workplaces, which privilege the 'the norms of male embodiment' and do nothing to accommodate pregnancy. I also note the inconsistency between the medical approach to pregnancy, in which pregnant women are constructed as 'being in a "condition" in which they must take special care to protect the well-being of the fetus' (Longhurst 2001: 54), and employers' approach to pregnancy, in which pregnant women are encouraged to suppress the symptoms of pregnancy in order that they may 'carry their weight, and their usual workload' while looking 'smart' (Holland 2007: 1).

'Norms' of male embodiment at work

The notion that paid work is primarily associated with healthy male bodies has been put forward by a range of feminist scholars (Höpfl and Hornby Atkinson 2000; Longhurst 2001; Puwar 2004; Thomas 1999; Swan 2005). The concept of masculinity is seen by employers not only as the 'norm', but as representing 'ideal' traits of solidity, predictability and rationality, both physically and psychologically. Healthy, heterosexual male bodies are seen to be the 'gold standard' in the workplace, and even the healthy, non-pregnant female body already falls short of this. Edwards and Wajcman (2005: 80) suggest that the 'labelling of the manager as male' gives to masculine bodies 'the sanction of custom', which has become institutionalized and is therefore difficult to oppose. In this context, Höpfl and Hornby-Atkinson (2000: 138–9) suggest that the notion of the female body in the office is acceptable only if women are able to successfully 'blend in' their female bodily characteristics with predominantly male cultures. Martin (1989) has applied similar concerns specifically to working-class women, observing how they are expected to conceal from the workplace the bodily manifestations of reproduction. Thus, mothers who are able and/or willing to keep their reproductive capabilities 'off-stage' may aspire to the status of 'inferior men' (Höpfl and Hornby-Atkinson 2000: 135). For pregnant women, such demands are almost impossible to meet – the pregnant body, after all, underlines women's sexual difference from the male 'norm' at work. Longhurst (2001:65) observes how the bodies of pregnant women are highly visible, and treated as 'matter out of place' when they enter the 'public realm' of the workplace. Thus, employed women are placed under pressure to disavow their pregnancy while at work. They are compelled by employers and 'experts' to try and 'blend in' with 'the norms of male embodiment' by consistently presenting, at work, a pregnant body which appears 'healthy', 'reliable' and 'sparky'. In order to achieve this, many women feel obliged to work to even harder than usual, attaining a standard of exceptional performance and attempting to conceal and to contain all bodily manifestations of pregnancy – especially in relation to leakage.

The leaky reproductive body

Longhurst (2001) has suggested that the pregnant body is unwelcome at work because it threatens the conventional social order of things. This, she argues, it is due to the metaphorical and material tendency of the pregnant body to 'leak'. Such threats of leakage and instability mean that women's bodies 'invoke suspicion because they are seen to signify women's 'inherent lack of control of [their] bodies' and consequently of themselves. Grosz (1994) introduces ideas of disgust and fear in relation to women's reproductive functions. In a seminal observation which has been cited in relation to employment and the maternal body by Gatrell (2007b) and Longhurst (2001), Grosz (1994: 203) observes how:

> Women's corporeality is inscribed as a mode of seepage ... The association of femininity with contagion and disorder, the undecidability of the limits of the female body (. . . in the case of pregnancy) leads to the social definition of women as liquid, irrational bodies and incites revulsion.'

Shildrick (1997: 34) also links women's 'otherness' to their 'leaky' bodies. She focuses on the indefinability of the feminine body – which at any moment may expand to accommodate another body within itself, or which may potentially leak fluid. Thus, the pregnant body is seen as a particularly hazardous threat to workplace stability. Martin (1989) and Longhurst (2001) further observe that liquids connected with reproduction are associated, by employers, with poor health and maternal unreliability, this obliging employed mothers to conceal leakage of any kind. Thus, the physical symptoms of pregnancy – nausea, vomiting, expanding waistlines which cannot easily be contained within business dress, the threat of breaking waters and leaking breasts – must be concealed from others at work. As Longhurst (2001: 41) describes: 'The enlarging of the breasts ready for feeding the infant, the swelling of the stomach, the threat of the body leaking fluids and splitting itself in two, all this marks women's sexual Otherness'. Longhurst (2001: 41) goes on to explain that: 'Pregnant women's body fluids pose a threat to social control and order. [Others] may try to confine the pregnant woman to the private realm because of the threat that her leaking, seeping body . . . and her splitting self poses to a rational [male] public world.'

As it grows, the pregnant body is itself is unaccommodated by workplace norms, a scenario vividly illuminated by Tyler (2000: 290) who is obliged to 'manipulate' her 'heavily pregnant' body into a workplace space which is too small, struggling to manage the discomfort of 'a foot caught in my ribs . . . back ache and tumescent ankles', alongside the fear that her 'massive', 'leaky' pregnant body might 'split apart at any moment' and she might 'pour [her]self onto the floor in bits'.

For employed, pregnant women who are attempting to manage the kind of pregnancy work described above, while concurrently meeting workplace requirements to contain and conceal their pregnant embodiment, the inconsistent demands of health advice and employers are a chasm which it is almost impossible to span. Research by Lagan et al. (2006: 17) suggests that pregnant women are increasingly turning to the internet for information, support and advice on how to deal with complex, contemporary problems of this kind: 'The internet is one of the fastest-growing resources of information on . . . pregnancy and childbirth for many pregnant women.' Lagan et al. observe that pregnancy discussion fora, followed by pregnancy web clinics, are the most popular form of internet resource utilized by pregnant women, and the views and experiences of other women on the web are seen as a 'trusted source' of information.

My own research on pregnancy websites reveals a hidden community of pregnant workers who support and inform one another, apparently regarding the internet as a 'safe forum' where the problems of combining pregnancy and employment can be discussed. Conversations between women on pregnancy discussion fora, and web-based pregnancy advice clinics, suggest that the pregnant body, pregnancy symptoms and any references to pregnancy are seen as 'taboo' in the workplace. There is a gulf between the outlawing of discrimination promised by law, and the everyday experiences of pregnant workers. Pregnancy discrimination is commonplace, and this occurs regardless of occupational status. Whether message board participants are in high-status roles such as medicine, or in low-skilled roles such as care assistants, employed pregnant bodies at work are likely to be treated as deviant from workplace norms. Seemingly, employers and co-workers are prepared to tolerate the pregnant body only on the condition that women contain and conceal the physical effects of pregnancy, so that workplace 'norms' are not disrupted. Thus, most pregnant employees feel obliged to conceal and to 'control' their pregnant bodies. Women feel pressured to hide pregnancy by keeping it secret for as long as possible and by keeping quiet about pregnancy at work. Pregnant women feel under duress to 'prove' themselves by working at least to their usual standard, but often much harder, often striving for a standard which I term 'healthy supra-performance' in order to try and blend in with workplace 'norms' associated with 'ideal' male bodies.

Of the many hundreds of internet discussions about pregnancy and employment, one of the most common topics is how and when to tell employers about the pregnancy. Almost all pregnant women joining in pregnancy website discussions are afraid of announcing their pregnancy at work. They are keen to hide from employers the news of their pregnancy and to conceal their pregnant state for as long as possible. This may be because message board conversations indicate that, once pregnancy is made known, the majority of women experience negative attitudes and behaviour from employers and co-workers. One (very typical) account of workplace reaction to pregnancy is provided by Tina, an office assistant who recounts how, ever since she announced her pregnancy, 'the atmosphere [in the office has become] unbearable'. Tina explains that she is now 'hounded' at work to the point that she is feeling 'at the end of [her] tether'. Tina says of her situation:

> I'm 16 weeks pregnant and yet no risk assessment has been carried out on me. I can't stand going to work and find that I am in tears nearly

every day due to the way they speak to me. Everyone expects a lot from me and yes, I work to a high standard, but at the moment I am not coping.

In keeping with the observations of Longhurst (2001:41), Tina describes how her pregnant body is treated as an 'ugly' object of disgust and abjection. Her expanding waistline is viewed with horror by colleagues and she is advised to cut down on her food intake, as if this might somehow contain her unpredictable and swelling body.

Pregnancy websites are crammed with advice pieces written by 'experts' on pregnancy and employment. Most of these advice pieces are presented as 'helpful' but seem, in their approach, almost to be colluding with negative employer behaviour by treating the idea of hostile workplace reactions to pregnancy as 'normal'. Women are advised to conceal and contain pregnancy, and to delay the announcement of pregnancy for as long as possible (What To Expect 2007; Verybestbaby 2007; Family Education 2007). Once pregnancy has been declared, pregnant women are discouraged from discussing it at work. Holland (2007: 2) warns mothers to 'put a lid on the baby talk' and Kilby (2007) advises pregnant women to 'keep things to yourself'. Holland (2007: 2) explains that maintaining silence about pregnancy is important because 'aside from being annoying', references to pregnancy 'could send signals to your boss that you're not taking your job seriously enough'.

Expectant mothers are further counselled to acknowledge that their pregnancy could cause 'real problems' at work (Verybestbaby 2007) and it is generally suggested that, once pregnancy is made known, pregnant women should make strenuous efforts to appease and accommodate employers, rather than the other way around: 'Make it clear that you will be as flexible as possible about time off for antenatal appointments and stress that as a healthy woman, you expect your role to be unaffected' (Kilby 2007).

Healthy supra-performance and the employed pregnant body

Most 'expert' advice exhorts pregnant women to strive for supra-performance at work, if they wish to remain employed. Pregnant women are encouraged to atone for their pregnant status by undertaking significant extra work *in addition* to the 'normal' productive labour of paid work by, for example, working long hours and 'proving' themselves to be reliable in spite of their pregnant bodies. Family Education (2007) advocates that pregnant women should do more than 'the norm', if they are to avoid 'hostility' from managers and associates. Babyworld suggests pregnant women may feel too tired to think, but should nevertheless at all times 'maintain a sparky professional front, in case anyone accuses you of not pulling your load. . . . Unfair, yes, but that's office culture. Fight back. . . . And walk and talk to colleagues – don't use lazy email!' (Kilby 2007).

Correspondence between women on pregnancy message boards suggests that such advice is in keeping with pressures exerted on pregnant women by employers and co-workers to 'prove' themselves by taking on an 'increased workload' (Babyworld 2006b), and many pregnant employees appear under to be duress to comply with these expectations. Tina, who provided the example above, and states that she is feeling 'exhausted', observes:

> I am working so hard, over and above my duties. . . . I am constantly on the go.

Rebecca, a community nurse, shares with others on another internet pregnancy forum the pressures she is under to gain additional qualifications in her 'spare' time

> I work full time, run a house and look after my [eldest], I already have one course on the go that they have sent me on, and now they've just enrolled me on another 4 month course to do all in my own time at home . . . I asked if I could do the course [later], but was told [I must] do this course – after all, it was being paid for and I should be grateful.

The notion of supra-performance is embodied and is associated with idealized notions of 'healthy' bodies. In order to be tolerated at work, pregnant women are expected to be 'supra-performing', and in order to achieve supra-performance, pregnant women are expected to put on a 'healthy' performance no matter how ill or exhausted they may feel. In particular, the maintenance of a supra-performing, healthy front, requires pregnant women to conceal the unpredictable physical symptoms of pregnancy to convince colleagues that they are able to sustain at least the same level of bodily function and stamina as they did prior to pregnancy. 'Expert' website advice recommends the management of the pregnant body so that it appears to behave in a manner which is predictable and reliable. 'Presenteeism' – in which workers are present in the office when feeling unwell – appears to be required of pregnant women and is completely at odds with health advice which constructs pregnancy as an illness, a 'condition' which requires 'care' (Longhurst 2001).

For example, Holland (2007: 2) argues that

> many pregnant women feel lousy but that's no excuse for easing up on the job or becoming grumpy . . . no matter how tempting it may be to [take time off] every time you feel under the weather, you really

need to fight through that . . . so try not to be derailed by hormonal issues.

The requirement to be present at work and to appear healthy means that some women find it difficult to take time away from work for essential antenatal and screening appointments, and strive to conceal these so they are less 'noticable' (Gatrell 2007a). This further places women in the situation where the requirements of fulfilling the health 'work' of pregnancy are incompatible with the requirement to present at work a 'healthy body'.

Inevitably, the 'healthy' supra-performance demanded of pregnant employees requires pregnant women to contain, and control the messiness of pregnancy – the physical symptoms of leakage which are associated with poor health and unreliability such as bleeding, nausea and sickness, (Warren and Brewis 2004). In practice, this may be problematic because, as Kitzinger (2003) points out, leakage in the most literal sense occurs throughout pregnancy, unpredictably and in a variety of ways, ranging from 'morning' sickness (which affects up to 75% of women, may occur at any time of day and may continue throughout pregnancy) to unpredicted bleeding, leaking colostrum and leaking milk. Week by week, the body changes shape, and as the baby grows it moves, pressing on the ribs, causing discomfort, and on the bladder, causing the need to go to the toilet more often. By the end of pregnancy, the 'waters' will break and, as Kitzinger (2003: 251) describes, 'this may happen suddenly with a rush of water, or more likely with a slow trickle of water. You may not be sure whether the bag of waters has burst or whether you are wetting your pants.' Hormonal changes mean that emotions are acutely felt and pregnant women maybe more prone to tears than usual – another form of leakage which is likely to be unwelcome at work.

Unsurprisingly, in these circumstances, women attempting to fulfil embodied norms in the workplace via 'healthy' supra-performance often fear the embodied betrayal of pregnancy through unpredictable leakage of bodily fluids. Robyn Longhurst (2001), for example, describes her own attempts to hide pregnancy sickness from colleagues, as if nausea in the workplace was a source of shame which she felt must be concealed. Longhurst (2001: 45) expresses her fears that nausea might cause her to be sent home from the workplace and that colleagues might respond with abject horror.

It would appear, then, that the pressure to present a 'healthy' pregnant body at work obliges women to suppress, cover up and control the bodily manifestations of pregnancy so as to inconvenience employers as little as possible. Regardless of whether pregnant employees are employed at 'professional' levels, like Robyn Longhurst, or in less skilled roles, like Tina, women appear to accept the notion that manifestations of pregnancy are 'taboo' at work and are prepared to comply with the pressures to conceal and control pregnancy. Pregnant employees appear to recognize the notion that they may be required to 'prove' themselves with a workplace performance more productive than before pregnancy.

In this respect, it appears almost as though an unoffical and unwritten but powerful policy – completely at odds with what is espoused in legislation – is in place. The main thrust of this 'policy' – with which women are encouraged, by 'experts', to comply – is that pregnancy may be tolerated in the workplace *only* if women comply with the conditions of concealment, silence and 'healthy' supra-performance. This form of pregnancy discrimination has reached the point that employed pregnant women can survive in the workplace only by abjecting themselves from their pregnant bodies. They are obliged to hide pregnancy and its symptoms, to maintain silence about pregnancy and to achieve a level of 'supra-performance' and presenteeism which is difficult to reconcile with the requirement to be absent from work for antenatal appointments. Pregnancy may be present, but the pregnant body is concealed by expectant mothers and disregarded by employers. The employed pregnant body, while present in the workplace is, also therefore, concurrently, absent.

Why should this be? One possible explanation why pregnancy is 'taboo' at work may be that conventionally, as Young (2005: 55) observes, 'discourse on pregnancy omits subjectivity, for the specific experience of women has been absent from most of our culture's discourse about human experience and history'. Young (2005: 46) argues that, in the context of Western medicine, 'pregnancy does not belong to the woman herself. It is a state of the developing fetus, for which the women is a container, it is an objective observable process coming under scientific scrutiny, or it becomes objectified by the woman herself'. Citing Kristeva, Young (2005: 46) observes that there are few 'treatises' which are 'concerned with the subject, the mother, as the site of her proceedings'. Western health practices thus construct the growing fetus as a separate and individual entity with needs which women, as expectant mothers, must meet by, for example, attending screening tests and relinquishing particular foodstuffs.

The tendency to alienate and separate women from their pregnancy is carried over into other aspects of life, and this applies to women who are combining pregnancy with employment. Young (2005: 55) suggests that 'A subject's experience or action is alienated when it is defined or controlled by a subject who does not share one's assumptions or goals'. The goals of employers related to productive labour are unconnected to the labour of pregnancy. For this reason, expectant women may feel obliged to accommodate the 'norms of male embodiment at work' (Hausman 2004: 276) by trying to 'blend in' with what Höpfl and Hornby Atkinson (2000: 137) describe as 'predominantly male [way of working], defined by men for men and established as the normative basis for working arrangements' throughout pregnancy.

Earlier on in this chapter, I suggested that, while there is a growing body of research on combining productive labour with new motherhood, which I consider below, research on the social experience of combining pregnancy and paid work remains limited. In effect, the 'absence' of the pregnant body at work is reflected by an absence of discussion about pregnancy and work in scholarly literature – especially in journals related to management and management practices. This, in its turn, is related to discounting of the labour of pregnancy, which tends not to be articulated as 'work', even though the performance of pregnant women is measured against complex and demanding health standards throughout.

Conclusions

The purpose of this chapter has been to argue for the articulation of pregnancy as a form of work, both in relation to the embodied work of pregnancy (in which the baby is supposed to come first) and the embodied work of employment (for which purpose the baby is supposed to remain hidden). The ever-present theme in the chapter has been the requirement for women to subjugate their bodies to the needs of others, prioritizing the needs of the baby in order to meet the requirements of 'good' mothering as defined within health guidelines, while concurrently suppressing and concealing bodily changes so as to meet employer expectations. The pregnancy work of the 'good mother' and the pregnancy work of 'supra-performance' within the workplace share two things in common. Both require women to put themselves at the bottom of the priority list and both have conventionally been hidden from view. Thus, the self-regulation and clinic attendance required to follow the advice of health practitioners is taken for granted, and obfuscated behind the discourse of 'good' mothering, while the pregnancy (and the following of health advice) must be concealed within the workplace, so as not to disrupt workplace 'norms'.

In conclusion, I suggest that pregnancy should be reconceptualized as an embodied form of women's work which is acknowledged, and included in 'the articulation of work activities' (Glucksmann 2005: 19; Truman 1996). I further argue that new attempts must be made to change workplace attitudes towards pregnancy, so that pressure is placed upon employers to accommodate the work of pregnancy. The situation where women are required to perform pregnancy work in secret in the workplace should be highlighted and should no longer be tolerated. Managing the work of pregnancy in late modern society is already difficult enough, and women should be able to do this without facing the kinds of constraints faced by Tina and others. Employed pregnant women should not, therefore, be expected to conform to 'embodied male norms' (Hausman 2004: 276) at work, but should be able to combine the labour of pregnancy with paid work without the requirements for silence, concealment and 'healthy supra-performance'.

5 'Love is not enough': Birth, new motherhood and employment

Introduction

In this chapter I explore the interrelated topics of women's reproductive and productive work, looking specifically at birth and breastfeeding. Key to my argument is the idea that notions of 'choice', in relation to birth and the embodied labour of new motherhood, are largely illusory. Thus, women are supposedly offered 'choice' in relation to how they give birth, but in practice opportunities for maternal decision-making about how and where to give birth are very narrow. In exploring ideas about motherhood and paid work, I acknowledge that this is an ongoing issue for women with dependent children of all ages. However, for the purposes of this chapter I focus on the time when women's embodied mothering work is at its most demanding: when children are of pre-school age and at their most physically dependent. In particular, I explore the relationship between women's embodied maternal work and the management of the maternal body in the workplace, through a discussion of breastfeeding practices. I suggest that in the rearing and nourishing of small children, and in the subsequent management of their new maternity in the workplace, breastfeeding women are constrained by a variety of social expectations which, as in the case of pregnancy work, are often conflicting. Thus, the pressure on women to breastfeed beyond the first year of babies' lives is intense, and breastfeeding initiation and duration rates are measured by health services. However, breastfeeding is seen to be a 'natural' element of mothering, and is thus not articulated as 'work' – nor is it accommodated within the context of employment.

As I observed in the previous chapter, the labour of reproduction – of bearing and raising children – is still, arguably, regarded as a more 'appropriate' form of women's work than the labour of production and employment, even in developed, late modern societies, especially if women are well educated and middle-class. While the responsibility for reproduction may lie with women, however, the manner of giving birth and raising children is rarely left to mothers' discretion and women are bombarded with a confusing and often conflicting range of health guidance and social opprobrium in relation to every aspect of the labour of birth and motherhood. In a society which draws upon notions of individualization and agency (Beck and Beck-Gernsheim 1995), mothers are often informed by health agencies, policy-makers and employers that they have 'choices' about how to perform the labour of birth, and how to rear and nourish their children. In practice, however, maternal 'choices' are very limited and, as in the case of pregnancy, maternal discretion and decision-making with regard to birth and infant feeding are constrained by pressure to conform to the expectations of others, including health professionals and employers. Mothers are often expected to perform the work of birth, and subsequently childcare, to the most exacting of standards in the context of oppressive narratives about 'good' mothering (Miller 2005) and (especially in the case of breastfeeding) social imperatives about what constitutes acceptable, public, embodied behaviour (Kitzinger 2005).

Birth 'choices'

In relation to birth practices, conflicting opinions exist as to how the notion of choice may be interpreted. These differing viewpoints tend to focus on arguments around the benefits of supposedly 'natural' birth versus the advantages of more technological approaches. In particular, concerns are raised about the disparity between what appears to be the range of 'choices' offered to women by health agencies, and the experiences of birthing women in practice. Cultural feminist Della Pollock (1999) suggests that women who wish to make active birth 'choices' will find these difficult to achieve if they conflict with obstetric guidelines. Thus, she alludes to the idea of birthing 'choices' in military terms – as 'resisting the alienating effects of hospital', using 'guerilla tactics and subterfuge' and 'going in there and fighting' (Pollock 1999: 21).

Since the 1970s, in both the UK and the USA, there has been a growing concern with birth practices and the notion of maternal birth 'choice' both from a biomedical perspective and from a feminist viewpoint. 'Birth' has been a focus for feminist scholarship since the 1970s and early 1980s, when writers such as Rich (1977), Oakley (1981) and Rothman (1982) expressed concerns about the medicalization of childbirth in Britain and the USA. Research on the politics and practices of birth has developed since then, because changing health practices and technologies (such as IVF) have transformed social understandings and individual experiences of reproduction since the 1970s. Nevertheless, 'birth' (by which I mean not only the biomedical approach to child-bearing, but also the range of embodied and social practices associated with birth) continues to be the subject of intensive debate, to which concerns expressed in the 1980s about 'choice' and mothers' lack of autonomy remain central.

This is because, while birth technologies may have altered since the 1980s, birth practices remain remarkably resistant to change – at least in UK and North American contexts. Thus, in 1984, Ann Oakley argued that mothers should be able to take greater control of the birth process, and expressed dissatisfaction with the notion that 'the wombs of women are containers to be captured by the ideologies and practices of those who . . . do not believe that women are able to take care of themselves' (Oakley 1984: 292), an argument which is still the main focus of discussion among scholars and birth campaigners such as Sheila Kitzinger (2003). Kitzinger, who has been described as the 'high priestess' of the birth movement (Kitzinger 2006), has sought for years to question technocratic birth cultures. She challenges what she regards as the requirement for women to surrender, to medical institutions, control of their pregnant bodies, for example giving birth to suit hospital timescales while 'tethered' to a hospital bed. Kitzinger and the National Childbirth Trust in the UK, and Pollock (1999) in the USA, have also contested the notion that women who resist medical interventions such as scans and amniocentesis are irresponsible and negligent.

It is over twenty years since Kitzinger's first book was published, yet in relation to notions of maternal 'choice' very little appears to have changed and the arguments put forward in Kitzinger's early work differ very little from the discussions in her most recent volumes (Kitzinger 2006). This is in spite of the fact that Kitzinger's arguments are apparently in keeping with the promises made by government health agencies such as the UK NHS, which proclaims its 'commitment to offer all women and their partners a wider choice of type and place of maternity care and birth . . . and . . . opportunities to make well informed decisions about their care throughout pregnancy, birth and postnatally' (Department of Health 2007: 5).

However, research suggests that such choices appear, in practice, to be very limited. For example, Miller (2005: 94), in her study of new mothers' embodied experiences of giving birth, and using similar terminology to that of Pollock (1999), observes that 'although [mothers] initially adopt strategies that question and resist expert practices, eventually they succumb as choices apparently run out'.

The idea that women should have 'choice' with regard to the manner and place of birth is important because, as women writing on childbirth have argued for many years, birth practices have important and long-term consequences for women's health. As Oakley (1981: 2) argued: 'The beginning of motherhood is immensely important and the way in which a birth is managed could influence a woman's whole experience of being a mother'. More recently, and in a similar vein, Kitzinger (2006: 4–6) has observed how birth practices which focus on the biomedical, but not the social and emotional needs of women have far-reaching consequences. [Birth] is likely to affect the way a woman feels not only about herself but about her baby and her partner. It can have catastrophic effects on relationships. Care needs to be changed [so that] post-traumatic stress after birth can be prevented.

In the twenty-first century, the conflicts between biomedical concerns around 'safety' and discourses about 'natural' childbirth, and the tensions between birth 'choices' which are available in theory, but which are impossible for many women to access in practice, are evident. Thus, women who seek to give birth vaginally and in a hospital setting may be able to exercise some 'choice' around the detail (for example, health professionals are likely to support the desire for lavender oil or relaxation tapes), but women who want a home birth, or seek who a Caesarean delivery for personal (as opposed to biomedical) reasons, are likely to meet resistance.

The relocating of childbirth from a midwifery-led, home-based setting to an obstetrics-led, male-dominated hospital context has been well documented. Since the 1970s, when midwifery and childbirth came firmly under the control of obstetricians – who even now are often male, (Pringle 1998) – many feminist writers on pregnancy and childbirth have interpreted the medical management of childbirth as being linked with the idea of living in a society which is inherently patriarchal. The 'male' control of the female birthing body has been seen (Rich 1977; Oakley 1981; Rothman 1982; Kitzinger 2005) as symbolic of the wider oppression of women by men in society. Pollock (1999: 13) argues that the desire to technicalize birth is also classed, and that this is driven by both men *and* women. She suggests that

> the history of birthing in the United States is part of the larger history of industrialization, a history driven by general confidence in the advantages of scientific and technological 'progress'. Men and women shared this vision. Both were driven – although perhaps for different reasons – to perfect the birth process. Both were deeply invested in what has been generally characterized as a 'masculine' ideology of control over the body as a material object: a machine, literally a means of production. Indeed the rise in reproductive technologies – from the use of anesthesia and forceps to cesarean section . . . has been fuelled by a middle class eager . . . to maintain lines of biological descendance and inheritance [and] to exercise its rights and power to purchase within what would become an industrial economy of (re)production.

Whether we believe that the technolgizing of birth is due to the male oppression of birthing women, or the result of the growing industrial economy in which men and women hoped that new technologies would make the labour of birth safer and less painful, or, as I conclude, a mixture of both these elements, it is certainly the case that by the mid-1970s, most women in Britain and America gave birth in hospital, and not at home. Today, to the dismay of the home birth lobby, some hospitals in the UK deliver as many as 8,000 babies per year within large and high-tech maternity units which are part of larger hospital buildings (Bosanquet *et al.* 2005). Rates of home birth in the UK dropped sharply from the 1970s onwards and have remained low ever since. Since the 1980s the number of home births in the UK has remained low varying between 1% and 2.7% (Bosanquet *et al.* 2005). These figures probably overstate the situation, since all births which do not take place in hospital are classed as 'home' births. Thus, births which were unplanned emergencies (occurring, for example, in a car or ambulance on the way to hospital) are included in the 'home birth' statistics. There are some industrialized countries where home birth is more common than in it is in the UK and the USA. In the Netherlands, for example, home birth rates have traditionally been much higher at almost 30%, but the indications are that there, also, home birth rates are falling in favour of hospital births.

Among proponents of 'natural' birth, in which women give birth without drugs or monitoring systems, preferably at home or in a homely setting, hospital birth is seen as symbolic of, and synonymous with, the idea of birth as a form of production. Kitzinger (2006: 4) claims that many women in childbirth, in hospitals, are 'treated like products on a conveyor belt, their labours are obstetrically "managed" [by others] and technocracy distorts the birth experience'. The requirement for women to perform the labour of birth in accordance with hospital regimes 'in situations where they are helpless and trapped' (2006: 3) has been cited as the cause of post-traumatic stress disorder among some women (Kitzinger 2006: 2–3, 5, 152–3). This suggests little improvement upon the situation described by Ann Oakley over 30 years earlier, in which she described the medical management of childbirth in similar terms (Oakley 1981).

Following prolonged campaigns, women's groups such as the Boston Women's Health Book Collective (USA) and the National Childbirth Trust (UK) have attempted to enhance and improve women's knowledge about, and autonomy in the context of, birth. Birthing partners are now allowed to be present during hospitalized labour and birth – which Pollock (1999) sees as a mixed blessing – and women are now rarely obliged to undergo the humiliation of enemas and the shaving of pubic hair (Wolf 2006). Nevertheless, as Kitzinger argues above, it remains the case that for many women who give birth in hospital, any real sense of 'choice' is constrained by obstetric protocols.

In theory, steps have been taken to try and change this situation. In the UK, at the end of the twentieth and the start of the twenty-first century, there have been a range of government initiatives with the stated aims of making childbirth more 'woman centred', in particular *Changing Childbirth* (Department of Health 1993) and *Maternity Matters* (Department of Health 2007). Both of these documents purport to extend women's choices around the choice of place, and type of delivery.

However, despite promises made within these government reports that women should be able to make 'choices' about how and where they give birth, it is arguable that birth choices have in practice become increasingly restricted. For example, the Department of Health (1993) noted with concern the dwindling number of small, midwifery-led birthing centres available in the UK, and challenged the increasing trend for women automatically to be booked into large maternity units within district general hospitals. The *Changing Childbirth* report advocated the benefits for some women of giving birth in small birthing centres, in privacy and away from home, but in a smaller and less medicalized setting than a hospital. It was suggested that, in small birthing centres, care could be individualized and driven more by mothers' needs than by the collective regimes of large hospital maternity units. Retaining and/or extending the option of the small birth centre was seen, in 1993, as especially important in circumstances where space in mothers' homes was limited and there were already other children, and also in relation to ethnic minority women, who it was felt might benefit from the more relaxed and personal approach. Fourteen years after the publication of *Changing Childbirth*, the Department of Health (2007: 12) continues to advocate 'Birth supported by a midwife in a local midwifery facility such as a designated local midwifery unit of birth centre . . . These units promote a philosophy of normal and natural labour and childbirth.'

Birth outcomes in small birthing centres are good. A study of over 12,000 women in the USA who delivered their babies in birth centres showed that death rates, and the rates of health problems for mothers and babies, were similar to those in larger hospital settings, but with less medical interventions (Rooks *et al.* 1992). Similarly, in 2000, in a case study of the London-based Edgware birth centre, women were shown to be less likely to need Caesarean sections, or other medical procedures, than would be usual in a large maternity unit (Kitzinger 2006). Small birth centres might, therefore, appear on paper to be an attractive compromise between the impersonal nature of a large hospital and the idea of giving birth at home, which might feel very risky to women brought up in a society where hospital birth is the 'norm'.

In practice, however, for most women the option of going to a small birth centre may be difficult to take up. Despite the 1993 recommendations, the number of 'small' midwifery-led maternity units in the UK has continued to fall (Walsh 2006). According to Department of Health figures, the number of small birth centres fell from 527 in 1973, to 341 in 1996, and to 188 in 2003 (Bosanquet *et al.* 2005). At the same time, the centralization of maternity services has increased, with nine units delivering between 5,000 and 6,000 babies per year and one unit (Liverpool Women's Hospital) delivering more than 8,000 babies per year (Bosanquet *et al.* 2005: 12). The Department of Health (2007: 12) acknowledges these problems in its qualifying remarks: 'The [small birth unit] might be based in the community, or in a hospital; patterns of care vary across the country to reflect different local needs. Women will be able to choose any other available midwifery unit in England.' In other words, it is perfectly possible that the midwifery-led care associated with small birth units might either be situated within a large general hospital, or be located so far away from the mother's home that giving birth there is totally impractical – as Kitzinger (2006) points out: 'The trouble is that a woman is fortunate if she has a birth centre near her.' Small birth centres where midwives operate independently of district general hospital services are so rare, that Powys, in Wales, which does offer midwifery-led care in a small birth centre, is described by the *RCM Midwives Journal* as being in the 'unique position of providing a purely midwife-led service without a district general hospital or medical team' (Lewis and Langley 2007).

Home birth

The reduction in opportunity to give birth in small units has not been replaced by the 'choice' of giving birth at home. This might seem surprising because in government policy documents, the option of home birth continues to be foregrounded, and is presented as if it provides a realistic option for mothers. In 1993, *Changing Childbirth* advocated that some women would benefit from the opportunity to give birth at home, with a midwife taking the role of lead professional and without medical interventions. Calling for health services to make home birth a viable option, *Changing Childbirth* acknowledged that mothers' emotional and psychological needs were often not met in general hospital maternity units. The report argued that this was because larger units, even with the best of intentions, often orientated maternity care to accommodate the needs of the hospital, not the needs of individual women. *Changing Childbirth* thus emphasized the importance of meeting mothers' psychosocial needs, as well as providing a high standard of physical care. The document suggested that mothers should be offered the choice of giving birth at home: 'the policy of encouraging all women to give birth in hospitals cannot be justified on grounds of safety' (Department of Health, 1993: 1).

Advocates of 'natural' and or 'normal' labour and childbirth such as Kitzinger (2006) argue that planned home births can be very satisfying for mothers, partners and midwives because the home setting means that mothers are less constrained by hospital protocols and are likely to have more say in decisions about how they wish their labour to be managed. In a qualitative study, and in line with Kitzingers's arguments, Longworth *et al.* (2001) argue that home births are more likely to result in a natural birth, free from interventions and 'allowing nature to take its course'. Kitzinger (2006) and Longworth *et al.* (2001) further suggest that home births are a more emotionally satisfying experience than are hospital births. In this context it is interesting to note that (as observed earlier) in the Netherlands, 30% of births take place at home and this is associated with low Caesarean rates (Odent 2003).

It is important to recognize here that while home birth might offer some women a sense that they are in control of their own labour and birth, and that the atmosphere of home might feel very comforting and intimate for some women, this is not the case for all. The discussion about home birth is classed, and the prospect of giving birth to a child in accommodation which may be cramped and poorly furnished is less inviting than the thought of labouring in a comfortable bedroom with en-suite facilities. Furthermore, for women with large families, the time spent in hospital with the new baby may be very precious. One woman, Elsa, who took part in my own recent (unpublished) research on the maternal body stated:

> I said to [the hospital staff] please don't send me home, I have got three children now and when I go home I'll have to do everything. I need this space, please don't send me home yet, and I cried and they let me stay for three days.

Equally, it is acknowledged that for some women, in keeping with the views of Kitzinger (2006) and Rothman (1982), home birth is far preferable to the idea of labouring and giving birth in hospital. It is also important to recognize that, given the reduction of small birth centres, home birth would for many women be the only option other than a hospital birth. In this context, it is interesting to observe how, despite the lack of progress, since *Changing Childbirth*, in making home birth a viable option, the *Maternity Matters* report foregrounds home birth as if this were a realistic 'choice' for many women and it is stated (Department of Health 2007: 5):

> Depending on their circumstances, women and their partners will be able to choose between three different options. These are:
>
> - a home birth
> - birth in a local facility, including a hospital, under the care of a midwife
> - birth in a hospital supported by a local maternity care team including midwives, anaesthetist and consultant obstetrician, For some women this will be the safest option.

As in the case of small birth centres, however, while home birth might *appear* as an option in policy documents, it remains the exception. Of the approximately 700,000 births registered annually in England, Scotland and Wales, only around 2% take place at home (Bosanquet *et al.* 2005: 12) – slightly more than in 1993 but indicating (as noted earlier) that home birth is still a rare event. It has been argued by Longworth *et al.* (2001) that these figures do not reflect the potential demand for home birth because a high percentage of women may not be aware that this option is available to them. Longworth *et al.*'s (2001) study explored UK women's preferences for place of delivery and found that 42% of mothers surveyed had not been given any information regarding alternative locations for giving birth other than their main, local hospital unit. The situation in the USA is similar, with most births taking place in a hospital setting (Pollock 1999). Health services are often resistant to the idea of home births for a range of reasons. These include fears of problems and litigation, fears about attending home birth (midwives who are unfamiliar with delivering babies outside large hospital settings become less confident about supporting home births) and fears about safety. As Bosanquet *et al.* (2005: 12) suggest, 'the justification for this centralisation [of maternity care] has been to save money and improve patient safety but the effect has been to remove patient choice'. In the context of my own research, it is apparent that persuading the 'authorities' to facilitate home birth is not easy and those women who do manage to achieve a home birth tend to be those who are articulate, relatively affluent and, often, those who have medical knowledge – perhaps because they are already qualified nurses or doctors.

Thus, for the vast majority of women in the UK – and also in North America (Pollock 1999) – the only available option in relation to 'choice of place of birth' (Department of Health 2007: 5) is a hospital birth, possibly in a large maternity unit serving 4,000 or more women per year. This may reduce the opportunity for midwives to focus on women's individual needs, and on this basis Kitzinger (2006: 17) argues that, following a hospital birth, many new mothers still feel as if they have been shoehorned into 'a social system that regulates her behaviour ... a bureaucracy designed to conformity and obedience and a hierarchical management structure that punishes deviance and rewards uncritical adherence to the rules and protocols it dictates'.

Kitzinger's remarks reflect an extraordinary situation, where apparently open and flexible offers of maternal 'choice' mask highly restrictive practices on the part of health services. The UK Department of Health (2007: 2) expresses a desire to offer 'choice over where and how to give birth' in the knowledge that, for most women, the range of options will be limited to their local hospital. Miller (2005) has highlighted the pressures faced by expectant mothers in the UK and USA, where the technicalization and medicalization of birthing practices has become the 'norm' in late modern society, to conform to prescribed notions of labouring and giving birth. Miller (2005: 51) observes that 'The lowering of both perinatal and maternal mortality rates and issues of safety and perceptions of risk have become inextricably bound up in . . . the shift to hospital based deliveries and the expert management of pregnancy and childbirth', with obstetricians using the language of safety and paternity to explain the need for mothers to give birth in hospital.

Notions of safety, and the idea that every pregnant woman and her baby are 'at risk' until the baby has been delivered without incident, have for years been central to the justification of the hospitalization of birth, and the requirement for women to conform to hospital regimes (Oakley 1993: 135). The UK Department of Health (2007: 5) promises women 'wider choice' while simultaneously using the notion of 'safety' to circumscribe this offer. 'Safety' is wielded as the weapon which persuades women to comply with hospital protocols, and this is intricately wrapped up in the ideas about 'good' mothering which I discussed in the previous chapter. In hospital, notions of 'good' mothering are closely associated with the idea that women will follow professional advice and protocols without argument. This puts women in the situation where any challenge to obstetric guidelines may cast them in the role of 'bad mother'. In this context, Kitzinger (1992: 73) has argued that obstetricians (often men) use the suggestion of 'risk' to enable them to retain control of childbirth, women who question medical advice being regarded as irresponsible and foolish. As such, the birthing mother is subject to 'Emotional blackmail. . . . In childbirth she may be warned that she must accept hospital protocols and obstetric decisions for the baby's sake . . . [thus] obstetric power is legitimized' (1992: 73). 'For many women, childbirth is an ordeal in which they are disempowered. Control of their bodies is torn from them' (1992: 68). As one woman puts it: 'The professional team was very efficient. The baby is lovely. But I don't feel a whole person' (1992: 74).

Narratives of 'natural' motherhood

One of the (presumably unintended) effects of campaigns to detechnicalize birth, has been to increase the pressure of the work involved in giving birth by raising women's expectations that they 'should' be able to deliver babies 'naturally' – in other words, without drugs, anaesthetics or medical interventions. Both birth experts and health professionals urge birthing women to aspire to narrow and demanding ideals in which 'good' and/or 'natural' births (and consequently 'good' motherhood) are defined by mothers' ability to labour and give birth within a hospital setting, but without medical assistance. Thus, health agencies call for 'all women to be supported and encouraged to have as normal a pregnancy and birth as possible' (Department of Health 2007: 2), and the Royal College of Midwives has established the Campaign for Normal Birth. Miller (2005: 89) has observed how mothers feel pressured by narratives of 'natural' motherhood to 'act responsibly through interactions with experts and expert practices [in hospital]' while concurrently striving for 'natural' deliveries, drawing upon 'essentialist ideas of women's natural capacity to give birth and instinctively cope'.

This expectation that women should give birth 'naturally' or 'normally' within a hospital setting is ironic, since it has been long established that hospitalization often leads to intervention, for example forceps or ventouse deliveries, narcotics and epidurals.[1] Many contemporary women delivering vaginally in hospital will, thus, still find themselves in the position described by Adrienne Rich in 1977: 'No more devastating image could be invented for the bondage of woman: . . . drugged . . . and her legs in stirrups at the very moment when she is bringing new life into the world' (Rich 1977: 171).

As Miller (2005) suggests, 'relinquishing' oneself to medical assistance in this way involves mixed feelings for women. Most mothers who have given birth to a healthy child are grateful. However, feelings of gratitude are accompanied by resentment and a sense of failure and defeat as women struggle to prove themselves as 'natural' mothers who do not 'need medical help' (Miller 2005: 95) while performing the labour of childbirth in a hospital setting. Thus, ideals of 'good motherhood', in relation to the work of labour and birth, have become a confusing mixture of essentialist ideals about 'natural motherhood' (in which women are responsible for quality and the birth is a product in its own right), combined with the notion that giving birth is unsafe unless a woman labours within a large-scale hospital, in which the baby is the 'product' and a healthy child (and not the performance of birth) is the measure of success.

Given that contemporary interpretations of maternal 'choice' regard the acceptance of medical intervention within hospital maternity units as indicative of failure, it is unsurprising that some women who have Caesarean sections regard themselves as having 'failed'. In a newspaper interview, the actress Kate Winslet expressed her deep feelings of inadequacy on having her baby delivered by Caesarean (Atkins 2004). Although Caesarean deliveries are now common in developed countries (in the UK the rate is around 22%, Royal College of Obstetricians and Gynaecologists 2001), this is regarded as an unhealthy trend and as a result, the World Health Organization has a mission to reduce the numbers of Caesarean sections worldwide and has stated that 'there is no justification for a caesarean section rate of higher than 10%–15%' (Cheung *et al.* 2006). I do not intend, here, to explore the debates for and against Caesareans on clinical grounds, other than to observe that Caesarean

---

[1] Forceps and ventouse deliveries involve giving birth with mechanical assistance – forceps are used to pull, and ventouse to suction the baby's head out of the vagina. An epidural is a regional anaesthetic which blocks the nerves in the spine so as to numb the pain of labour. Narcotics such as pethidine may be used to reduce the pain of labour, but this may also reduce women's sense of control and lead to longer labour (Stoppard 2005).

birth, like so many other aspects of birth, is an emotional issue about which health professionals and others have very strong feelings. Thus, protagonists for and against Caesarean sections do an excellent job of mustering the evidence to suit their own particular arguments, meaning that convincing arguments may be found on both sides.

What concerns me here is the notion of maternal 'choice' which, while it may in theory cover the type and place of birth (Department of Health 2007: 5) does not seem to extend to a right to Caesarean section on maternal demand. Arguably, essentialist ideals of 'good' and 'natural' motherhood' provide part of the explanation for why Caesarean birth by maternal request is usually excluded from offers of 'choice' in relation to birth. Women who request Caesarean sections as their birth of choice are thus likely to be denied this option unless they can prove 'clinical need' – in other words, give a biomedical reason for seeking a Caesarean. Women who seek a planned Caesarean section for personal reasons (i.e. because it is their preferred choice) may thus be denied this request. Those who seek Caesarean deliveries because they are afraid of giving birth vaginally, because they wish to organize birth around their working schedules, or because they fear damage to the pelvic floor are likely to meet resistance from health professionals and are also likely, as summed up by journalist Isabel Oakeshott (2007), to be 'derided by natural birth pedagogues as "too posh to push" '. Maternal 'choice' may thus be seen on paper as 'the opportunity to make informed choices throughout pregnancy and birth (Department of Health 2007: 12) but, in relation to Caesarean section, maternal requests are seen as something which should be 'managed in accordance with [official clinical] guidance' (Department of Health 2007: 12).

Early motherhood

Breastfeeding work – nourishing the next generation

Just as the labour of birth is defined and circumscribed by health advice, and by social attitudes about 'good' mothering, so is the embodied work of new motherhood. In the context of 'parenting' children of all ages, it is often mothers (rather than fathers) who are the subject of criticism, and measured against Taylorist-style standards of 'good' mothering (Gatrell 2005). Mothers with dependent children of all ages may be under scrutiny from schools, relatives, employers and health and social services in relation to how well they are perceived to be performing the role of mother. Marshall (1991: 69–70) has observed how the 'standard' for 'good' mothering allows only positive accounts of mothering to be acknowledged, this meaning that women who do not meet the 'standard' are seen as 'faulty'. More recently, Miller (2005) and Mullin (2005) have pointed out that 'standards' associated with 'good' mothering are unrealistic and incompatible with contemporary lifestyles, but that they remain oppressive to women in late modern society.

In relation to the supposed 'standards' of good mothering, I propose to examine what happens during the early stages of mothering, when mothers are undertaking the very physical labour of caring for young children. In particular, I focus on the embodied work of infant feeding because this issue highlights the pressures imposed on mothers by external agencies in the context of 'good mother' narratives, and concurrently illustrates the disparity between notions of maternal 'choice' and health advice. My focus on new maternity reflects, furthermore, the growing level of scholarly interest in breastfeeding, from the relative perspectives of health and medicine, and feminist accounts. The issue of breastfeeding is also pertinent here because it underlines the tensions, both in the UK and in the USA, between social expectations about how mothers should behave in public and at work – what Young (2005) describes as acceptable 'breasted' behaviour – and health guidance on the benefits of breastfeeding young children, which often draws upon the narrative of the 'good' mother.

I begin the discussion by providing a brief outline of what breastfeeding involves. This is because, although some readers may be familiar with the literature on breast- and infant feeding, or may have had the experience of breastfeeding, or both, some information about infant feeding might be useful for readers who are less familiar with this process. Babies may, from birth, be fed breast milk directly from the breast. Establishing breastfeeding may be difficult and painful, causing cracked and bleeding nipples. This discomfort may be exacerbated by the postnatal pain of medical procedures. Women who have had Caesarean sections will, at least for the first 24 hours after birth, be lying in a hospital bed with attached intravenous lines and a catheter, and women who have had assisted (forceps or ventouse) deliveries may be recovering from episiotomies, where the vaginal wall is cut to facilitate the birth, meaning that sitting down to breastfeed is extremely uncomfortable and mothers are often in pain and in a state of stress and distress (Kitzinger 2006).

In the first three days after the birth, the breast produces 'colostrum', a substance which assists in building up infant immunities. Subsequently, the breasts are filled with milk which is produced 'on demand' – thus, in theory, the more the baby feeds, the more milk is produced in the breast. If mothers are not able to feed their babies when their breasts are full, this may be painful and is likely to cause leakage. Once breastfeeding is established, breast milk may be expressed, refrigerated and stored for later use, when it can be fed to infants from a bottle or a feeder cup. Women who wish to express milk often use a breast pump for this purpose, but may find expressing difficult because, in the absence of the baby, the body's 'let down' reflex may not respond as productively as when the baby is present. Furthermore, the process of pumping breast milk usually requires the use of a machine which makes a loud whirring noise, which mothers often find hugely embarrassing (Boswell-Penc and Boyer 2007). As an alternative to breastfeeding, babies may be fed from bottles with commercially produced, dairy or soya-based, formula milk. This involves the purchase of powdered milk which must be mixed with boiled, cooled water in carefully sterilized and prepared feeding bottles. Formula milk may be stored for a limited time in a refrigerator, and if not used within the given time-frame must then be disposed of and reformulated. It is possible to buy cartons of ready-prepared formula, but these are expensive and take up a good deal of space, so for many mothers who are bottlefeeding, these would be used only on occasion, and would not provide a regular substitute for the work involved in preparing bottlefeeds.

At present, the pressures on mothers to breastfeed their babies are intense. Breastfeeding is regarded by health services as part of the work involved in 'good' mothering as it is considered to provide the best infant nourishment available. This is because current health research suggests that, clinically, both for children and their mothers, breastfeeding offers significant health benefits (Galtry 1997). It has been argued that breastfeeding increases infants' immunities and protects them both in childhood and in later life from health problems such as asthma and infections (Raymond 2005), diabetes (Jackson 2004) and even behavioural problems (Berger *et al.* 2005). Health research also suggests that mothers who breastfeed beyond 6 months benefit healthwise, substantially reducing the risks of breast cancer and osteoporosis. Women who breastfeed for over 2 years are said to reduce their risk of breast cancer by half (Wolf 2006).

As Wolf (2006) observes, the emphasis on increasing breastfeeding rates relates not only to initiation rates, but also to duration rates of breastfeeding. Thus, it is no longer seen as sufficient to breastfeed for the first few weeks of a baby's life, but into toddlerhood. It is recommended that babies should be fed exclusively on breast milk for 6 months, and on a combination of breast milk and solids beyond the age of 1 year – preferably for up to 2 years. In the breastfeeding information pack which was distributed to UK health professionals in 2005, the Department of Health (2004a: 2) stated: 'Breast milk provides all the nutrients a baby needs for healthy growth and development for the first six months of life and should continue to be an important part of babies' diet for [at least] the first year of life'. The American Academy of Pediatricians recommends breastfeeding minimally for one year and preferably well into the second year of life (Witters-Green 2003).

Bailey and Pain (2001) and Ortiz *et al.* (2004) have observed that breastfeeding duration rates in the UK and USA are lower than health agencies would wish. Thus, in 2004, in a drive to improve children's health, the British NHS attempted to increase not only the number of mothers who initiated breastfeeding but also the length of time these women continued to breastfeed. Health campaigns to promote the initiation and, especially, increasing the duration of breastfeeding in the UK and USA are aimed at individual mothers, rather than organizations. In the literature produced by the British NHS for midwives and health visitors (Department of Health 2004b), it is explained to health professionals that the 'target audiences' for the promotion of breastfeeding are individual mothers. In the documentation, while mothers' need to breastfeed 'in public' is considered, this is discussed only in the context of occasional visits to libraries and shops, with no mention of the workplace. Thus, the weight of responsibility for infant nutrition through breastfeeding lies with the individual mother. As I explain below, however, this poses a problem for employed breastfeeding women, because organizational and social attitudes towards breastfeeding are discouraging and unhelpful. This means that mothers are likely to be the subject of opprobrium if they do not breastfeed, but that they are equally likely to experience overt criticism if they perform the work of breastfeeding anywhere other than within the home. Furthermore, while health agencies focus on the need for mothers to breastfeed, in order to maximize infant health prospects, little attention is given to the intensive labour required of breastfeeding mothers, or to the difficulties of establishing and continuing breastfeeding work while feeling tired and ill.

Breastfeeding duration and initiation rates

Research into the effectiveness of campaigns aimed at promoting breastfeeding among new mothers indicates that women are knowledgeable about the positive effects of breastfeeding on children's health and that these campaigns have had a positive impact on the number of women who initiate, or attempt to initiate, breastfeeding (Bailey and Pain 2001; Earle 2002). Nevertheless, it remains the case that *duration* rates of breastfeeding in the UK and in the USA remain low (Bailey and Pain 2001) because many mothers who do establish breastfeeding switch to formula when children are between 3 and 9 months of age. Bailey and Pain (2001) observe that 66% of new mothers in the UK initiate breastfeeding, but that this drops to 27% by the time babies are 4 months old and 14% at 9 months. In the USA, while 69.5% of mothers initiate breastfeeding, only 17% are still exclusively breastfeeding when their babies are 6 months old, and fewer than 5% are breastfeeding when babies reach 1 year. Only 10% of mothers who work full-time are still breastfeeding babies at 6 months, this figure rising to almost 30% for 'stay at home mothers' (Boswell-Penc and Boyer 2007).

Breastfeeding initiation rates are related to age and social class. Recent Department of Health guidelines on infant feeding and child nutrition state that only 59% of women in manual occupations in the UK initiate breastfeeding, as opposed to 85% of women in higher social classes. Age and levels of education play a significant part in women's decision to breastfeed, with 51%

of women who leave full-time education before age 16 choosing to breastfeed, compared to 88% of women who continue education until at least 19 years (Department of Health 2004a). The NHS regards low rates of breastfeeding among women from disadvantaged communities as 'an important equality issue' (Department of Health 2004a: 3). Murphy (2003) argues that low-income mothers are just as aware as more affluent women of the promoted health benefits to babies of breastfeeding. In this context, Murphy (2003) and Bailey and Pain (2001) have observed that not all women enjoy breast-feeding and suggest that some women find attempts by health agencies to encourage breastfeeding intrusive, oppressive and totally incompatible with social expectations and lifestyles. Murphy (2003) observes how women may be forced to adopt strategies of subterfuge and concealment in order to be able to escape the pressures incumbent on them to breastfeed. In keeping with Murphy's findings, I suggest that the idealization of breastfeeding as the one 'best' source of infant nutrition, and the concept of breastfeeding as an essen-tial (and arguably, essentialist) form of women's embodied labour, places unbearable pressures on some women. In my earlier research on breastfeeding, women who attempted to breastfeed, but gave it up at an early stage, were haunted by a sense of failure to nourish their children to the standard set for them by health agencies. This caused them distress for years to come – even though their children appeared to be in good health.

Two mothers, Sam (an academic) and Sonia (a nurse manager), found breastfeeding difficult and ceased after 3 days and 2 weeks, respectively. Sam and Sonia's knowledge about the medical benefits of breastfeeding exceeded their experience of the process of breastfeeding a new baby. Their clinical knowledge was also wrapped up in essentialist ideals about breastfeeding as a 'natural' maternal quality, when in practice it is a skill which must be learned, which involves time, patience and hard work even for women who are well, and which may be difficult to achieve if women are feeling ill and distressed following a difficult birth. Like some of the mothers who participated in Bailey and Pain's (2001: 311) research, Sam and Sonia had assumed that childbirth and breastfeeding ought be 'innate skill[s]'. They were shocked to find that breastfeeding was associated with severe pain and difficulty. Each stopped breastfeeding, in spite of her understanding that this was 'best' for child health, and each experienced a long-term sense of guilt that she had not con-tinued to breastfeed. The guilt felt by these women was individualized, and in no sense did it appear to be shared, or alleviated, by the health professionals who were caring for the women at the time. Sam recalls:

> The birth was such a shock. I wanted a natural birth, I never expected to be all drugged up and battered. And I thought I would be a natural, breastfeeding mother but my nipples were bleeding and so painful, and when I tried to sleep they kept shaking me awake and saying

'your baby needs your breast'. So I gave up in despair and he went on to formula, so I feel dreadful because I know that breastfeeding is best and I wanted to be good at it.

(Quoted in Gatrell 2007b: 397)

Sonia recounted:

I had this dreadful, shocking hospital delivery, then enormous problems breastfeeding him, so I didn't enjoy it and gave up. But I felt so guilty about not giving him the best and not being a natural breast-feeder, which contributed to me not enjoying having a baby, so then I felt even worse.

(Quoted in Gatrell 2007b: 397)

Another research participant who struggled to breastfeed, was so deeply affected by the 'breast is best' discourse that she was afraid to be seen in public feeding her new infant from a bottle, and thus confined herself to her house during the early months of his life.

Breastfeeding duration: cultural and personal factors

Having established that breastfeeding can be difficult to initiate and get established, I now turn to breastfeeding duration. The sharp decline in feeding once babies are 3 months old may be accounted for by both practical and cultural factors including maternal exhaustion, worries about whether the baby is getting enough milk, and the attitudes of others towards breastfeeding. In practical terms, women may move from breast- to bottlefeeding because (as in the case of pregnancy work) discourses about the 'natural' qualities of breastfeeding obfuscate the fact that it requires energy, time and attention. Hungry babies who are fed 'on demand' may require feeds every 2–4 hours, and each feed may take half an hour or longer. As Kitzinger (2003: 401) notes, mothers may feel 'very drained when nursing is long and drawn out and if [mothers] are tired and the baby is constantly demanding to be fed'. The embodied work of breastfeeding may thus be difficult to sustain with only one baby to care for, and someone else to help with shopping, cooking and household labour. For women with more than one child and/or for those women who are doing all the housework by themselves, the labour of feeding an infant from the breast may become impractical and overwhelming. The work of motherhood and domestic labour is difficult enough when women are feeling well and are not bereft of sleep. For mothers who are feeling exhausted and trying to cope either with first babies, or with new babies and other children, moving from breast to bottle may seem like the only manageable option.

Dykes (2005) further attributes low breastfeeding duration rates to mothers' lack of confidence in their biomedical ability to nourish their infants. She argues that, before motherhood, women's understanding of 'production' is associated with ideas of efficiency and disembodiment. The embodied experience of breastfeeding, and the unpredictability of babies' and mothers' bodies, explains women's lack of trust in their own embodied ability to feed their infants. Dykes's proposition concurs with Kitzinger's (2003) reports of mothers' fears that breast milk will be insufficient to satisfy and nourish their children.

Most influential, however, is the general social aversion, in the UK and the USA, towards breastfeeding mothers, who are expected to nurse babies as a private, hidden act, rather than as a public activity (Kitzinger 2005). Kitzinger (2005: 40–1) argues that women who breastfeed outside the home may be seen as 'immodest' and 'exhibitionist', failing to 'conform to normal standards of decency'. Mothers who breastfeed are expected to conceal this as though they are partaking in a 'shameful' act, and babies are expected to be equally discreet: 'Not only must the breast be hidden but the baby's behaviour must be kept muted so that no-one is aware of the act'.

While concealment may be possible when babies are under 3 months old, it becomes increasingly difficult as children grow older, when mother and child may find themselves the focus of public jibes and criticism. In a UK television programme, which filmed women breastfeeding in a market square, members of the public were uncomfortable. One interviewee was quoted saying: 'It shouldn't be allowed' (Channel 4 2006). Both Young (2005) and Giles (2004) have psychologized male aversion to breasteeding, suggesting that men feel threatened by the possibility that maternal satisfaction in breastfeeding will displace heterosexual desire, thus some men may resent the attachment of female babies to their breastfeeding mothers. In this context, Giles notes how lesbian mothering causes outrage among men because this involves a further displacement of women's erotic relationship with men.

Whatever the reasons behind the public aversion to breastfeeding, and despite apparent attempts through policy and legislation to establish women's right to breastfeed in public, plus the pressure on women to accept the notion that 'breast is best' for infant nutrition, breastfeeding remains an activity which women are expected to conduct in private. Thus, mothers who breastfeed in public have found themselves the subject of overt criticism. One mother, Estelle, who took part in my own research on the labour of new mothering, found herself ejected from a café where she had been a customer for many years.

> I used to go into this café which I had previously supported. But one day I breastfed my baby daughter in there. And they asked me to leave and not to come back . . . Like I should be ashamed of myself, breast-feeding my own daughter. And I can't tell you how furious I was but

how absolutely, I mean I have never felt so disabled in my whole life as that point, ever . . .

(Quoted in Gatrell 2007b: 400)

The same woman recalled an instance when she attempted to feed her baby in a public art gallery and was approached by a member of the public, a woman, whom she had never met before and told to 'go home'. Estelle states:

These are examples of the tremendous kind of pressure on mothers who want to give the best start to their children but aren't allowed to be *seen* feeding *anywhere*.

(Quoted in Gatrell 2007b: 401)

Estelle is not the only woman to be criticized for breastfeeding in an art gallery, an activity which has in the past attracted national press coverage. Renaissance oil paintings of virgin mothers breastfeeding might be socially acceptable, but the materiality of living women breastfeeding living babies is not, as testified by the ejection of a nursing mother from the National Gallery in London (Griffin 2004; Laurance 2005). In England and Scotland, national policy has been introduced with the intention of making breastfeeding in public legal. However, this comes with various caveats and would not, presumably, prevent shop owners or institutional bodies from refusing to allow breastfeeding on 'other' grounds should they disapprove and wish to forbid it on their premises.

After maternity – breastfeeding and employment

I have already suggested that, if they seek to breastfeed in a public setting, women may be heavily criticized. As the experience of British and Australian MPs Julia Drown and Kristie Marshall suggest (as noted in Chapter 2, both were asked to leave the premises when attempting to breastfeed babies in parliament), this problem may be exacerbated if the 'public setting' concerned happens to be the workplace. McKinlay and Hyde (2004), Bailey and Pain (2001), Galtry (1997) and Ortiz *et al.* (2004) all contend that the constraints imposed upon employed mothers may negatively affect the duration of breastfeeding. They consider that maternal cessation of breastfeeding can directly be attributed to the unsupportive attitudes of employers. In this context, the requirement to conform to organizational expectations regarding what Young (2005) terms 'breasted' behaviour has obliged many women who have established breastfeeding to cease this on their return to employment. McKinlay and Hyde (2004) have argued that mothers wishing to breastfeed infants, or to express milk in organizational spaces, face hostility and discouragement.

Witters-Green (2003) explains that this is due partly to employers' lack of knowledge about the health benefits of breastfeeding (for both children and mothers), and also partly to organizational ignorance about the practical needs of nursing mothers. Employers are antipathetic towards breastfeeding and/or expressing breast milk at work because they fear this might interfere with employees' duties, it might cause other employees to feel 'discomfited', and it might induce employed mothers to think about their children when they should be concentrating on workplace tasks (Witters-Green 2003: 424).

Höpfl (2000) suggests that organizational antipathy to breastfeeding is due to deep-seated fears about women's bodies which are regarded, by employers, as unreliable and unpredictable, in a way which does not apply to the bodies of male employees. Höpfl focuses on the difficulties of trying to assimilate the post-childbirth body into the workplace, and observes how physical manifestations of maternity, such as breastfeeding, are unwelcome: 'the organization [is] not a place for women with physical bodies which produce . . . blood, breast milk and maternal smells' (2000: 101). On returning to employment, therefore, new mothers are expected to render their maternal bodies as shadowy as possible, and breastfeeding mothers especially are required to discipline their 'leaky' bodies (Shildrick 1997), keeping infants and breastfeeding separate from workplace activities (Puwar 2004; Gatrell 2005).

The prospect of managing their lactating bodies in the workplace (especially leakage and the expressing and storing of milk) is sufficient to persuade many women to give up breastfeeding before returning to work (Bailey and Pain 2001; Gatrell 2007b). For some mothers, the move from breast to formula is seen as a change for which they are 'ready', and which is accepted, or even welcomed. For other women, however, this decision is much harder, and these women might have continued breastfeeding for longer, had they not been required to return to work. For example A-level maths teacher Lianne explained how she needed to make her body 'fit in' with the male environment at her school:

> Breastfeeding? In *school?* Putting breastmilk in the staff fridge? You're *joking.* You can smell the testosterone when you walk in the door and you have to fit in, which obviously you can't do if you're breastfeeding. I hated giving up and [baby] cried because she wanted me, but I had to get back to work and the Head was not best pleased with me anyway, being off on maternity leave. So I needed to work at fitting back in, so breastfeeding was out of the question.
>
> (Lianne, quoted in Gatrell 2007b: 398)

Women who do breastfeed at work are likely to find, with rare exceptions (Boswell-Penc and Boyer 2007), that health advice about the requirement to breastfeed infants beyond the first year is ignored by employers (if they are aware of it at all) and the onus appears, usually, to be on 'employees (rather than employers) to procure requisite space and time . . . "It is up to you to work out where to pump, where to chill and store your milk and how to schedule work breaks that coincide with let-down times" ' (Boswell-Penc and Boyer 2007: 561). Significantly, in the information packs provided for midwives and health visitors to help promote breastfeeding, little mention is made of breast-feeding and employment. The Department of Health (2004b) directs health initiatives to promote breastfeeding primarily at individual mothers rather than employers. Perhaps unsurprisingly, in this context, few employers offer breastpumping or feeding breaks and few offer a suitable space for feeding infants or expressing milk. Thus mothers who try to combine paid work with putting babies directly to the breast are likely to be required to leave the premises in order to give feeds (Gatrell 2007b). Mothers who wish to express breast milk are likely to have to do this in the lavatory, which is hardly the most conducive or the most hygienic location for this process. This suggests that ability and access to combine breastfeeding with paid work is class-based. As Estelle (quoted in (Gatrell 2007b: 401) recalls, unless women have access to personal office space, the lavatory is likely to be the only available option:

> what I find amazing looking back at it, is that I just got on with it. Like I can imagine being squeamish about it and thinking 'Oh God how on earth can you express milk for your baby in a toilet . . .?' But I didn't want to feed her anything else . . . so that's what I did, and I was still doing it 18 months later.

Boswell-Penc and Boyer also focus on the class-based, and racialized, aspects of breastfeeding. Lactating women require not only suitable space to express milk, but also sufficient autonomy in the workplace to be able to leave their post for the time it takes. Thus, women in low-paid, low-skilled jobs – often black and minority ethnic workers – may have less opportunity to manage the expressing of milk than professional and highly educated women, who might have more opportunities to manage their own timetables. One of Boswell-Penc and Boyers' research participants, for example, 'a 21 year old woman of color' was unable to breastfeed even though she worked in the childcare centre where her daughter was placed. This was because she was working with pre-school children, while her daughter was cared for in the baby room and staffing schedules did not allow for this mother to leave her post, even for a short time. The mother concerned was thus obliged to move her daughter from breast milk to formula, at least during the working day (Boswell-Penc and Boyer 2007: 558).

Even if women do manage to express milk at work, there are rarely any specially dedicated facilities for storage. Among my own research participants, although some employers provided fridges for the general use of all employees, these were often dirty, old, and packed with cows' milk (for coffee and tea) and sandwiches. No employer offered refrigeration specifically for the purpose of storing expressed breast milk. The experiences of my research participants, in the UK, coincide with those of women who took part in Boswell-Penc and Boyer's (2007:560) study, in which women expressed 'anxiety . . . about storing milk in communal refrigerators'. Given the lack of facility and encouragement at work, it is unsurprising that women feel obliged to hide from colleagues the fact of their breastfeeding. All of those who took part in my research on combining the work of infant feeding with employment (Gatrell 2007b) experienced pressure to present themselves in the workplace appearing, and behaving, as they had prior to childbirth. In accordance with the observations of Giles (2004) and Kitzinger (2005: 40), Julie (quoted in Gatrell 2007b: 402) was forced to treat her breast milk as a 'shameful . . . waste substance', while foregrounding the organizational requirement that her newly maternal body must 'look smart'. Julie recalls:

> I was expected to present [myself] at work looking and behaving as I had done before I had children. This was almost impossible [and] 6 weeks after I went back there was this conference which meant being away . . . and they insisted I went. I was gone for three full days and that was a long time because I was still breast feeding, trying to look smart and not leak, so I just had to take a pump, run out, and go and stand in the bath and throw (all) my milk away, which was really upsetting.
>
> (Quoted in Gatrell 2007a: 402)

Interestingly, Julie and one other mother, public sector manager Louise, wished to continue breastfeeding at work. Louise felt that this would, however, be 'unacceptable in any form' at work, and, like Julie, regulated her milk flows so that her body produced milk only at night, this allowing her to lie to colleagues that she had ceased to breastfeed, when in fact both Louise and Julie continued to do this until their children were 2 years old.

> [Breastfeeding] was unacceptable in any form . . . but I was determined. So I breastfed for two years . . . every night even though I was working (and I couldn't express, that was out of the question). . . . And my body just learned to regulate itself. And I didn't have any problems physically with that. It learned, it probably knew, that it was just at nights. So I didn't have leakage at work. (Louise)
> The expressing thing at work was just difficult really. So I was really only feeding him at night [from 7 months onwards]. . . . And it's amazing, your body really does adapt, you can *make* it adapt. And

it's not just me, my cousin is doing it [too]. . . . Her body *knows* it's only at night. (Julie)

(Quoted in Gatrell 2007b: 402–3)

Conclusions

In conclusion, it would thus appear that, as in the case of pregnancy, the conflict between the maternal work of infant feeding in the context of the health ideals about 'good' mothers, and expectations regarding appropriate 'breasted' behaviour in the workplace are irreconcilable. Although governments and organizations may espouse the concept of equal opportunities for women, the *underlying* implication of employer attitudes is the notion that women should breastfeed their children, but that breastfeeding should take place only at home. Thus, in the past, influential bodies such as the UK Institute of Directors have not been afraid of suggesting that: 'It is a biological fact that it is women who give birth to children and are best equipped to look after them, especially in the early years' (Malthouse 1997). In the present, little seems to have changed. The 'politics of banishment' and the 'narratives which encode women's biological productivity as shameful' continue apparently to prevail (Boswell-Penc and Boyer 2007: 563). The maternal labour of infant feeding (whether by formula, breast milk or a mixture of the two) is discounted and not articulated as 'work', even though there are tremendous social pressures to perform infant feeding in accordance with late modern, Taylorist-style standards and measurement of what is 'best' for children. Infant feeding provides an especially pertinent example of how women's work is not 'differentiated out or recognised as activities separate from the relationships . . . within which they are conducted' (Glucksmann 2005: 19). In this case, the labour of infant feeding is obscured within the narrative of 'good' and 'natural' mothering. The maternal work of infant feeding has become 'hidden' labour in the most literal sense, with breastfeeding mothers under pressure to conceal feeding activities from the public gaze, and some bottlefeeding mothers feeling so oppressed by the opprobrious views of others that they, also, confine themselves to the private sphere.

As I shall argue in Chapters 6 and 7, even if mothers succeed in concealing their maternal status with regard to infant feeding, their experience of being 'unwelcome' at work does not seem to diminish. This is because the bodies of small children, even if they are breastfed in secret and outside the workplace, are associated with ill-health and are regarded as an integral and inseparable extension of women's maternal bodies. Thus, Morgan (1996) argues that sick infants are automatically regarded as mothers' responsibility and Cockburn (2002: 185) suggests that employed women with small children are associated with unpredictable and expensive absences. Some employers may regard mothers as a 'severe nuisance', bringing an 'unwelcome . . . whiff of the nursery into the workplace'. Cockburn (2002: 185) reports how some managers feel 'fed up to the back teeth' with maternal employment, resenting the 'continual absences of women for one thing and another. Now it's the clinic, now the baby's due, now the youngest has measles.' As Boswell-Penc and Boyer (2007: 563) argue, 'We need to expand the limits on what kind of bodies belong at work, and allow a broader range of living to occur there'.

More particularly, there is a need to 'differentiate out' the work of birth and of new motherhood, recognizing these activities as 'separate from the relationships . . . within which they are conducted' (Glucksman 2005: 19) – in other words, to reconceptualize these forms of maternal labour as 'work' rather than an integral element of 'natural' motherhood. The articulation of pregnancy, birth and breastfeeding as forms of work could have two positive consequences. If maternal and reproductive labour is defined as 'work', then mothers may be in a better position to articulate and negotiate terms and conditions, especially in relation to supposed 'choices' about where and how to give birth. In addition, the articulation of birth and infant feeding as 'work' might assist in exposing the chasm between health and social definitions of 'good' mothering, and workplace expectations that the practices of mothering should take place in secret and should not infringe on the workplace, or be seen to disrupt workplace practices.

6 'To honour and obey': A history of women's productive work

Introduction

In the following three chapters, I focus on women's productive work, exploring the boundaries between paid and unpaid work, and formal and informal labour. I explore who establishes and maintains the boundaries in relation to what choices and opportunities are available to women, and I compare women's options in relation to the opportunities on offer to men. Before attempting to analyse which kinds of work are 'included' within debates about formal and informal labour markets, which I do in Chapters 7–9, I felt it would be helpful to give a short consideration of women's historical position, from Victorian times to the present, with regard to embodied boundaries and productive labour (observing, for example, how middle-class women were often effectively confined within the home). The purpose of this discussion is to show how, until the later twentieth century, women were excluded from public life, had fewer legal rights than men and had consequently much less autonomy than their male counterparts. As well as focusing on women's economic situation, my overview includes a description of the role of the female body within marriage, with regard to embodied practices and male domination. It is intended that this contextualization of women's traditionally disadvantaged position may help to explain (but not to justify) the background to present-day inequalities such as the gender pay gap.

The social role of women

For centuries, women have been excluded from the social opportunities offered to men because their bodies place them within the social and biological category 'female'. At the same time, women have historically been allocated (and, as I argue in Chapters 7 and 8, are still allocated) particular duties, these tasks often involving embodied practices specific to their female gender, for example, mothering, domestic work and nursing. The embodied practices described are often associated with concepts of 'selfless', ideal womanhood – the antithesis of the 'selfish feminist' described in twentieth-century popular culture (Tyler 2007).

Debates about patriarchy and selfless womanhood may be traced back to the nineteenth century, when the vision of women as 'angels in the house' was articulated by British Victorian poet Coventry Patmore, who in 1956 published a poem which articulated the characteristics of the supposedly 'ideal' woman – selfless and compliant – 'gentle', 'sweet', and 'virtuous' (Patmore 1856: 169). Patmore's popular but controversial poem, *The Angel in the House*, portrayed a middle-class wife who achieved perfection by devoting herself to her home and her husband, a theme that became highly politicized. Anstruther (1992: 65) has observed how:

> One of the burning topics of the [Victorian era] was the role of the wife and . . . whether [she should] follow her husband meekly or insist on equal partnership. Coventry Patmore wrote in favour of the former, seeing in [his wife's] obedient love a deeply religious, moving [devotion]. [*The Angel in the House*] became a kind of manual of matrimony. The title itself became a catchphrase which entered into the English language. To be an 'Angel in the House' acquired its own particular meaning, that of a perfect, docile spouse.

Most specifically, the poem's title became the catchphrase for those Victorians who opposed women's claim to independence and sought to challenge the campaign for women's suffrage and the Married Women's Property Act. The title perfectly conveyed the feelings of those who believed that 'a woman's place was in the home' (Anstruther 1992: 7) and that husbands should make financial and political decisions on women's behalf. This is important in the light of the fact that, in the nineteenth century, whether married or single, women had few political rights in Britain and America because only men were entitled to vote (Phillips 2004). Following a long and bitter fight, women in America were given the vote only in 1920, women in the UK achieving equal voting rights with men only in 1928 (Phillips 2004). Women's suffrage was seen as the thin end of the wedge in relation to the feminization of politics. The notion that women might, in addition to gaining the vote, move to represent their constituents in parliament, was seen as a scandalous threat to the Victorian social order, not only by men, but also by some women. In 1884, the UK magazine *Punch* published an unflattering depiction of Lydia Becker, a prominent campaigner for women's rights, supposedly making a speech in the UK House of Commons whilst knitting a blue stocking. The cartoon was entitled: 'The Angel in the House, or the result of female suffrage'.

"THE ANGEL IN 'THE HOUSE;'" OR, THE RESULT OF FEMALE SUFFRAGE.
(*A Troubled Dream of the Future.*)

Reproduced from the original cartoon featured in Punch magazine – image supplied by Lancaster University Library.

This vision of a woman MP (published at a time when women did not even have the vote) was captioned: 'A Troubled Dream of the Future'. It left the reader in no doubt about the strength of the views of those who opposed women's suffrage, interpreting women's social position as angelic, and firmly within the household – not within the powerhouse of politics (Anstruther 1992).

The metaphorical 'angel' in the house(hold) has been described, by Virginia Woolf (1979) and Ann Oakley (1993, 2002) as symbolic of a social ideal of unselfish femininity which has constrained the development of women's careers, and retains a negative influence on women's position within the home and the labour market. I argue in Chapter 8 that this argument remains pertinent because the association between's women's embodied, sacrificial role as unselfish houseworker and carer in the home, and the idea that women who undertake such roles as paid jobs should seek minimal reward, has transferred into the late modern labour market.

Dependence on men

The nineteenth-century 'angel in the house' referred to by Patmore (1856) was by implication a middle-class married woman who, it was assumed, would be financially supported by her husband (a notion which excluded working-class, or single middle-class, women). Victorian Britain was a patriarchal society in the literal and legal sense. At the beginning of the Victorian era, social structures combined to enforce women's dependence on men. For working-class women, 'dependence on men . . . was reinforced by low rates of pay. It was assumed from the start of their working lives that [women's] position as wage earners was only temporary' (Rowbotham 1997: 19).

Rowbotham (1997) observes how, at the turn of the nineteenth century, working women in the UK were paid so little that some sort of union with, and reliance upon, a man was almost obligatory if they were to afford to live – even if this barely served to raise them above subsistence level. The alternative was to enter domestic service, where food and accommodation were paid for, but personal freedom was severely limited and the prospects upon retirement were often grim. Working-class women could also earn money as factory or shop workers, or as seamstresses, but in all of these occupations, as Roberts (1972: 57) observes, 'the work was hard and tedious, the hours painfully long, the pay pitifully low and the treatment frequently harsh'. As a consequence of such limited options, Roberts (1972: 57) suggests that many lone women 'took their chances with life on the streets'.

It was expected that middle- and upper-class women would marry, and be financially supported by men. Thereafter, their only permitted forms of 'labour' would be to manage the household, satisfy their husbands in bed, bear children and fill their time with embodied activities deemed acceptable for women to undertake. Greer (2006: 137) quotes a father's advice to his daughters in 1809 to learn needle-work and knitting 'not on account of the intrinsic value of all you can do with your hands . . . [but] to enable you to fill up, in some tolerably agreeable way, some of the many solitary hours you must necessarily spend at home'.

The assumption that women would be financially supported by husbands was all very well, but it failed to take account of the number of single women in Britain in the mid-nineteenth century. The 1851 Census showed that 29%

of women were either widowed or unmarried (Philips 2004; Peterson 1972). This has been ascribed to a number of factors, including higher male mortality rates, male emigration to America and Australia, and the probability that middle-class men would not marry until they felt could afford to support a wife and children in a 'suburban villa' with staff (Phillips 2004: 20). This was a serious problem for middle- and upper-class women with no income and no prospects of marriage, because the labour market opportunities for such women were very limited, due to the social unacceptability of paid employment combined with the fact that they were qualified to do very little. Poorly remunerated work as a paid companion, or a governess, was almost the only role available to 'genteel' women, such employment being considered 'appropriate because, while it was paid employment it was within the home' (Peterson 1972). The roles of governess and companion offered food and accommodation, but were badly paid (if at all) and neither offered any security if relationships with employers went awry, or on retirement. The American author Edith Wharton, writing in 1905, provides an evocative description of the impoverished circumstances of the single and orphaned Lily Bart, whose aunt withdraws financial support when Lily fails to fulfil the role of obedient niece and companion to her aunt's satisfaction (see Wharton 1997). Peterson (1972) describes the social and financial pressures of being employed as a governess, in which pay was low, and did not include provision for clothing, laundry, travel, medical care or a pension. Peterson (1972: 8) suggests that, even in 'the best of circumstances, a governess's income left her on the very edge of gentility, with no margin for illness or unemployment'.

Women in wedlock

Although most women had few financial alternatives other than marriage, wedlock was in itself no easy option. In many respects, marriage disempowered women even further than spinsterhood. This was because, during most of the nineteenth century in the UK, only the male body within marriage could legally 'own' money or property. As Phillips (2004: 27) describes it, 'married women had no separate personality at all. Property, earnings, liberty and conscience all belonged to their husbands.'

As such, in Britain until 1882, when the second Married Women's Property Act came into being (Phillips 2004), married women were legally and economically disenfranchised from the moment they made their marriage vows. Wives were obliged to relinquish control of all their material possessions and lost their rights to any property, money or income that they may have possessed prior to marriage, their assets passing automatically into the ownership of their husband. This also applied, subsequently, to any money that women might earn, or inherit, during their married lives. Married women were further forbidden to enter into legal contracts of any kind, this effectively excluding them from earning their own living and closing down any possibility that they might leave a violent or unhappy relationship. Although they were expected to bear children as part of the marriage contract, women and had no legal rights over their own children, who 'belonged' to the male partner if the child was born in wedlock. Husbands had entire custody and control of their off-spring and, if the marriage broke down, a man could personally bar his wife from access to children. Even following the Infant Custody Acts, which were enacted in 1973 and 1880, separated women were afforded only very limited rights to appeal for custody, and in practice were unlikely to have any part in children's upbringing unless estranged husbands permitted this (Phillips 2004).

Once married, women lost control even over their own bodies because the wedded female body became, in the legal sense, the property of her husband, and women's work involved fulfilling male conjugal rights. In the Church of England, marriage ceremonies included pledges of female obedience and women had to promise to love, honour and obey their husbands. Obedience in this sense implied the subjugation of the female body to male desire. Men were entitled to sex within marriage as a right, and while men could file for divorce from women who committed adultery (from 1857), women were not legally permitted to divorce unfaithful husbands. Thus, as women's rights campaigner Helena Swanwick wrote in 1913, during the nineteenth and early twentieth century, a man could legally 'enforce marital rights and insist on his wife's faithfulness while enjoying his own licence' (Swanwick 1913, quoted in Phillips 2004: 213).

Violence within marriage was considered to be a private affair between husband and wife until 1878, when women were able, in theory, to obtain separation orders if their husbands beat them, this being extended in 1886 to include desertion. In practice, however, even in the context of violent mar-riages, separation orders were difficult to obtain and it was highly problematic for separated women to gain maintenance from husbands who did not wish to provide this. As noted earlier, there were few opportunities for women in the labour market and presumably these would be even more circumscribed for estranged wives, possibly with children, who were qualified to do very little.

This lack of qualifications was a difficult problem to resolve. Should women – single or otherwise – have wished to gain some sort of qualification in order to fit them for employment, this would have been very difficult prior to the mid-twentieth century, especially if they sought to gain a degree.

Women and education
Women who sought financial independence through training would have found it virtually impossible to access formal education, even if they could afford to pay for it. Becoming qualified in order to gain employment was problematic for working-class men, but almost unheard of for women of any

social class. Before the Second World War, therefore, most women were poorly educated in comparison with men. Some working-class girls would have been able to attend elementary schools where they would be taught by trained teachers, but those middle-class women who received any kind of education at all were often taught at home by unqualified governesses (Peterson 1972).

Whatever the educational experiences of school-age girls, grown women were limited in terms of what they could do. Towards the close of the nineteenth century, a small number of opportunities began to open up for women to train as secretaries or clerks (Phillips 2004), but until the mid- to late twentieth century, women were explicitly excluded from entering universities. While early feminists fought for women's right to a university education, anti-feminist activists campaigned vociferously against higher education for women, using essentialist discourses about women's physical fragility, and the need to prioritize childbearing, to substantiate their arguments. Thus, it was argued by Dr Edward Clarke of Harvard College that women must be forbidden from studying at degree level because too much cerebral activity could damage women's reproductive organs and might, as a consequence, compromise their abilities to bear healthy children. In 1873 Dr Clarke published *Sex in Education*, a slim but influential text which hypothesized that higher education would 'destroy the reproductive functions of American Women by overworking them at a critical time in their physiological development' (Showalter and Showalter 1972: 41).

Despite the arguments of campaigners like Clarke, which were widely disseminated and debated at length in the press (Showalter and Showalter 1972), opportunities for women to access higher education gradually began to open up. Girton College was established in 1869 as the first residential college for women. However, it was not officially part of the University of Cambridge, meaning that while the opportunity to *study* for a degree became possible for a small number of middle- and upper-class women, only men were permitted to graduate (Dyhouse 2006). Although women were awarded their degrees from Oxford from 1920, women students from Cambridge were barred from graduating until 1948. In 1998, more than 400 women who had been denied the right to graduate returned to Newnham College travelling from as far afield as Indonesia, Israel, New Zealand and Zimbabwe for their long-delayed graduation (BBC News 1998).

Even when women were allowed not only to attend Oxford and Cambridge, but to collect degrees at the end of their years of study, the numbers of women at university remained very small in comparison to the number of men. Dyhouse (2006) suspects that quotas were introduced to protect higher education as a male preserve. She observes how reasons for limiting the number of women students (to around 20%) were attributed to apparently insoluble problems such as the limited number of student rooms available to, and appropriate for, women students. The number of women students attending university began to increase only in the late 1960s and early 1970s. Dyhouse (2006) relates this rise in the numbers of women to a variety of factors including the founding of new universities, the equal opportunities legislation which challenged the idea of gender 'quotas', and the increased expectations of young women following the impact of second-wave feminism.

Just as they were excluded from education, women were also, until the mid-1970s, legally excluded from many forms of employment. During both the First and Second World Wars in Britain, and during the Second World War in the USA, windows of employment opportunity opened up to women while men were away fighting as women of all social classes (especially in 1939–45) were encouraged to substitute for men employed in lower-ranking positions (though even during wartime, senior posts were reserved for men). However, women were expected to withdraw gracefully from the labour market when soldiers returned, allowing homecoming men to reclaim available jobs. Thus, once men were demobilized (and especially if women were married) it was assumed that women would relinquish their paid work in favour of men who had been away fighting, but were returning from the front (Summerfield 1998).

Phillips (2004: 308), describing Britain after the First World War, suggests that:

> With the end of the [War], women's new prosperity shuddered to a halt. Many were sacked [and] jobs were kept open instead for returning soldiers. Because of the carnage at the front, there was now an enormous number of surplus women, as a result almost one in three had to be self supporting. But public opinion assumed that women could still be supported by men and . . . the women did not want to stand in the way of the returning soldiers.

With reference to America, Sheila Rowbotham has described, similarly, how: 'When the men came . . . home, most Americans assumed that women were going to return to being housewives. Indeed, a substantial number of people thought women with husbands who could afford to support them should not be allowed to work' (1997: 268). 'American mothers who were in paid work were therefore accused of neglecting their families and told that children who felt abandoned could become the juvenile delinquents of tomorrow' (1997: 321).

Following the Second World War, however, and despite the pressures from government and the media to give up work and take on the Parsonian role of wife and homemaker (as described in Chapter 2), the number of women participating in the labour market began to creep up (Rowbotham 1997). Thus, in the USA, women made up 25% of the labour force in 1940, rising to

41% by the 1970s (Morris 1990). In Britain in 1948, 33.6% of the labour force were women, this figure increasing to 41.7% by 1980. Increases in women's labour market participation did not mean, however, that they were offered the same opportunities as, or paid equally with, men (Morris 1990).

Legal inequalities

Prior to the enactment of anti-discrimination laws and policies, it was perfectly legitimate to dismiss a woman from paid employment if she married, or if she became pregnant (Gatrell and Swan 2008). It was also legal to pay a woman substantially less than a man for doing an equivalent job. In the recent publication of the wartime diaries of Nella Last (dating from 1939 to 1945), an appendix at the back of the book gives the average wages of men and women, doing equivalent paid work, as £4.96 and £2.22 respectively (Broad and Fleming 2006: 308).

As more women entered the labour market, however, the notion of a 'legal' gender pay gap was seen as increasingly unacceptable to women, and in the 1960s and 1970s feminist activists began to campaign for equal pay and conditions for women. The women's liberation movement and some politicians (in Britain, Barbara Castle MP was the leading campaigner) began to fight for equal employment opportunities for women, and these campaigns began to have a serious impact on public consciousness in both Britain and America (Rowbotham 1997). For example, in 1970, the British feminist Germaine Greer published her seminal text *The Female Eunuch*, in which she raged against the unfairness of unequal pay and conditions for women. Greer argued that working women should be paid the same as men who were doing equivalent jobs and quoted a range of instances where women's career progress was limited, and/or where they earned less than men in same employment. In relation to equal pay, Greer (2006: 136) noted that 'women working in banks have an incremental scale that stops at £800 p.a., while men's rises to £1,100: hardly more than one women in thirty earns even as much as the average man's wage'. Greer (2006: 136) also observed how 'Bus conductresses [who sold tickets] were lured into the [transport] industry by [the offer of] equal pay when staffing became a problem, but they cannot become drivers, garage managers or inspectors: When one-man buses come in they will be laid off or employed at lower wages in the canteens'.

Bruley (1999) notes that Asian women in the UK were especially poorly paid during the 1970s compared with men and with other women. For women from a Pakistani or Bangladeshi background, the notion of employment outside the home was culturally unacceptable. Thus, many of this group of women were obliged to contribute to household economies by undertaking manual work in isolation, within the home, for very low wages.

In their respective analyses of women's social role during the twentieth century, Lydia Morris (1990) and Sue Bruley (1999) have both suggested that the gender pay gap has been perpetuated partly due to the propensity of some trades unions to protect the position of male members at the expense of female members, based on heteronormative assumptions that male earnings should provide the principal household wage. Bruley (1999) reports how one group of female cleaning staff felt unsupported by their union, which appeared unwilling to help organize collective action for better pay, even though the same organization was considered quite militant in relation to male members' pay and conditions. As I describe in Chapter 10, this argument remains pertinent because the idea that some unions continue to prioritize male members at women's expense is still a subject for debate. This issue has been brought to bear in the context of a present-day campaign to equalize women's pay within local government (Brindle and Curtis 2008).

Women's employment since 2000

In theory, the social position of contemporary women should be very different now than it was in the decades following the Second World War. Equal opportunities legislation came into force in Britain and America in the mid-1970s and was supposed to protect women from unequal pay and discrimination on grounds of their reproductive capacity (Rowbotham 1997). Since 2000, women and racialized minorities, both male and female, should be able to expect fair and equal social treatment, as should disabled citizens. Yet the number of women who hold positions of power remains very small and, as Puwar (2004) and Gatrell and Swan (2008) note, the number of black or disabled women in high-profile and/or influential positions is tiny. On average, women at all stages of their career, and women of all classes, earn consistently less than men, even in professions such as higher education, where the number of women employed equals the number of men (Association of University Teachers 2003).

Furthermore, in the home, despite women's increased labour market participation, women in heterosexual relationships still undertake the lion's share of domestic labour (Martin 2007; Womack 2008) and, as I discuss in Chapters 3 and 8, the social expectation that women should provide physical care for children and elderly relatives prevails. Regardless of whether or not they are employed, a lack of state provision in capitalist countries continues to ensure that women carry the burden of care for ill and/or elderly relatives with limited support (Morgan 1996). In 1991, 20% of women aged between 45 and 64 were providing such care (Jackson 1997).

Moreover, women's legal rights to own property, the decline of marriage, and rising divorce rates have failed to prevent the controlling, by some men, of women within heterosexual relationships, through violence. Within some heterosexual relationships, although in theory husbands may no longer enforce conjugal 'rights', women appear still to be coerced into having sex with abusive male partners (Kelly 1988). In 1992, over 420,000 incidents of domestic violence involving female victims were recorded by the British Crime Survey, and Maynard and Winn (1997) estimate that over 90% of domestic violence is perpetrated by men on women. Women are often expected to accept threatening behaviour within marriage/cohabitation and 'often find themselves caught between their own experiences of behaviour as abusive and the dominant beliefs which define such behaviour as normal or inevitable' (Maynard and Winn 1997).

Maynard and Winn assert that domestic violence is racialized as well as gendered, and that this is more of an issue for black women than for white women. They attribute this to the concern that black women may be even more reluctant than white women to report violence from male partners, due to fears that enforcing agencies may fail to take them seriously. Thus, although divorce is more easily available now than in the late nineteenth and early twentieth centuries, some women remain trapped in unhappy and possibly violent relationships because they are too frightened to leave. Furthermore, as Smart and Neale (1999) observe, many women with children remain in unsatisfactory relationships if they feel that staying married offers the best option for the children.

In addition (while there may be occasional 'celebrity' exceptions to this rule), women often face serious financial disadvantage on divorce, especially if they are mothers who have given up paid work when children are very small. For women with low qualifications who have been out of the jobs market for some time, obtaining paid work may be difficult, especially if they need to organize and fund childcare, and some men prove to be unreliable with maintenance payments – if they pay anything at all on relationship breakdown (Smart and Neale 1999). Thus, even in contemporary marriages, while the legal situation offers married women more freedom now than in the past, the 'choices' on offer to some women may in practice be limited, with the gendered, embodied and economic power balance remaining in favour of the male partner. The extent of contemporary male economic domination within marriage/cohabitation is perhaps best illustrated by the fact that, until 2000, married/cohabiting women's paid work did not 'count' in the same way as men's. Government statistics measured the characteristics and social standards of heterosexual couple households by recording only the occupation of the 'head of household' – usually a man. Thus, until the beginning of this century, for married or cohabiting heterosexual women, statistical studies about class and social mobility defined women's occupational status through the male with whom she was living (Grint 2005).

The labour market and the gender pay gap

Furthermore, while it is true that women's labour market participation has increased since the 1970s, and that the opening up of university education has provided job opportunities for women at the higher end of the job market, in Britain and America at least, it is often still men, and not women, who hold the senior and most highly paid posts (Gatrell 2005; Edwards and Wajcman 2005; EOC 2007a; Economist 2005). This is particularly likely to be the case in professions which have conventionally been open only to men, such as medicine, academia, finance and the law. Thus, in UK higher education, the number of women professors remains low in comparison to the number of men; and in politics, the number of female MPs remains consistently less then the number of male MPs, with only around 20% of seats in the British House of Commons held by women (EOC 2005b).

Furthermore, while women should, in theory, receive the same pay as men in an equivalent job, a marked gender pay gap continues to exist in practice. On average the gender pay gap is just under 17 % in the UK for full-time women workers and up to 38% for part-timers (EOC 2007a). In the USA the average gender pay gap is even higher, at around 20% for full-time female workers and rising to 25% for college-educated women aged 30–45 – a figure which has not changed in ten years (Leonhardt 2006; Padavic and Reskin 2002). Figures provided by the Women's Bureau of the US Department of Labor demonstrate that qualifications do not necessarily reduce the gender pay gap. In 2003, in America, men with a bachelor's degree or higher qualification earned a median weekly wage of $1,131. Women qualified to bachelor's degree level or higher earned a median weekly wage of $832 dollars – so as a percentage, highly qualified women are earning 26.4% less than men (US Department of Labor 2005: 33–4). The gender pay gap affects black and minority ethnic women even more severely than it does white women. For example, in the USA in 1998, as a proportion of men's wages, white women earned 73%, African-American women 63% and Hispanic-American women only 53% (Seager 2005).

Women who attempt to challenge unequal pay will not find this an easy prospect. Whether they are in highly paid professional or low-paid manual jobs, women who take legal action to redress wage inequalities will often experience this as an unpleasant and protracted process, with claimants under duress to drop their case (Griffiths 2008). Even if they succeed in winning back pay and a better wage, women seeking equal pay may be accused of causing (often male) job losses, if employers suffer financial losses as a result of having to fund back pay as well as paying women a fair wage. Such charges may be laid not only by employers but also, apparently, by their own unions which, instead of backing women's claims to equal pay, have been accused of trying to persuade women members to accept low settlements so as to protect male jobs (Brindle and Curtis 2008).

The gender pay gap affects more than just day-to day living, adversely impacting other aspects of women's lives, in the context of education and occupational segregation. For example, women in Britain are financially disadvantaged, in comparison with men, if they attend university. Girls now outperform boys at A level, and at present, in many subjects, more women than men are registered at university. However, women will be expected to pay for their university education for many more years than equivalent male students. This is because the gender pay gap, together with the possibility that they make take time out of the labour market to have children, means that it will take women on average 5 years longer than men to pay off student loans.

In the UK, the Women's Work Commission (2006) demonstrated a high level of occupational segregation, with men occupying the better-paid roles such as plumbing and firefighting, while women (as considered in Chapter 8) tend to be concentrated in the lesser-paid roles such as care work. This form of occupational segregation has been described by Hakim (1979) as horizontal segregation, with women clustered into the lower-paid occupational roles. In the case of uniformed and traditionally masculine occupations, such as firefighting, employers have launched campaigns aimed specifically at recruiting more women. However, the numbers of women firefighters, both in Britain and America, remains on average very small – often well below 5%. It has been suggested by Baigent (2007), in relation to firefigting, that this may be due to male resistance to women's entry to occupations which conventionally enhance men's own sense of their masculinity. Baigent and O'Connor (2007) claim that 'firemen are effectively limiting the amount of women firefighters at token level [by] . . . harassment . . . the purpose is to marginalise women and ensure they recognise they are not welcome'.

The unwelcome and unworthy maternal body

It is thus apparent that, even in the twenty-first century, women's bodies may still be 'unwelcome' in certain occupational contexts, just as it is also apparent that employers continue consistently to ascribe less economic value to women workers than to men. One reason why employers are able to maintain this discriminatory position is that the process for contesting discrimination is prolonged and difficult. For example, as I noted in Chapter 4, women continue to be subject to discrimination and dismissal if they become pregnant – despite thirty years of legislation which is supposed to protect them from such unfair treatment. In the UK, research undertaken by the Equal Opportunities Commission has shown that around 220,000 pregnant women each year experience some form of disadvantage or discrimination at work, of whom 30,000 are dismissed from their jobs due to pregnancy. This affects women working at all levels of employment, but mothers in professional and management roles are particularly vulnerable, with one-third experiencing discrimination, as opposed to one-fifth of pregnant women overall (EOC 2005a). In two recent cases, senior and highly paid women were demoted, harassed and finally dismissed from their jobs due to becoming pregnant, one woman's manager stating that he felt 'betrayed' by her pregnancy, which he considered rendered her 'useless' in the workplace (Griffiths 2008). However, pregnant mothers are reluctant to take action to assert their rights. In the UK, only 3% of those who lose their jobs will seek redress at an employment tribunal, and less than one in 20 will seek any form of advice (EOC 2005a). This is partly because women who do go to court claiming sex discrimination (following pregnancy or for other reasons) may win their case, but may then find themselves unemployable, as they are then regarded as troublemakers, to whom no employer wishes to offer a job. As journalist Sian Griffiths (2008) has observed, women who 'stand and fight face not only the stress of a legal battle but also the knowledge that [their actions will] make it more difficult to get a job in the future.

Conclusions

The consideration, in this chapter, of women's historical and contemporary position with regard to embodied boundaries and productive labour (observing, for example, how middle-class women were historically confined within the home) has shown how policy and legislation, while they have improved the situation for women in some respects, have not proved a panacea. The social conventions which traditionally excluded women from public life and afforded women fewer legal rights than men have in theory been outlawed. In practice, however, it appears that old habits die hard, and women's lack of autonomy within the home and in the labour market continues, to some extent, to be maintained through social attitudes and behaviour. Furthermore, the evaluation of the role of the female body within marriage, in the context of embodied practices and male domination, suggests that divorce laws and women's increased labour market participation have not automatically transformed all heterosexual partnerships into equal partnerships. Some women continue to make their reproductive and labour market decisions in the context of relationships which may be violent and confining. In such circumstances, men continue to set the boundaries in relation to what 'choices' are available to women.

Similarly, although women's labour market opportunities and participation have increased, the situation whereby men hold the most senior and influential roles remains constant. Women's bodies, while they may be allowed entry to some roles within the labour market, are still excluded from others – often the best paid and most secure roles, with the best pension schemes, such as firefighting. As in the past, women's bodies are afforded less economic value than men's, and although the gender pay gap is now illegal, it remains firmly in place. Finally, women continue to be unfairly expelled and excluded from the labour market if they have children, in a manner which does not apply to men – if men are expectant fathers, the chances of their being dismissed for that reason are small.

In conclusion, it appears that women's ability to establish and maintain the boundaries between home and work, and between paid and unpaid, and formal and informal work are better now than they were in the nineteenth century. In practice, however, women's opportunities are still circumscribed in comparison with those of men. As Walby (1990) has argued, private forms of patriarchal control, exercised by individual men within households, have been extended to encompass paid employment, in keeping with women's increased labour market participation. The embodied conventions which traditionally afforded men power and privileges within the labour market and within heterosexual relationships remain a source of reference for contemporary social conventions, which appear in some respects to have as much in common with nineteenth-century behaviour and belief as with twenty-first-century legislation and policy. Thus, there are circumstances where the maternal body may still be subject to negotiation, oppression and discrimination, which it may be difficult, disadvantageous and even dangerous for women to challenge (Griffiths 2008).

In Chapters 7–9, I attempt to analyse how women's work is understood in relation to debates about inclusion with regard to paid and unpaid work, and formal and informal labour markets. Hopefully, the overview of women's traditionally disadvantaged position in society given in this chapter (while it does *not* justify discriminatory practice) will pave the way for understanding women's productive work in the present day.

7   Angels in the (power)house: Women in senior roles

Introduction

In May 2007, I visited an exhibition of photographs in London's National Portrait Gallery. The photographs were by photo-journalist Nick Danziger, and were taken as a documentary of the political decision-making process leading to the invasion of Iraq by British and American troops. The photographs are a thought-provoking record of the run-up to a controversial war. I was struck by one thing in particular. The bodies captured on film, and the power that they were so visually portrayed as wielding, were almost exclusively male. The bodies of women, if they appeared at all, were in 'supporting' roles – as wives, secretaries, or junior press officers. The photographic exhibition was a particularly evocative display of how few women hold centre-stage roles within politics.

It is acknowledged that there have been, and continue to be, occasions when women are appointed to very senior roles in the UK and the USA. However, even the election of a woman prime minister in the UK has not produced a major shift in the gender imbalance in politics, at either a junior of a senior level, and the majority of elected political decision-makers continue to be male. This observation is not limited to the world of politics. An examination of the board of any major company or organization in America or the UK will predominantly reveal bodies which are male and white. Similarly, within the professions and within family businesses, women's bodies in the context of leading, well-paid and influential roles are in the minority – if, indeed, they are represented at all.

In this chapter, I evaluate women's absence and presence in the context of productive paid work at the high end of the formal labour market. The chapter has three parts. I first look at the numbers of women in senior roles and observe how paid work in senior political, professional and business contexts is associated with male bodies. I suggest that there appear still to be unwritten embodying, and gendered, boundaries in relation to the formal labour market which privilege the male body, and I observe how women may have infiltrated middle to lower levels of political and professional hierarchies but are rarely to be seen in the most influential roles.

Having established the lack of women in leading roles, I then consider what happens to women who do, as Puwar (2004) describes, 'invade' traditionally male 'spaces' such as the House of Commons and the corporate boardroom, thereby manifesting the 'troubled dream of the future' predicted in the nineteenth century, when it was feared that the angel in the house-(hold) might aspire to become an 'Angel in the House' of Commons (Anstruther 1992). As Puwar (2004: 8) acknowledges: 'Formally, today, women and racialised minorities can enter positions that they were previously excluded from'. However, in practice, while the opportunities for women in senior roles may on paper be limitless, invisible boundaries constraining women's progress continue to exist. Furthermore, women's work at senior level appears to be measured differently, and more harshly, than men's work. I report how, when women do invade the male arenas of Parliament and the boardroom, they become subject to extreme, and very public, 'Taylorist' forms of measurement which are not applied to men in similar positions. Senior women are exposed to a level of scrutiny which is only made possible due to their small number, and in this respect I suggest that very senior women may experience both isolation and pressure to blend in with male embodied norms within the workplace.

Finally, I attempt, through the lens of the body, to understand *why* so few women are able to break through the 'glass ceiling', despite initiatives dating back to 1995 to try and increase the number of women at senior levels in politics and organizations. In this context, I consider the continued existence of the 'glass ceiling' in relation to the masculine 'norms' of the workplace relating to long-hours cultures and antipathy to part-time employment. I then question the supposed 'unreliability' of the maternal body, a concept which I argue is unfairly and inaccurately used as 'evidence' for arguments about women's inability to make rational decisions and their consequent unsuitability for top-level roles in politics and business.

Lack of women: the 'glass ceiling'

As noted in the previous chapter, legislation protecting women's position in the labour market, and supposedly assuring them of the right to equal pay, has had some effect. Today, there are more women politicians, managers and professionals employed within the formal labour market than there were prior to the equal opportunities agenda. Nevertheless, there remain deep inequities within the labour market, which become increasingly evident at the most senior levels in politics, business and the professions. *The Economist* describes the situation thus: 'Open the door of any boardroom . . . and the chances are that most people around the table will be men. For years, there have been plenty of talented women coming up in business, public life and politics – but those who reach the top are still the exception' (EOC 2005b: 1).

As Bradley *et al.* (2000) observe, the concentration of women in the lower tiers of occupational hierarchy – what Hakim (1979) terms 'vertical segregation' – remains a problem. Women's vertical segregation within the workplace has been described as the 'glass ceiling' – a barrier which is transparent but impenetrable, so that women can see the top of the management hierarchy, but may not reach it. For black and minority ethnic women, the situation is even worse, as women in these groups are likely to experience unfair treatment not only due to their gender, but also in relation to their ethnic background. In their research on women's professional identities, Bell and Nkomo (2001) acknowledge the existence of the glass ceiling as a barrier to promotion for all women, but argue that black and minority ethnic women are also faced with a 'concrete wall', meaning that they are prevented, through unfair organizational practices, from even seeing the top of the career ladder, never mind climbing it.

Bradley *et al.* (2000: 82) thus observe that 'The persistence of vertical segregation means that even if women make inroads into an organizational category they do not reach top positions within it.' This is despite attempts by government agencies to enhance opportunities for women at senior executive levels. In 1995, the US government established the Glass Ceiling Commission, for the purpose of facilitating women's entry to the most influential levels in business and society. In the UK, the Equal Opportunities Commission (EOC 2005b) has campaigned to open up to women senior jobs leading to top-level posts, calling for strenuous action by politicians and others already in senior roles to recruit and retain more women at high levels. In spite of these initiatives, however, the number of women in the most highly paid and influential jobs remains very small. *The Economist* (2005) reports that although women account for 46.5% of America's workforce, less than 8% of America's top managers are women. In the UK the situation is similar. While approximately 45% of the UK workforce is female (Bradley *et al.* 2000), very few women command top-level positions. In the corporate world, the number of women appointed as 'executive' directors with voting rights and share options is very small. In 2005, the number of women executive directors of FTSE 100 (top British) companies was only 14 – this in comparison with around 400 men in equivalent positions (Singh and Vinnicombe 2005). As to non-voting directorships of FTSE 100 companies, only just over 10% are held by women, and 22 companies have no women directors at all (Singh and Vinnicombe 2005). The UK's Equal Opportunities Commission (2007a, 2007b) has voiced concerns that the increase in the number of women entering top jobs has stalled, and fears have been expressed that this may even go into reverse. Similarly, it has been observed in *The Economist* (2005) that, in the USA, the number of women in very senior roles has altered very little since 1995 when the Glass Ceiling Commission was set up.

If women are appointed to 'executive' positions in business, they are unlikely to earn as much as men in equivalent roles. The gender pay gap appears even greater at executive level than it does for women in middle-ranking management positions. While one may have more general issues with the extraordinarily high levels of executive pay on offer to senior bankers and company executives, it remains evident that women holding leadership roles in business are paid substantially less than their male peers (Webb 2007). Thus, despite years of equal opportunities policies and initiatives, women who scale the highest peaks of the 'corporate summit' remain 'rarities' (Economist 2003: 64). As *The Economist* stated in 2005: 'The glass ceiling . . . is proving particularly persistent. The corporate ladder remains stubbornly male and the few women who reach it are paid significantly less then the men whom they join there' (Economist 2005: 67–8).

Women in family businesses: the tradition of male primogeniture

This picture of women's poor representation at board level extends beyond the corporate boardroom and the world of 'blue chip' companies and into the arena of family business. Hamilton (2006) and Mulholland (1996) have both observed how, within family businesses, the boundaries between women's paid and unpaid work are blurred and, as a consequence, women's contribution is undervalued. Women are thus underrepresented at board level within family businesses and are paid less than male relatives. Mulholland (1996) demonstrates how women in affluent and productive family firms experience discrimination in terms both of pay and career opportunities even more explicitly than if they were employed in the corporate sector. She observes how women's efforts may be 'appropriated by male kin' as women are 'marginalised and excluded' from decision-making processes (Mulholland 1996: 78). Sons are seen to be the natural 'heirs' of family firms, with daughters afforded only supporting roles. Daughters are often poorly remunerated in comparison with sons and may be obliged to make the difficult choice between fighting for equality within the family unit, or accepting the status quo for the sake of stability, in the context both of the business and family relationships.

Hamilton (2006) has, similarly, also observed the application of the principle of male primogeniture within family business. Daughters may be 'passed over' in the line of succession in favour of brothers and male cousins, and women are often excluded from the social and economic rewards of family business, sometimes working without official status and for no pay. Women's role within family business may be understood through Glucksmann's (2005) concept of 'embeddedness' – or Truman's (1996) notion of women's 'hidden' work – in a context where women are expected to take a back seat so as to allow male relatives to appear to be taking the lead. Women's work is thus hidden from view and is neither included nor articulated in the same manner as men's work within the family business context. Where women do achieve board status and economic equality in family firms this is unusual, and often involves a struggle, with daughters required to spend years 'proving' themselves in a manner which is not expected of male family members. Hamilton (2006: 15) observes that frequently the traditional 'constructs/discourse of the "heroic" male owner manager and the invisible woman [is drawn upon] to present the business to the outside world as a particularly recognisable form of organisation'.

Hamilton (2006) has found that the retention of this 'heroic' male narrative is seen by both family members and external agencies (e.g. banks) to enhance the status of the family firm within the business environment. In this way, the articulation of women's work activities within family businesses is downplayed, in order to enhance the idea of men's contribution to family labour, because the narrative of the male owner manager is seen to be better for business.

Such failure to articulate women's contribution within family businesses, and the poor representation of women in executive roles, is highly significant in relation to the undervaluing of women's work. This is because, while the influence of family businesses on global economies is often unrecognized (due to the focus on large corporate organizations) the contribution of family firms to global business is, in practice, massive. Howorth *et al.* (2006) contend that family firms of varying shapes and sizes represent between 75% and 95% of firms registered world-wide, and assert that family businesses account for up to 65% of gross domestic product. Thus, if women are underrepresented and underpaid in the context of family business, the implication is that they are being seriously disadvantaged on a large scale and in a global context.

Politics and the professions

The situation within the corporate and family business sectors, where women are underrepresented at senior levels and their work undervalued, is mirrored within the political field. In politics in the UK and USA, as I observed at the start of this chapter, while women are gradually beginning to enter political 'space' at some levels by, for example, becoming involved in local politics (Bruley 1999), there are far fewer women than men in parliament. The number of 'Angels in the House' of Commons is still small in comparison with the number of men and, as Anne Phillips (2004: 224) has observed, 'the overall statistics on women in politics continue to tell their dreary tale of underrepresentation'. There are also very few women at senior ministerial or senatorial level.

Arguably, women are even more poorly represented in the 'professions' than they are in parliament, particularly at the most senior levels. As I established in the previous chapter, more women in the UK, America and Europe are educated to degree level than in the past. Nevertheless, in most professions, it is men, and not women, who continue to hold the most prestigious roles (Gatrell 2005; Edwards and Wajcman 2005). This is especially likely to occur in professions which have traditionally been male 'preserves' such as medicine, academia, banking and the judiciary, in which, in 2007, less than 10% of women had achieved the status of judge (EOC 2007a).

Thus, although women may be well qualified, and might work in organizations with policies purporting to offer equality of opportunity, the career ladder for women in large companies is often foreshortened, while the male ladder extends to the top of the career tree. Women are often moved laterally and may be 'hived off' into specialist or gendered positions, with limited opportunities, such as human resources – known as the 'velvet ghetto'. Black and minority ethnic women who become 'professionals' in the political or business world are particularly likely to be offered roles which take them sideways, rather than upwards, for example being asked to take responsibility for 'diversity' in organizations, often in addition to existing managerial loads and without any attendant prospect of promotion or improved pay (Gatrell and Swan 2008). Thus, women in political, professional, corporate and family business roles are still constrained vertically in terms of career progress and are eased horizontally into particular jobs that are seen as less valuable than those which lead to top-level posts such as a voting seat on the company board, or to a ministerial role in politics.

In the final part of this chapter, I consider why this should this be the case, even though over 30 years have passed since anti-discrimination legislation was enacted. Before searching for an explanation for the lack of women in top roles, however, I consider what happens when women *do* succeed in breaking though the glass – or even the concrete – ceiling. I thus examine what happens when women's bodies, as Nirmal Puwar (2004) puts it, 'invade' corporate and political spaces which have traditionally been 'reserved' for men, and enter the Houses of Parliament and/or the corporate boardroom, in the role of Member of Parliament and/or director, rather than as cleaners or office assistants.

'Angels' invading men's space

Puwar's (2004) research highlights the tensions which become apparent when the female body is no longer confined to subservient roles historically assigned to women such as cleaner or secretary, which involve 'embedded' or invisible work, and which reflect the traditional notion of the deferential, metaphorical 'angel in the house'. Puwar's focus is British politics, and in *Space Invaders* (2004) she analyses what occurs when women enter the House of Commons in

the visible and influential role of MP. Puwar observes how women (and especially women who are from racialized minorities) contest, though their very
presence in the House, the 'somatic norms' of leadership, which are traditionally associated with white men (Elliott and Stead 2008). Puwar observes how,
while women may be entering the UK House of Commons in small numbers,
their embodied presence still does not afford them the 'undisputed right to
occupy' this previously all-male and influential political space (2004: 8). She
asserts that women are still 'matter out of place' and that their presence 'institutes a whole series of processes which signal that they are "space invaders" '
(2004: 10). Thus, Puwar recounts how the black MP Diane Abbott was mis-
taken for a cleaner when she was first elected to parliament. Similarly, a senior
woman in another male-dominated industry (electronic engineering), quoted
in Watson's (1994: 197) research, was obliged to remind colleagues that she
was 'not a secretary or a tea maker'.

Puwar further observes how the debating or enactment of any legislation
relating to women's bodies (such as health screening) leads to the public derid-
ing of women MPs by male politicians in the House. She observes how the
small number of women MPs, combined with the notion that they are invad-
ing male spaces, makes them very visible. They are 'marked' out by their difference from the male 'norm', and this exposes them to different and more intense
forms of scrutiny and criticism than apply to male colleagues.

The glass cliff

The exposure to scrutiny and criticism observed by Puwar in relation to
women MPs is not restricted to female politicians, but is also experienced by
senior women who break through the 'glass ceiling' in the corporate world.
Earlier in this chapter, I noted how the number of women on corporate boards
remains very small (especially in voting or executive roles). When women do
achieve director-level posts on corporate boards they are, like female MPs, very
'visible' (Puwar 2004). Ryan and Haslam (2007) have argued that the limited
number of executive female board members makes them a focus of negative
attention in a way that does not apply to men. Executive women on corporate
boards are thus singled out and individually scrutinized by shareholders, colleagues and the financial press. For example, in November 2003, Elizabeth
Judge (2003) writing for *The Times*, questioned the competence of the few
women operating at board level in top UK companies. Judge produced a report
in which she claimed that, when women are appointed to the boards of FTSE
100 companies, share performance declines. Judge (2003) lamented: 'So much
for smashing the glass ceiling and using their unique skills to enhance the
performance of Britain's biggest companies. The triumphant march of women
into the country's boardrooms has instead wreaked havoc on companies' performance and share prices.'

Judge bases her argument on an analysis of figures published annually by Singh and Vinnicombe of Cranfield School of Management, which classifies FTSE 100 companies by the number of women on their executive boards. Judge asserts that those companies with the highest percentage of women directors had performed badly in comparison with companies with only male directors on the board. From this analysis, Judge concluded that 'corporate Britain may be better off without women on the board'.

Ryan and Haslam (2005, 2007) have challenged Judge's findings as misdirected and unfair. They argue that her figures are inconclusive and that her statistical analysis is flawed, observing, for instance, that she fails to take into account the performance of some male-only boards where share prices are low, and that the measures linking women's appointment to corporate boards with falling share prices are too crude to be convincing. However, in their close examination of Judge's methods and her conclusions, Ryan and Haslam (2007) have also discovered another, more sinister phenomenon in women's appointment to FTSE 100 boards. They term this trend the 'glass cliff', and suggest that women may be offered seats on corporate boards *only* when share prices are wobbly and corporate performance is suspect. In such circumstances, it is argued, male job applicants are likely to reject an offer of a seat on the board, but women are likely to accept it – either because they are less well informed than male colleagues who are part of 'old boy' networks, or because they see it as the only opportunity on offer to them. As Ryan and Haslam (2007) point out, an alternative account of the association between the appointment of female directors and falling share prices would simply involve turning the argument on its head – in other words, rather than the appointment of women leaders hastening a drop in company performance, the prospect of a company's problems becoming public knowledge could precipitate the appointment of women to the board. Thus, women may find that their only opportunity of getting to the top of the 'corporate summit' (Economist 2003: 64) is to take on a role eschewed by men, at a point where the company they are joining is experiencing problems. Women executives thus risk being allocated the 'blame' for poor performance and, presumably, the possibility of bankruptcy or takeover.

Unequal pay

Women in top-level roles are not only disadvantaged in relation to the kinds of jobs they are offered, which may consist only of those posts which men have rejected. They are also disadvantaged in the context of pay. Babcock and Laschever (2003) underlined the importance, for women, of contesting the gender pay gap at an early stage because a narrow gap at an early stage in a woman's career will widen as she gets older. Webb (2007), similarly, suggests that for a woman earning a starting salary of £25,000 (while a man may begin his career on £28,000), the lifetime pay gap will be £300,000. Babcock originally ascribed the executive and managerial gender pay gap to women's apparently 'natural' reticence to ask for more money and suggested that this problem could be solved by a change of attitude on women's part. In an interview in *Kiplingers Personal Finance* (Siskos 2004), Babcock asserted that women were

> less comfortable negotiating to advance their own interests [than men]. In our society, it's not as acceptable for women to be assertive as it is for men . . . women should research salaries ahead of time so they can ask for more money in an informed way . . . employers expect women to concede more in negotiating, so it's important to start out with a higher initial target.
>
> (Siskos 2004: 29)

In 2007, however, Bowles *et al.* published their follow-up research on women's salary negotiations, which showed that women may have good reason to feel nervous about attempting to negotiate a better salary. Bowles *et al.* (2007) demonstrated that, while senior men are expected (and maybe even encouraged) to seek higher pay, women who ask for greater financial reward are regarded negatively by both male and female colleagues and line managers. Women who seek pay awards in line with male peers may thus be shunned and criticized by employers and colleagues, who regard them as selfish, pushy and 'less nice'. This may discourage women from attempting to negotiate pay packages which are similar to those received by male colleagues (Vedantam 2007).

'Selfish' executive women

Accusations of selfish and/or pushy behaviour are not restricted to situations where women seek to attain equality of pay with male colleagues. Desmarais and Alksnis (2005: 459) have argued that all women who 'defy the traditional female gender path by taking on leadership roles' may be subject to hostile treatment. This, they argue, is because women in leading and leadership roles are already failing to meet social expectations about appropriate, embodied female behaviour. Merely by being in a leadership role, women are challenging gendered 'norms' since ideas about leadership are, conventionally, associated with men (Elliott and Stead 2008). Senior women (whether executive, professionals or politicians) are thus likely to be singled out for criticism whatever their personal circumstances. Consequently, women who are not in a heterosexual relationship may find themselves under scrutiny, especially if (as discussed in Chapter 2) they have no children. Conversely, women with male partners and children may be accused of 'selfishness' if they appear to be foregrounding paid work, as opposed to focusing on the needs of male partners and children (Davidson and Cooper 1992).

Unsurprisingly, given the small number of women in top-level roles, female executives may find themselves feeling isolated and excluded, their position as perhaps the only very senior woman in an organization making it hard to relate to either male or female colleagues (Marshall 1995). Women working in predominantly male environments may find themselves with little apparent alternative other than to 'adapt to the organizational culture' by adopting a management approach which is associated with a masculine style of management (Fielden and Cooper 2001: 5) This is not to suggest that there *are* essentialist differences in the way in which men and women manage – rather, as Wajcman (1998), Bradley *et al.* (2000) and Kerfoot and Knights (1993) suggest, there are considered to be gendered management *styles* which are associated with appropriate masculine and feminine *behaviour*. Bradley *et al.* (2000: 79) explain how gendered management styles are 'not equivalent to men and women' but are seen as part of the appropriate performance of 'male' or 'female' manager because they are 'associated with gendered norms in the workplace'. Thus, a 'feminine' approach to management may be thought of as consultative and empowering, while a masculine approach may be seen as directive and decisive. However, while men with a masculine management style tend to be congratulated for adopting a 'feminine' approach when the situation demands it, the same does not necessarily apply to women (Brewis and Linstead 2004). Psychologists Cooper and Davidson (1982: 36) observe how women who exhibit characteristics commonly associated with a masculine performance of gender at work (e.g. adopting an authoritative style) may, instead of being praised for their decisiveness, be labelled 'bossy', whereas a man in the same situation would be more likely to be applauded for his 'leadership qualities' (Cooper and Davidson 1982: 36).[1]

In summary, then, there are uncomfortable consequences for women who invade spaces formerly 'reserved' for male workers, through attaining forms of paid work within the formal labour market which have conventionally been associated with male bodies. Arguably, women in very senior roles have crossed the boundaries of the kinds of work associated with the maternal body (or the angel in the household), by ensconcing themselves in work activities within the formal labour market which were formerly carved out as male territory. Women whose paid work is articulated as 'senior' and/or 'executive' are likely to be small in number and this makes them highly visible. They cannot

---

[1] Kerfoot and Knights (1993) and Connell (1995) observe that the stereotypical 'norms' of male management styles at work may be oppressive for some men. They observe how the 'norms' of masculine management styles privilege men who are heterosexual and able bodied. Thus employed gay, disabled or minority ethnic male managers may be disadvantaged by what Puwar (2004) describes as the 'somatic norm' at work – the notion of 'ideal workers' as able-bodied heterosexual white males.

mingle with the male crowd and may be singled out for scrutiny or blame. Finally, women in executive roles are still ascribed less economic value than equivalent male workers but, if they seek equal pay, will be seen as 'pushy'.

Why so few in number? Women, maternal bodies and work

So far, in this chapter, I have suggested that women in professional, political and business careers experience vertical segregation, and are often blocked or steered away from 'top' jobs in family and corporate business, politics and the professions. I have also considered what happens to women who do 'break through' glass ceilings and corporate walls. I have observed how they are treated as bodies 'out of place' (Puwar 2004) while concurrently being subject to very public forms of measurement and scrutiny.

In this next section, I attempt to understand *why*, over 30 years after equal opportunities legislation was first enacted, senior women in politics, business and the professions should remain so few in number. I suggest that the explanation for this relates to both social and embodying traditions, which are inextricably linked. In this respect, I turn to the work of Judith Butler regarding heteronormative assumptions about gender, and I consider such assumptions in the context of views about women's supposedly low work orientation, especially in relation to part-time working. I move on to explore ideas about women's maternal bodies as supposedly unreliable, in relation not only to pregnancy but also to menstruation and the menopause.

Social assumptions about gender and work

As I have discussed in Chapter 6, women who seek careers in politics, business and the professions are battling with deeply ingrained social and gendered conventions about what the social role of women 'ought' to be. As described in Chapters 2 and 6, the role of women in Anglo-American society has historically been associated with heterosexuality, wifehood, motherhood and home-making. The Parsonian definition of male and female behaviour (described in Chapter 2), in relation to the gendering of reproductive and productive labour, provides a useful explanation for how the stereotypical blueprint for the gendered division of labour continues to be so enduring, and so firmly located within heterosexual norms. However, given the feminist critiques of, and challenges to, the gendered blueprint, and women's increased labour market participation, this does not entirely explain *why* the gendered stereotyping of women's work has remained so durable. I now put forward ideas about why senior women seem to be so constrained by conventional and heteronormative notions about the social role of women. I investigate social misconceptions about women as uncommitted workers, and question assumptions about women's bodies as too unreliable for senior positions within the labour market.

I begin by drawing upon the work of the post-structuralist feminist writer Judith Butler, who (as noted in Chapter 2) has offered a convincing explanation regarding why social expectations about women's social role are so enduring and so difficult to disrupt. Butler (1990, 1993) has investigated traditional power structures, and the concept of male heterosexual hegemony, by deconstructing essentialist notions of gender. Butler draws upon the idea of 'performativity' as an explanation for why traditional social notions of what male and female embodied behaviour 'ought' to be, remain resistant to change. Butler suggests that 'gender' is not a characteristic which men and women 'have' or own. More accurately, 'gender' is something that men and women 'do', or 'perform', the performing of gender being underpinned by the social foregrounding of heterosexuality as the 'norm'. According to Butler, however, the doing of gender along conventional social lines involves more than a single performance, or even a series of performances. In order to express masculinity or femininity in keeping with long established social 'norms' such as the Parsonian notion of male economic providers and female housewives and child-bearers, men and women must *continually* and constantly perform their gender, time after time, in order to maintain it. Thus, the doing of gender goes beyond the notion of performance, because it is ingrained from birth, and must be repeated until death. The expression of gender, therefore, is the result of repeated gendered 'performances' which follow a set of social rules and behaviours which are shared (and in this sense legitimated) by a high proportion of men and women in society. The performance of gender, therefore, becomes 'performativity'. Crossley (2005) offers a useful illustration of how the performance of masculinity becomes performativity, and I quote this example below, but adapt Crossley's words so they may apply to womanhood:

> I might claim to express my [femininity by restraining my gait, growing my hair long and styling it], dressing as I do and so on. [As such] gender is nothing but the cumulative effect of these various behaviour patterns, it exists entirely through them and, as such is 'done' by them. [Gender] is performed and exists only in this performative mode. More to the point, because it exists only in the 'doing', it is never 'done'. It is never completed but must be continually repeated. For example, I never become ['female']. I just keep on becoming [female], or, rather, I keep on 'doing' my [femininity] and my [femininity] consists entirely in the process of doing.
>
> (Adapted from Crossley 2005: 208)

The purpose of Butler's work is not merely to observe, but to challenge and disrupt conventional gender norms. However, Butler acknowledges that this is difficult to achieve on an individual basis, given that performativity is not merely a matter of choice, but might also be a question of habits which are learned in infancy. Furthermore, as argued by Gatrell and Swan (2008), if individuals find themselves responsible for disrupting the conventional gender norms through their own personal life trajectory, they may be personally challenged and threatened. Thus, women (and sometimes men) whose lives do not follow heterosexual gendered 'norms' because, for example, they have no children, or have children but are also in employment, or are in single-sex relationships, may find themselves facing opprobrium, criticism and even violence (Gatrell and Swan 2008). In the workplace, as described earlier in this chapter, women can find themselves disrupting social norms simply through inhabiting a role previously associated with the male body – for example, as a political leader or an executive director, in which case such women may be subject to scrutiny and individualized, often negative, attention.

The gendering of workplace commitment: women's supposed low work orientation

While it cannot 'solve' the problem of discrimination against women, the notion of gender as performativity provides a helpful explanation as to *why* social and economic expectations, and some social research approaches (Hakim 1996), appear to continue to associate women's bodies with the domestic sphere, perpetuating the traditional notion of what Hakim (1996: 179) has described as 'the sexual division of labour which sees homemaking as women's principal activity . . . in life'.

As described in Chapter 2, the hypothesis that homemaking and unpaid productive labour are gendered, and that domestic labour should be central to an understanding of women's work, is used by some scholars as the foundation upon which to build the argument that employed women are less committed to paid work than men. In 1996, for example, Hakim (1996: 179) qualified her claim about the sexual division of labour with the argument that 'The acceptance of differentiated sex roles underlines fundamental differences between the work orientations, labour market behaviours and life goals of men and women'.

More recently Hakim (2000) quantified this assertion, suggesting that women's commitment (or otherwise) to paid work can be explained through preference theory. The underlying assumption here is that women have a 'choice', supposedly unhindered by social circumstances, about whether or not to undertake paid work. Without taking into account arguments about gender regimes and patriarchy (e.g. the views of Walby 1990), Hakim concludes that only 20% of women are employment-oriented, with 20% home-oriented and the remaining 60% of women in the labour force treating employment as a 'job' rather than a 'career', which they can adapt around home and family, perhaps by working part-time. Having put forward the notion that women's gender is accompanied, for 80% of women, by either a low or a compromised employment orientation, Hakim focuses particularly on mothers, whom she claims may lose interest in paid work once children are born.

Part-time working and low employment commitment

The link between motherhood, part-time working and supposed low commitment to paid work has been seized upon by those who appear to believe in the essentialist nature of gender and gendered practices. Scholars such as Tooley (2002) continue to promulgate the idea that 'there are gender differences in the way men and women respond to domesticity' and employer-oriented organizations such as the UK Institute of Directors appear to feel comfortable about endorsing such views:

> Increasingly, [women] are refusing to make choices [between career and children] insisting that they must have it all, loading the consequences on to employers instead. The government is encouraging this selfish and irresponsible attitude [which] tarnishes those many working women who have not lost sight of the reasonable limits to self advancement [of combining] work and family.
>
> (Lea 2001: 40)

The public articulation, by the Institute of Directors, of employed mothers' desire for 'self-advancement' as 'selfish' helps to shed light upon the reason why stereotypical norms continue to preclude women from leading social roles within the formal labour market. As occupational psychologists Desmarais and Alksnis (2005: 459) suggest: 'The idea persists that women should be responsible for [the home] . . . [thus] all working women are violating the normative assumptions of the role of women to some degree'. The notion of women's ambition as selfish also suggests that women's labour market contribution is classified differently from than that of men, who (whether or not they are fathers) are regarded as legitimate (and presumably unselfish) contributors to the economy.

Feminist and equal opportunities campaigns to alter the gendered articulation of executive-level 'work' so that this embraces women – including mothers who wish to work flexibly (EOC 2005b) – are constrained by a lobby against change. This is especially relevant where motherhood and part-time working are concerned. It seems ironic, given the pressures placed upon highly educated women to reproduce (discussed in Chapter 2), that women's professional careers are blocked if they become mothers. Nevertheless, Arber and Ginn (1995) have asserted that, despite increased labour market participation, women with children remain disadvantaged because motherhood is linked with assumptions about low commitment to paid work. Ideas about women's low work orientation are particularly bound up with negative employer attitudes towards part-time working, especially among senior women (Gatrell 2005). Singh and Vinnicombe (2004), Birnie *et al.* (2005) and Desmarais and Alksnis (2005) all argue that this is because, despite alternative evidence and regardless of work–family policies claiming to support the *principle* of part-time working, organizations persist in regarding women employed on a part-time basis as less committed than full-time employees.

Why should this be? The EOC (2005b) challenged negative employer attitudes towards part-time working among senior women. The EOC launched an initiative highlighting the low percentage of women who hold executive roles in the UK and advocated the need to accommodate senior mothers who work less than full-time. However, these attempts by the EOC to improve work–life balance for women are taking place in a cultural context where only full-time work and, increasingly, long hours and 'presenteeism' are considered to be the 'norm' (Collinson and Collinson 2004; Lewis and Cooper 1999). The need to conform to the embodied and 'normative basis for working arrangements' (Höpfl and Hornby Atkinson 2000: 137) requires men and women working in top-level roles to manifest bodily presence at work for extended periods. 'Commitment' to paid work is thus interpreted as requiring full-time presence in the workplace. Women who work part-time cannot always be present when others are at work, and through their child-related bodily absences are marked out from the 'ideal', meaning that they are 'violating . . . the [traditional] assumption that commitment [to employment] equals full-time, undivided attention to the firm' (Blair-Loy 2003: 94). Consequently, regardless of anti-discrimination legislation, mothers working part-time are disadvantaged in labour markets in the UK and North America, and the combination of motherhood *and* part-time working is regarded by many employers as being particularly incommensurate with senior-level employment (Williams 2000; Blair-Loy 2003). Professional mothers who work part-time (even for a short duration) are unlikely to be promoted to senior roles and are expected to be prepared permanently to 'sacrifice upward mobility' (Blair-Loy 2003: 92). They are, consequently, placed on the 'mommy track', a route which requires ability and experience but which is 'lacking [in] career advancement possibilities' (Blair-Loy 2003: 92). This situation is summed up neatly by Desmarais and Alksnis (2005: 459), who state that 'organizations . . . continue to hold the implicit assumption that the ideal worker is a white man who is employed full time'.

In my own research on part-time working arrangements among women in managerial and professional roles, all participants had the qualifications and the experience to progress to senior levels within their organization, and all worked in places where policies promising equal opportunities to part-time employees existed. In practice, however, mothers found that part-time working was available only to women who were prepared step onto the 'mommy track' and, in some cases, to accept demotion. Some women who were offered the 'choice' between full-time work in their existing post, and part-time work in a downgraded post, decided to work part-time and pay the price of being demoted. There was no suggestion of any route off the 'mommy track' should women seek later to return to full-time work. Thus, the decision to work part-time appeared to close off permanently any possibilities for career advancement at very senior level. For example, Sarah-Jane, a hospital doctor in the UK NHS, was obliged to relinquish her status as a hospital consultant when she returned to work as 80% of a full-time equivalent. She recalled:

> It was made clear when I was pregnant with my second child that I would not be expected to take extended maternity leave and there would be no reduction in my hours. They were quite firm on that, they said: 'if you are not full-time, then you are not fully committed to the [health] service so we cannot employ you as a Consultant. You will have to come back on a staff grade.' And I am so angry that I have had to give up my Consultant status . . . but I felt I just couldn't stay at work till 9pm *every* day, like it wasn't my choice any more, my choice was governed by [my] children. But [the NHS] wants you to pretend that your children are not there, they want you to be a woman who behaves like a man and when you are working 80 per cent you can't do that any more, so you are de-valued because you are a mother.
>
> (Quoted in Gatrell 2007a: 470)

Sarah-Jane's demotion appears to be linked not just to the issue of her part-time status, but to her employers' belief that part-time working must inevitably signify lowered commitment on Sarah-Jane's part to her paid work. Consequently, once Sarah-Jane had accepted a part-time contract, her employers ceased to value her as highly as when she was employed five days per week. Having been forced to 'give up' her consultant status, Sarah-Jane felt sure that she would no longer progress up the career ladder – even though she had 25 years of her working life remaining. It would thus appear that women's part-time working, for a multiplicity of reasons, precludes opportunities for promotion within organizations. This is because, regardless of work–family policies claiming to support the *idea* of part-time working, organizations persist in perceiving women employed on a part-time basis as less committed than full-time workers. This provides part of the explanation for the exclusion of women from senior roles within organizations.

The unreliable maternal body – pregnancy, menstruation and menopause

It is apparent that, in Sarah-Jane's case, her employers were uncomfortable not only with her wish to work part-time, but also with her maternal absences from work due to pregnancy. Part of the reason for women's exclusion from executive roles in management may relate, therefore, to their 'troubling talent for making other bodies' (Harraway, quoted in Tyler 2000: 298). I have already observed (in Chapter 4) how, when women become pregnant – whatever their age or social class – their social and financial capital drops. It has been argued that this is because, in the workplace (and especially at senior levels in traditionally male institutions), pregnancy is regarded as 'a deviant condition' (Young 2005: 10) because it underlines embodied female difference from the norms of the male 'ideal worker' (Williams 2000: 70). This argument is especially pertinent at senior and executive levels, where women are few in number, and their female bodies thus already mark them out from the 'norm'.

In my own research on pregnancy and professional paid work, mothers found that the behaviour and attitudes of workplace colleagues changed as soon as their pregnancy became apparent. Even women working in director-level roles noticed that, in circumstances where they had achieved high career status, their 'executive' capital fell once their pregnant embodiment became visible. Amanda, an architect who directed her own company, recalled how clients questioned her competence when her pregnancy became visible:

> Pregnancy poses a problem with client relationships. People were over-sensitive to my potential birth once I started to show. And there I was, running my own business and I would go to meet a client with my [junior] business partner Nicky. And I would say: 'here is my colleague who is *not* pregnant, also a woman, we work together on this'. And I said to Nicky: 'you should have gone without me, even though it's my business . . . because [my pregnancy] . . . undermines us. And I lost a couple of existing clients. Because other people's perceptions of pregnant women are inaccurate.
>
> (Quoted in Gatrell 2007a: 468)

Likewise, Beth, an academic, recalled how the possibility of promotion was instantly rescinded when she announced her pregnant status:

> When I did tell [my line manager], she sat down . . . like she was in shock and said 'Well, that's the *last* thing I wanted to hear. That is *very* disappointing'. Then she said: 'Well, I had intended to recommend you for promotion, but obviously now [you're pregnant] that can't

happen.' She barely spoke to me after that, other than to dump vast quantities of work on me.

(Quoted in Gatrell 2007a: 468)

These arguments correlate with the EOC's contention that many employers associate pregnant bodies with lowered employee commitment, instability, ill health, workplace absence and contamination, one manager describing his pregnant colleagues as 'soiled goods' (EOC 2005a: 11). Given that employers make links between pregnant bodies and unattractive employee characteristics such as low motivation and unreliability, it is unsurprising (if unjust and illegal) that they also disqualify pregnant women from the category 'executive', preferring instead to appoint bodies which appear to represent healthy and 'ideal' masculinity.

Pregnancy is not the only reason why employers equate women and the maternal body with unreliability. Wajcman (1998), examining the situation of women managers, has argued that non-motherhood does not result in women being treated on an equal basis with men. The possibility that a woman might, at some point, give birth is enough to disadvantage her in the workplace. Wajcman (1998: 143) suggests that women with no children 'face the same prejudices as other women even though they have refused the mantle of mother'. Similarly, as noted in Chapter 1, Cockburn (2002) has reflected that women's reproductive status makes them a focus for discrimination. The views of Cockburn and Wajcman accord with two confidential surveys undertaken in 1997 and 2003 by the UK Institute of Directors which revealed that, respectively, 45% and 66% of IoD members would have reservations about employing woman of child-bearing age, due to the possibility that they might become pregnant (Malthouse 1997; Griffiths 2008). Similarly, in 2005, the Equal Opportunities Commission (2005a) estimated that employers' antipathy toward the possibility of pregnancy may be even higher than previously thought, with up to 80% of human resources professionals admitting that they would 'think twice before employing women of childbearing age'.

Menstruation and menopause

Employer notions of unreliability and the maternal body extend beyond women's capacity for pregnancy. As Martin (1989) has observed, menstruation (which begins in teenage years and may continue well into women's fifties) is regarded by employers and sometimes by women themselves as 'messy', 'gross', 'disgusting' and symbolic of the fragility and unreliability of women's bodies. Martin (1989: 93) notes how 'problems arise' for women in locations where menstruation 'does not belong', with women having to 'manage the host of practical difficulties involved in getting through the day of menstruating' without letting it 'show'. The hidden aspect of menstruation, and the menstrual cycle, adds to social fears about what Grosz (1994) describes as the 'undecidability' of the maternal body. Women are socially bound to conceal menstruation from view – thus, employers who (as I describe below) associate periods and menstrual cycles with poor judgement and ineffective management will have no idea when women's 'subversive' bodies are, secretly, bleeding (Shildrick 1997: 164). Menstruation thus is both metaphorically, and literally, associated with the idea that women's bodies are leaky and unpredictable, and with the notion that women's leakiness is manifested through irrational and unpredictable feminine behaviours.

Thus, despite research showing no statistical differences between women's absenteeism when overall menstrual days and non-menstrual days are compared, assumptions are made that women may take sick leave from work while they are menstruating (Bates Gaston 1991). Furthermore, myths abound relating to menstruation and the impairment of women's intellectual performance in the workplace. Women's abilities to make sensible decisions are seen by both women and men as likely to deteriorate the week before a period, due to pre-menstrual tension (Bates Gaston 1991), which is believed to cause 'forgetfulness, lowered judgement, lack of co-ordination and difficulty concentrating' (Martin 1989: 121). It is acknowledged that medical research does identify PMT as a health issue for some women (Martin 1989), and I would not wish to downplay the importance of PMT for this group. However, other studies have shown no consistent mood fluctuation across the menstrual cycle for the majority of women, with some research even suggesting that women may be more creative in the pre-menstrual stages of their cycle than at other times (Bates Gaston 1991). Nevertheless, in a survey undertaken by Bates Gaston (1991) about the workplace performance of menstruating women, 71% of male managers and 62% of female managers believed that performance was impaired by menstruation. In this context, it is perhaps unsurprising that universalizing notions about PMT as a cause of impaired mental capacity among 'women' have been foregrounded in arguments against the employment of women at senior levels where they are 'center stage in the paid workforce' (Martin 1989).

Describing the work of Laws (1983), Martin suggests specifically that the recent focus on PMT by employers and the media is an attempt to combat feminism. This notion, Martin (1989: 121) suggests, is made all the more convincing 'by the conjunction between periods of our recent history when women's participation in the labor force was seen as a threat and, simultaneously, menstruation was seen as a liability'. The view that PMT may be foregrounded in arguments against the employment of women is further substantiated by the fact that men's health issues are rarely brought to bear in arguments against the employment of men. As Grosz (1994) and Holiday and Hassard (2001) have pointed out, men also experience health and bodily issues which they must manage during the working day – but male bodily secretions and/or health issues are much less likely to be exploited as part of essentialist discourses against the appointment of men in senior political roles.

The menopausal years

Negative workplace attitudes towards women colleagues continue as women enter their menopausal years, usually involving gradual physical changes, with women's periods ceasing on average around age 51, but sometimes much later (Bates Gaston 1991; Ortiz *et al.* 2006). The abilities of menopausal working women are often framed within a medical context. Notions about women's decision-making and other intellectual job requirements are linked to medical research about the unreliability, fluctuating hormones and irrationality experienced by some women, who are symptomatic during some part of their menopause (Bosworth 2004; Freeman *et al.* 2004). Women who experience in the workplace physical symptoms associated with menopause, such as hot flushes, may be questioned about these (Reynolds 1999), and the heat of their bodies compared with irrational and moody behaviours, while male colleagues, unencumbered by heat and perspiration, are seen as 'cool, calm and collected' (Martin 1989: 172).

Although, as with PMT, the menopause does sometimes cause health issues for a number of women, there is evidence that only a small percentage of women 'report severe menopausal symptoms' (Bates Gaston 1991: 75). Bates Gaston (1991) reports scant evidence to substantiate the idea that the menopause 'causes [all] women to be physically and mentally incapacitated' and cites her own study which found that, on average, the workplace performance of menopausal women was superior to that of younger women, a finding which she attributes to maturity and experience. Negative attitudes, on the part of both men and women, towards the workplace performance of the menstruating and menopausal body appear to bear little relation to the everyday experience of many women. As Bates Gaston (1991: 69) observes: 'The research evidence is overwhelmingly against the incapacitated, unstable and weak model of menstruating [and menopausal] women which [remains] a stereotype within our society.'

The framing of women's organizational and intellectual capabilities within a biomedical framework of unreliability and failure (Nettleton 2006; see also Chapter 2 above) provides the final part of the explanation, in this chapter, for why women continue to be excluded from leading social roles in politics, business and the professions. As Bates Gaston and Martin have argued, the drawing upon biomedical discourses which equate menstruation and the menopause with 'failure' has perpetuated the myth that the maternal body cannot adequately fulfil the role of 'colleague, fellow worker or reliable functionary' (Martin 1989: 169). Evidence that menstruation and the menopause have impacted on the health experiences of only some women, some of the time, has not prevented the utilization of medical research evidence to give backing to discrimination against all women. As Bates Gaston (1991: 67) observes, medical discourses about women's menstrual and menopausal symptoms continue to be used to legitimize unfair and insubstantial arguments that women are unemployable (especially, presumably, in leadership roles) due to their 'raging hormones'.

Conclusions

In this chapter I have considered women's productive paid work at the high end of the formal labour market from three perspectives, looking first at the lack of women in senior political, professional and business contexts, then at the experiences of women who do 'invade' traditionally male workplaces, and finally at the factors which block women's career progression.

In all three of these perspectives, I have observed that there are still unwritten embodying and gendered boundaries relating to the understanding of the formal labour market which privilege the male body. Apparently, women in leading social and business roles continue to manifest the 'troubled dream of the future', when it was predicted that the angel in the house(hold) might aspire to become an angel in the House of Commons (Anstruther 1992). Unsurprisingly, in this context, while the opportunities for women in senior roles may on paper be limitless, invisible boundaries constraining women's progress continue to exist in practice, these including antipathy towards the maternal body and to practices associated with maternity, such as part-time employment. Women who do reach senior levels are often isolated and scrutinized in relation to their workplace performance, which may in itself be calculated via the lens of the menstruating, menopausal maternal body. As I have observed, there are no similar, health-related measures of men's intellectual capacity. This substantiates the argument made earlier in this chapter that women's work at senior level is measured differently from, and more harshly than, the work of men in equivalent roles.

In conclusion, I suggest that notions about the supposed 'unreliability' of maternal bodies (whether pregnant, menstruating or menopausal) are substantiated though the use of medical and biomedical research which is referenced out of context. This research is conveniently and inaccurately drawn upon as 'evidence' of women's unsuitability for top-level roles in politics and business. Although this line of reasoning has, according to Bates Gaston, been distorted, it is nevertheless accepted by many women, as well as by men. Perhaps women have become so used to being negatively assessed and measured in biomedical terms that they have begun to take for granted notions about menstruation/menopause and lowered performance. If this is the case, it seems important that we question and challenge these assumptions, as well as the idea that the performance of employed women should be viewed through the lens of their reproductive health – when the same measure is not applied to men. It is incumbent on society to shift outdated views about women and menstruation/menopause, in this way challenging the justification of inequalities through discourse about women's biology.

Having examined women's work from the top end of the employment market, in the next chapter I consider women's work from the other end of the spectrum. I examine the understanding of women's work 'across the boundaries between paid and unpaid work . . . formal and informal sectors' (Glucksmann 2005: 19) in relation to domestic labour and the labour of care. I consider how women's household and care work has transferred into the workplace and extend the metaphor of women as embodied 'angels in the house(hold)' beyond the private sphere, and into the labour market.

8   Angels in the house(hold): Cleaning and caring

Introduction

In the previous chapter, I examined what occurs when women employed as co-workers – not as cleaners or secretaries – enter occupational fields of power where male bodies are firmly entrenched. I now consider women's embodied role as 'angel in the house(hold)' from a more traditional perspective, in which women perform domestic work both within the home and the labour market, where it is usually poorly paid. The title of the chapter originates from the poem *The Angel in the House*, written in 1856 by Coventry Patmore and discussed in Chapter 6. As I have already noted, the image of Patmore's unselfish and feminine 'angel' has been drawn upon by feminist scholars (Woolf 1979; Oakley 1993, 2002) as a metaphor for social expectations that about the ideal women. Oakley (2002: 85–6), wrote:

> Angels are epitomies of sacrificial femininity, always thinking about other people . . . The iconography of family life remains firmly wedded to these angelic images and wares. It's one reason why it's so hard to see the hard labour that goes on there . . . everyone plays the great twenty-first century game of The Equal Division of Labour. But the game is a form of cultural warfare and its battles and secessions explain a lot of other politics as well.

In this chapter, I consider first how women's unpaid household labour is articulated as 'work'. I extend beyond the private sphere the metaphor of women as 'angels', exploring how notions of women's embodied sacrifice have transferred into the labour market in relation to women's (often poorly paid) work as cleaners and carers: domestic workers, nannies, nursery nurses, care assistants and nurses. I critique the notion of the 'angel in the house' as classed. In this context, I suggest that images of women as 'angelic' beings have contributed to the situation where working-class women, especially those with low qualifications, who are caring for the bodies of others, are expected by society to perform such paid labour for low pay because it is 'women's work'. I further suggest that women who are seen as performing their so-called femininity 'properly' are expected to do such work without complaint and with little acknowledgement. I first consider the role of women in relation to unpaid domestic labour and care, then I consider the position of women domestic workers/cleaners and carers within the labour market.

Housework

In Chapter 4 of this book, I highlighted the unrecognized nature of 'pregnancy work', suggesting that this should be acknowledged and accounted for as women's work. My argument in relation to pregnancy work has elements in common with the arguments put forward by materialist feminist writers such as Ann Oakley (1974) and Edmond and Fleming (1975) as they attempted to gain recognition for unpaid labour performed by women within the home. I consider first how the notion of 'housework' was defined in the 1970s, and then examine how far things have changed today. I suggest that, although the gendered nature of housework is now acknowledged in research terms, in practice the notion that women 'do' housework remains unchanged. I critique some of the contemporary notions that men are doing 'more', suggesting that men's enhanced contribution is often limited to areas which are incentivized, either because they provide a return on investment, or because they are less routine and more closely associated with notions of masculinity than are repetitive domestic chores. I observe that the gendered division of household labour is especially likely to occur when men and women are in married heterosexual relationships and note how, for women in lesbian partnerships, the picture appears to be fairer.

Oakley (1974) considered the situation of middle-class women who were 'responsible' for household cleanliness and were unlikely to be employed as cleaners in other people's houses, but who probably did not have the resources to 'buy in' domestic labour for their own purposes. Oakley defined 'housework' as encompassing the main physical chores required to keep a household going – principally cleaning, laundering, cooking and shopping for food. She then attributed to housework the following three gendered characteristics. Firstly, Oakley identified as a characteristic of housework the problem that it is 'not socially counted as work' (Oakley 1974:100) or 'labour' in the conventional sense. Oakley thus observes the 'status [of housework] as non-work', arguing that it is not seen as ' "real", i.e. economically productive, work'. Secondly, Oakley observed that housework was regarded as the responsibility of the adult woman within a household. Whether women were single or in partnerships and regardless of whether or not they were employed, the responsibility for housework rested with women alone. Oakley (1974: 1) notes that 'the characteristic features of the housewife role in modern industrialized society are its *exclusive allocation to women*, rather than to adults of both sexes' (emphasis in the original). Finally, women's lone responsibility for housework was seen to be associated with a lack of authority within heterosexual partnerships. Thus, women were seen to have 'autonomy' with regard to domestic chores because these were often carried out when women were alone and isolated within the household, meaning that cleaning was therefore undertaken without supervision. In practice, however, Oakley suggested that women were under pressure to perform domestic chores within the household to particular standards, meaning that notions of 'choice' were highly circumscribed. The order in which chores were performed might, therefore, be flexible, but leaving housework undone (or hoping that someone else might do it!) was not an option if women – especially married women – were to fulfil social expectations of the role of 'wife'. Furthermore, since domestic labour was implemented when women were alone, it remained a 'hidden' task, observed and 'counted' by no one other than perhaps pre-school children. Thus, in heterosexual relationships, when adult males returned home following a day's paid work in the public sphere, the ideal household would be spotless and tidy, the 'angelic' wife having apparently worked magic in order to attain such cleanliness, the embodied nature of the work of cleaning going unacknowledged and unrecognized. Betty Friedan (1965), writing about American suburbia, offers a similar picture of (by implication, affluent) wifehood, with women's work involving the sole responsibility for the manual labour of cleaning the home and physically servicing the domestic needs of others within the household. Central to Oakley's thesis, and that of Friedan, was the notion that women's work within the household was solitary, embodied, and not recognized as 'work'. Women were responsible for domestic labour which must be undertaken silently and without thanks, acknowledgement or pay, as women serviced the needs of others within the household. Oakley (1974) and Friedan (1965) argued that the embodied labour of housework should be acknowledged, and they also challenged the notion that housework should be closely associated with the female body, while men were not expected to perform domestic labour. Concepts of embodied feminine 'mystique' (Friedan) and magic were associated with the notion that domestic labour should be hidden from view and performed without apparent effort on the woman's part. These ideas contributed to the notion that unpaid domestic labour did not, and should not, count as 'work'. In this respect, as noted in Chapter 2, the 1960s television series *Bewitched* depicted a woman alone in her home (except for her child), achieving through magical powers, for the benefit of her husband, the illusion of domestic perfection.

It is acknowledged, here, that 1960s and 1970s feminist understandings of housework were classed and racialized – many black and working-class white women at the time would have been responsible for cleaning not only their own homes, but also those of others, and their issues were not considered in depth until later decades. For example, the black feminist academic bell hooks (1986: 136) points out that if 'poor women had set the agenda for the feminist movement . . . class struggle would [have been] a central feminist issue'. It is thus acknowledged that materialist feminist research of the 1960s and 1970s focused on issues more pertinent to middle-class white women than to working-class white women, or black women. However, it is also important to recognize the contribution of these studies in redefining unpaid domestic labour as 'work' because this has facilitated the inclusion of cleaning and caring work (both paid and unpaid) in more recent scholarship and debates around women's work – including this book.

Women's embodied responsibility for housework today

Several decades on, some changes are apparent. The first thing to note is that, although the household labour performed by women in heterosexual partnerships remains unpaid, it is now recognized and counted as 'labour'. Whereas in the past the unpaid labour of housework was neglected in official audits of productive labour, the concept of 'work' – including housework – is now measured more broadly. Thus 'time budgeting' accounts have been developed, the purpose of which is to measure and render visible the contribution made by women and men to productivity, not only in terms of paid employment, but also in relation to unpaid household labour. Concurrently, housework and the gendered division of labour have become legitimate subjects for research in the context of family practices, economics and occupational psychology (Seager 2005). Thus, the changes sought by feminists such as Oakley (1974) in the context of rendering housework more visible have, to some extent at least, been achieved.

In relation to equalizing the gendered division of labour, however, conventional heterosexual family practices whereby women, especially those in heterosexual relationships, do most of the domestic and care work in the home, remain resistant to change. Studies across the globe demonstrate that women and girls everywhere have greater responsibility for housework then do men and boys. Worldwide, 65% of women's total work time is spent doing unpaid work, while the average for men is around 30% (Seager 2005). In some geographical areas, such as rural India and Japan, men do very little in comparison with women and have a much greater share of 'free' personal time. In rural India, in a survey completed in 1999, it was shown that women slept on average 2 hours less than men and spent ten times longer doing household work than men (Seager 2005). In Japan in 2001, women spent on average 29 hours on housework each week, while men spent only 4 hours (Seager 2005).

In Western countries, while some men do make a contribution to housework, this is on average still small in proportion to the amount performed by women. In the majority of cases, married and cohabiting women retain the responsibility for domestic labour within households, while those men who do make a contribution continue to define their role as 'helping', leaving the liability for housework with female partners (Delphy and Leonard 1992; Maushart 2002; Gatrell 2005). Thus, in the USA in 2001, women spent on average 27 hours per week doing housework while men spent only 16 hours per week on domestic labour (Seager 2005), and in the UK in 2004, women were found to be spending on average over 10 hours per week more than men doing housework (National Statistics Online 2004). In 2007, the Equal Opportunities Commission reported that women spent 78% more time overall on housework than men (Equal Opportunities Commission 2007b). Even in Sweden, which was in 1995 appointed by the United Nations 'the most gender equal country in the world' (Evertsson 2006), a 2001 time budget survey demonstrated that men spend on average 9 hours less per week than women doing housework. Evertsson (2006: 416) relates the inequity of household labour to social expectations and to behaviours learned from infancy. She observes that

> children get their first impression of how family life can and/or should be organized by watching their parents. As a consequence, most children conceptualize 'male' and female' household tasks already at a young age [thus] if housework is also perceived of as a gendered activity among children the likelihood is great that an unequal division of work will be reproduced among them.

Evertsson explains how, although men's time spent doing housework has increased in Sweden, women still do the majority of housework. She demonstrates that, among girls and boys aged 10–18, girls do on average a higher proportion of household work than do boys. Thus, the cycle of the gendered division of labour repeats itself across generations and it remains the case that it is usually mothers, even if they working and especially if they are heterosexual and have a male partner, who bear the main burden of household work.

Heterosexuality and housework

At the dawn of the twenty-first century, despite women's increased presence in the labour market, changes in the pattern of responsibility for domestic labour, especially in the context of heterosexual marriages, appear to be limited. Shannon Davies conducted a study of 17,636 men and women in 28 countries (Jayson 2007). Her research demonstrated that, while men were in cohabiting relationships with women, they were more likely to contribute to housework than married men (though cohabiting men in heterosexual relationships still did less housework than their female partners). On marriage, however, men assume less responsibility for housework, adopting, arguably, an almost essentialist view of the married female body as somehow biomedically programmed to take on responsibility for domestic labour. Conveniently (for them), married men judge the extent of their contribution to household labour 'against the centuries-old standard of what a wife [is expected to do]' (Coontz, quoted in Jayson 2007).

Thus, it remains likely that women in heterosexual relationships in the West, no matter what their social situation, carry a far greater domestic burden than their male partners (Crompton 1997; Brannen and Moss 1991; Scott 1999). The pattern of women's lead responsibility for household chores is replicated in both qualitative and quantitative research. Dryden's (1999: 32) research on the division of labour between heterosexual couples led her to conclude that 'whether women were working full-time, part-time or were full-time care givers and whether men were working full-time or were unemployed, it was in every case the women who had major responsibility for the home'.

Scott (1999: 73) notes that even where men and women in dual-earner households devote the same amount of time to their paid work, women undertake around 9 hours per week more housework than men. This trend is reproduced in Hochschild's (1997) study of family practices in North America and by the HRM Guide Network in Canada which notes that 'While the share of paid work done by young women is high, their share of unpaid work is even higher' (HRM Guide Canada 2001:1).

Motherhood, men and housework

The literature on family practices has long observed that heteronormative assumptions about women's responsibility for household work are exacerbated if women are married and if they have children. At the end of the nineteenth century Charlotte Perkins Gilman (2002) made the connection between motherhood and the increase in women's domestic unpaid labour, and in the late twentieth century Ann Oakley (1981: 1) observed, similarly, that:

> Motherhood entails a great deal of domestic work – servicing the child, keeping its clothes and its body clean, preparing food. The demarcation lines between this and house-or-husband work blur. It is a crisis in the life of a woman, a point of no return.

Delphy and Leonard (1992) argue that mothers are often left to do the housework and 'routine childcare (feeding, dressing and washing . . .) while men play with children and take them out. Employed women therefore generally end up working very long days, at the least favoured aspects of household work … even when they have "good" husbands' (Delphy and Leonard 1992: 240). Sullivan concludes that the free time remaining for women with small children who are also in employment is less than that available to their husbands/partners and notes that 'women's time is … more pressured in terms of intensity' (Sullivan 1997: 235). Sullivan observes that the stress induced by the pressure on time has serious implications for the quality of women's lives. This is in accordance with Chira's (1998: 248) study of working mothers in the USA, in which she observes that most mothers shoulder responsibility for the 'double load' of paid work and housework, with male partners seeing their role, at best, in terms only of 'helping'. Some writers do not see the picture in quite such bleak terms, especially where highly paid women are concerned. Doucet (1995) argues that research on the heterosexual division of domestic labour may not recognize the time spent by men on household and garden maintenance. This view is, to some extent, shared by Crompton (1997: 85), who nevertheless agrees with Doucet's view that heterosexual mothers of small children undertake high levels of household labour. However, Chira (1998) points out that car and household or garden maintenance involves a level of freedom not offered to mothers, who usually do housework and look after children simultaneously – while men using machinery (lawn mowers, drills and so on) are exempted from the care of small children on safety grounds.

Women participants in my own research on family practices (Gatrell 2005) have observed that undertaking occasional and conventionally masculine 'repair and maintenance' roles did not equate to the humdrum routine of housework which remains with women – an observation which is also made by the women participants in Watson's (2008) research. One woman, Eleanor, who still retained responsibility for housework (even though she worked full-time as a senior education manager while her husband was doing a part-time job) described this situation in very cogent terms:

> I think what's really important are not the things you have to do once every three to six months, but what has to be done every single day, what has to be done to keep the family and house ticking over. And it's my experience that women still bear the brunt of that, even women in professional jobs … they are not just thinking they have to have this paper written or seminar [organized], they're thinking: [we] haven't got any bread for the sandwiches in the morning, we've run out of bread, loo roll and that sort of stuff which is the humdrum detail of everyday life.
>
> (Quoted in Gatrell 2005: 122)

Thus, while domestic labour is at least now recognized as 'work', and the hours spent cleaning, laundering and cooking are calculated in sociologies of the household as a form of labour (Shove 2003), this responsibility remains inequitable within heterosexual relationships, especially where there are children. In marriage, especially, the burden of unpaid domestic labour continues to fall unfairly on women, with men still managing to limit the level of responsibility they will accept for domestic work through engaging with traditional and essentialist ideas about women's embodied responsibility for housework.

Among lesbian couples, the division of responsibility appears to be more equal. Dunne (1999: 72) has suggested that in lesbian partnerships 'many of the assumptions which shape heterosexual practices . . . [are] turned upside down'. Dunne suggests that women in lesbian relationships share more equally responsibility for housework, especially if they have previously been in heterosexual relationships where the woman carried the burden of household chores. Dunne observes how her respondents felt that their lesbian relationships offered them 'freedom from gender assumptions around the allocation of household tasks . . . they felt greatly advantaged by the absence of "gender scripts" to guide their relationships with women [and] contrasted [with previous heterosexual relationships] the ease with which domestic arrangements emerged in their [lesbian] partnerships' (Dunne 1999: 73). Dunne's research suggests that lesbian couples have negotiated new ways of living together, which include a fairer allocation of domestic labour. She argues that lesbian partnerships 'provide insights into a more egalitarian social world where gender seems to have lost much of its power to structure relationships along lines of difference and inequality' (Dunne 1999: 76).

Most significantly, perhaps, more recent research on lesbian coupledom (Goldberg and Perry-Jenkins 2007) indicates that, when one partner bears a child within the intact relationship, the gendered division of household labour remains equal and childbirth – in contrast with what occurs in heterosexual relationships – does not coincide with an increase, for the mother, in the hours spent on housework (though the same is not entirely true of childcare). Thus, 'the prediction put forward by gender theory that the division of housework is *not* dependent on biological motherhood, was supported' (Goldberg and Perry-Jenkins 2007: 306; emphasis added).

Class-based responsibility for domestic chores

In many Western countries, the number of women with children under 5 years who are also in employment has risen dramatically since the 1980s. In the UK and the USA, in particular, this increase is particularly significant among women who are qualified to degree level or above and who are employed in professional roles (Gatrell 2005). This increase in women's employment at professional level has been accompanied by an increase in private sector caring jobs such as childminding and cleaning, as household work is outsourced by high-earning women (Crompton 1997; Ehrenreich and Hochschild 2003). As Rosemary Deem (1996: 12) observes, the more women in middle-class jobs earn, the more likely it is that they will be able to 'afford domestic help'. Deem suggests that women in paid work might feel more entitled to 'claim' some 'leisure time' for themselves than if they were full-time house-workers. And as Deem (1996: 9) notes 'Their salaries provide them with economic resources' with which they can fund both the leisure activities and the domestic help required to free up the time.

More frequently, however, employed heterosexual middle-class women feel pressured into paying for domestic help with cleaning and laundry due to the dual difficulties faced by employed women in neo-liberal societies. The first difficulty relates to heterosexual masculine tendencies to abrogate responsibility for housework, leaving this burden with female partners regardless of whether or not they are in paid work (Dobson and Waite 2007). Thus, as Gregson and Lowe (1994) and Maushart (2002) have noted, even if women in 'professional' paid work manage household labour by paying for domestic help, they are usually obliged to organize and fund this. Most male partners continue, firmly and conveniently (for them), to perpetuate the convention that within heterosexual coupledom, housework – whether externally resourced or undertaken by wives and partners – is not a male concern but is associated principally with women and maternal bodies (Delphy and Leonard 1992). This is particularly likely to be the case among married men who, after the wedding, are said to 'revert to stereotype, with the woman taking on the great majority of tasks' (Dobson and Waite 2007: 1).

Outsourcing the housework

Thus, as Ehrenreich and Hochschild suggest, as more women participate at the higher end of the labour market, poorer women are employed 'to do the "women's work" . . . that affluent women are no longer able or willing to do. . . . the question arises: . . . Who will make dinner and clean the house?' (Ehrenreich and Hochschild 2003: 3). This observation was clearly reflected in my own research on heterosexual, dual-earner, parenting couples (Gatrell 2005). In this study, half of the respondent couples paid for help with cleaning, laundry and other domestic chores and in each case the responsibility for sourcing, managing and funding this lay with the woman. Outsourced 'help' with housework involved cleaning (especially of kitchens and bathrooms) and ironing, in which case it was always the mother's responsibility to ensure that items were washed, ready to be pressed on a certain day of the week. Two mothers described the situation thus:

> I manage it and I organize all the stuff that needs to be done and that amazes me how much time that takes. So I organize that the washing

is done, to leave out in the basket so that [it can be] ironed . . . and I
then put it all away and start again.

(Eleanor)

The responsibility for [cleaning, washing and ironing] is mine . . . I
can choose how I do that, I can pay somebody and do without something or I can have a bit of extra money in my pocket and not pay
them but the responsibility is mine. . . . I hate the chores, I hate laundry and the endless repetitive trips upstairs, empty the airing cup-
board, put stuff away, fill it with new things, put another wash on . . .
and then you look round and the linen basket's full and you've got to
start again.

(Angela, quoted in Gatrell 2005: 125, 124)

The association between the maternal body and housework within heterosexual relationships causes resentment between some couples, and, as
noted by Ehrenreich and Hochschild (2003), has consequences for those
working-class women to whom the domestic labour is outsourced. Collins
(2007: 422) explains the situation as follows:

the liberal market regime is characterized by long hours . . . so the
only way [middle-class] women in these regimes can access the labour
market and compete effectively with men . . . is to outsource and
commodify large sections of home life . . . [by] employing cheap
labour to replace their own labour in the home. This cheap labour is
often female.

While it is important not to try and conflate liberal regimes across nations,
as there may be significant differences between, for example, the UK and the
USA, it has nevertheless been argued by Collins that the pay gap between
professional and unskilled women creates a situation – also observed by
Crompton (1997: 82) – whereby some women can attempt to participate, on
male terms, in the professional labour market with men, *only* because other
women are willing to work for low wages in jobs which may be 'insecure'.
Ironically, therefore, it would appear that the more well-qualified women in
the labour are paid, the more likely it is that such women will be able to 'meet
their household needs from the market' (Collins 2007: 422).

Ethical concerns around the inequities of outsourcing housework have
been alluded to by women who acknowledge how, in order to facilitate their
own employment, they rely on other, lower-paid women (Gatrell 2005). The
culpability for the market in low-paid domestic work is often laid at the door
of employed mothers (but not fathers) because, by implication, cleaning and
other household jobs only exist because middle-class women are employed

outside the home and are thus unable to take personal responsibility for domestic chores. However, as Gershuny (2002) and Collins (2007) both imply, the responsibility for this situation must be shared by governments and by employed men: governments because they provide 'little public provision of support' for working women and few incentives for men to change their behaviour; and men because they use the notion of long-hours cultures as an 'excuse to avoid domestic responsibilities' (Collins 2007: 422).

Poorly paid work behind closed doors

Ehrenreich and Hochschild (2003: 4) have commented on the 'invisibility' of women who are employed as domestic labourers (and child carers) in the homes of others, often as part of informal labour markets where their work is barely articulated and (whether as part of the formal or informal labour market) poorly rewarded. They note how cleaners and nannies are working behind the closed doors of households and are often doing this alone and 'hidden from view'. Ehrenreich and Hochschild relate this, in part, to the possibility that, in the USA, such women may be migrants who are resident without official status and who seek therefore to keep a low profile – an issue which is probably also relevant in the UK. They further note that the bodies of women domestics in the USA may be treated by others as if they were invisible, and this may be even worse for working-class black and minority ethnic women than for working-class white women. Ehrenreich and Hochschild also suggest that the 'invisibility' of women employed to do domestic work within heterosexual households stems from the idea that cleaners are employed, partly, to preserve the idea of domestic perfection. The employment of cleaners within households also serves to perpetuate the myth of women who can 'do it all', keeping 'spouses contented' by running a home which is as clean and well managed as a smart hotel, while also maintaining a career. Women who perform domestic labour for others often, therefore, 'remain in the background' while achieving 'hotel-room' standards, on behalf of employers and rarely performing housework 'in company' (Ehrenreich and Hochschild 2003: 4). To fulfil the role of 'angel in the house' on behalf of other women, privately employed domestic workers are, therefore, expected to undertake their duties silently and alone and for very low rates of pay, while adult males are absent from the home.

The employment of cleaners within the household, and the subsequent invisibility of these women, perpetuates the middle-class myth of the embodied 'angel in the house' who is able and willing to achieve domestic perfection without thanks, and without financial reward, even if she is employed in a demanding job. When outsourced to other women, housework may be paid, but because it remains so closely associated with the female body and with notions of women performing housework, silently and without apparent effort, the remuneration for cleaning is poor. Housework, therefore, remains a hidden form of women's work. Furthermore, while it is, at least, now calculated and articulated as 'work' in social surveys and time budgeting studies, outsourced household domestic labour continues to be assigned a low social and economic value within the labour market. Cleaners may thus be employed as part of the informal labour market for very low pay, especially if they are impoverished citizens receiving state benefits, or migrant workers without official status in their country. These women will have little or no access to the legal and health standards and benefits offered formally to employees through policy, such as minimum wages, pensions, health and safety protection and equality of opportunity.

The notion that housework should be performed in solitude and behind the scenes is reflected in the organization of domestic labour within public and office buildings. Just as heterosexual women are usually, even in the twenty-first century, expected to take responsibility for maintaining familial space to an increasingly high standard of cleanliness and comfort (Shove 2003), working-class women have also for many decades been employed as cleaners of organizational and institutional buildings. In such circumstances, the bodies of women workers have long been permitted to enter workplace spaces which may be very traditional and very masculine – but only if undertaking domestic (or at best secretarial) chores, and only if these duties are performed away from public view. There are, of course, men who perform low-paid, service-related jobs. However, the male body – especially if it is white – may be represented at various levels in organizations whereas the employed female body (and especially the racialized female body) is likely to be represented mainly at the lower end of the organizational scale, particularly in relation to workplace spaces that are still, conventionally 'male' spaces, such as seats of government or executive boardrooms. As Puwar (2004: 40) observes, in the context of executive political and/or managerial space, 'the black/female body is [usually] allotted a place [only] in the hidden labour of domestic work, outside of the "seat of power" '. Women's embodied role as 'angel in the house', in which domestic work is performed in the background, for relatively low pay and with little or no acknowledgement, thus transfers seamlessly into the labour market. In the context of organizations, so long as women continue to perform silently the embodied domestic and work associated with maternal bodies and embodied sacrifice such as cleaning and secretarial work, they are tolerated within workplace spaces.

'Angels' and embodied nursing care

Notions of the 'angelic' woman's body, somehow biologically 'programmed' to perform housework in the position of either wife or paid worker, spill over into visions of women as 'angelic' and self-sacrificing carers, both in the home and in the labour market. In this section I consider the consequences, for women, of social assumptions that care work – both paid and unpaid – is women's work and vocational and that, as such, it should be performed for little or no reward. I then consider women's responsibility for childcare, and conclude with a discussion about fatherhood, in terms both of the traditionally gendered division of labour and in relation to 'involved' fatherhood.

The physical care of others – whether children, sick relatives or ageing parents – is often considered to be women's responsibility. Many women, at all levels in the labour market, struggle to balance the demands of care (often child and/or elder care) and paid work – what Williams (2001: 107) describes as the 'burdens of the double day'. Through a case study taken from her research on elder care, Isaksen (2005) illustrates how daughters and wives are often expected, by both male relatives and social services, to take responsibility for older relatives simply because they are women. Describing the situation of Brenda, an employed single parent who shared with her own ageing mother the care of her ill and incontinent father, Isaksen (2005: 117) relates how Brenda's brother would not assist with the physical care of their parents. The local welfare authorities had also refused to help on the basis that Brenda was female and therefore 'ought' to provide the physical care needed by her parents, in addition to looking after her daughter and continuing in her paid employment:

> The welfare authorities stressed [Brenda's] moral obligations as a daughter and woman to push her to take on more care responsibilities than she felt she could deal with . . . Brenda's family life reflects a social pattern in the lives of many contemporary people, including the lack of male participation in informal caregiving.
>
> (Isaksen 2005: 117–18)

In order to gain some relief from a situation which she was finding increasingly exhausting, Brenda was seeking her mother's permission to organize part-time care for her father in a nursing home. Undoubtedly, if she achieved this, Brenda would find herself sharing her fathers' care with other women, who may be paid for this role, but who would probably work long hours, and be poorly paid, for, as Williams (2001) suggests, women predominate in the care-giving industry, providing for low wages the vast proportion of non-familial elder care, childcare and nursing care. As Williams (2001:109) explains, 'paid care-giving is an outgrowth of women's traditional role, it is the result of sex-stereotyping which places women in jobs that are extensions of their personal lives'.

Such caring roles, which require the physical tending of the other people's bodies and are poorly paid, often also involve working lengthy and unsocial hours. This is especially likely to be the case for women who are employed in nursing and/or caring roles without qualifications, such as in privately run care homes for the elderly. Jervis (2001) and Wolkowitz (2006) both suggest that while 'professional' nurses move away from the kind of bodily work associated with intimate contact and bodily waste, less qualified workers (mainly women) are increasingly required to undertake such tasks and many of these workers regard their responsibility for dealing with human waste as symbolic of their lowly position in the care-giving hierarchy. Dahle (2003) suggests that the bodily nature of care work, especially for workers at the lower levels of nursing hierarchies, is likely to be intimate and physically demanding. Patients may need help with primary functions such as passing bodily waste products, eating, getting in and out of bed, walking and so on. Dahle observes a correlation between what she indicates is the demeaning nature of intimate body work, and the performance of this work by unskilled women. Anderson (2000: 142) has observed how the lowest-paid and most physical care work is often performed by migrant and/or ethnic minority female workers, and Jervis (2001) also notes, in the context of elder care in the USA, the relationship between the intimate and very physical care work associated with bodily waste and the low-skilled racialized female care worker, who is expected to perform her work with kindness but with little acknowledgement and for very low pay.

The recognition that the most physical kinds of care work are performed for poor reward by low-skilled women is not to suggest that being a qualified nurse and working in a hospital or a community setting rather than in a privately run care home, relieves women from all of the problems discussed above. Caring roles which have acquired the status of 'profession', in particular nursing, are still 'culturally coded as 'women's work' (Dahle 2005: 127). As Dahle suggests, 'nursing is an embodied practice and the most female connoted of all occupations'. Where men do enter the nursing profession, it is often regarded as a 'transition' to a more senior management position, where the embodied nature of nursing and the intimate nature of care associated with female nurses is minimized in favour of organizational roles. Thus, despite attempts on the part of nursing colleges to professionalize the nursing occupation, the role of nurse still carries with it the cultural subtext of female carer as 'angel', with the associated inferences of vocational calling, self-sacrifice, unsocial hours and (at least, in comparison with medicine), relatively low pay. In the context of vocation, nurses are expected to undertake extensive 'emotion work' as part of their roles (Bolton 2001), and emotion work is difficult to disentangle from the embodied work of providing nursing care for frail or sick bodies.

The outsourcing of childcare

It is not only, of course, sick bodies for which women are employed to care. As in the case of the outsourcing of housework, as more women enter the labour market, so the number of jobs involving the care of other people's children increases. Employed nursery nurses or nannies may be employed in the homes of others, in day care centres, or in their own homes as childminders. In comparison with other jobs, as gender economist Jacobson (2007) points out, paid childcare work is poorly remunerated. For some women from poorer countries, as Ehrenreich and Hochschild (2003) point out, undertaking paid work as a child carer might even imply being separated from their birth children altogether, as they seek jobs as nannies or domestic workers in wealthier western countries – particularly in the USA. Ehrenreich and Hochschild (2003: 3–4) observe:

> While the European or American woman commute to work an average twenty-eight minutes a day, many nannies from the Philippines, Sri Lanka and India cross the globe to get to their jobs. . . . [They] achieve their status only by assuming the cast-off domestic roles of middle- and high-income women in the First World – roles that have been previously rejected, of course, by men.

Nannies preserve the illusion of domestic perfection by feeding and bathing the children, cooking and cleaning and then magically fading from sight.

Thus, on the face of things, at least among professionally employed heterosexual women with children, there is little sense that fulfilling traditional maternal responsibilities in relation to childcare have vanished or been shared with men. Instead, childcare is outsourced, usually to other women who are paid to 'stand in' for employed absent mothers. In this context, whilst acknowledging that individual childcare workers are often poorly paid, and almost always women, I also observe how, for those who can afford to fund this, the 'shedding' of some of the embodied responsibility for the care of children's bodies comes at a price both financially and socially. As in the case of the outsourcing of domestic work, mothers are often themselves required to pay for childcare in order to be able to work (Gregson and Lowe 1994). It should be noted that, in financial terms, the funding of childcare often requires a significant amount of expenditure. In 2002, the Daycare Trust (2002: 1) noted that the average cost of a nursery place in the UK ranged from £6,200 to £7,500 per year, and in some areas of London considerably more (up to £15,000 per year). In addition, Parsonian ideas about embodied maternal duty to care for the bodies of small children remain strong in Western countries. Thus, while social critics may 'excuse' women with no alternative source of income for undertaking paid employment, employed mothers who apparently 'choose' to work instead of remaining in the home to care for their own children may be harshly criticized by relatives and friends, and more widely by others whom they do not know.

In 2002, a reader's letter was awarded a prize by a UK newspaper, the *Mail on Sunday* for the expressing the view that:

> You cannot call yourself a mother if you think one hour of 'quality time' before bed is all your child needs. Quality time is *any* time your child needs attention . . . Children need to wake at a normal time, [and] . . . not be dragged out of bed while it's still dark and driven miles to a childminder . . . I am aware that many women need to work to survive . . . Those who do not should stop moaning. Come on ladies, it's self-inflicted so stop asking for sympathy.

The pressure on mothers to continue to take personal responsibility for childcare work is exacerbated by the social association between masculinity, heterosexuality and paid work. In contrast to the expectation that mothers should prioritize childcare over paid work, fathers who wish to care for their own children within relationships are likely to find themselves in breach of social conventions. Just as, between the 1950s and early 1970s (Parsons 1971), Parsons located womanhood in the context of reproduction and household labour, he described masculinity in the social context of heterosexuality and paternity but with the proviso that, having fathered a child, a man would play a limited role in physically nurturing it. Paternal embodied identity was associated, by Parsons, with earned income, and employment within the external community (Parsons and Bales 1956: 13). Thus, the adult male body was connected to 'his job and through it [to] his status giving and income earning functions for the family' (Parsons and Bales 1956: 14–15). In late modern society, full-time employment continues to be associated with virility and masculinity, and the small number of men who officially downshift their paid work so as to spend more time with their children may find themselves the target of opprobrium or the butt of jokes, especially in the UK and the USA (Hochschild 1997). Furthermore, Hochschild (1997) and Gatrell and Cooper (2007) have found that, even where work–life balance policies are in place to allow 'parents' opportunities to work 'flexibly', fathers in Britain and America are in practice often discouraged, by employers, from seeking 'flexible' part-time work.

Unsurprisingly, therefore, Mayhew's (2006) study has shown that it is still the case, in Germany, the Netherlands and the UK, that for the majority of dual-earner heterosexual couples, full-time employment remains the norm for men even if mothers work part-time. In countries where mothers are likely to work full-time, this is unlikely to mean a reduction in fathers' hours at work and, significantly, when children are of pre-school age, while mothers are likely to reduce their hours of paid work, 'fathers tend to have higher employment rates and work longer hours than other men' (Mayhew 2006: 46). Thus, while fathers may be seen as 'free' to focus on paid employment, they are arguably less 'free' to seek a work–life balance that allows for part-time work and part-time childcare than are mothers. This perpetuates the situation whereby women retain the responsibility for the physical care of small children (and for any parenting deficit apparently resulting from maternal employment), the inference being that mothers 'do' childcare and some fathers sometimes 'help'.

Exceptions to the rule – 'involved' fatherhood

The notion that mothers 'do' childcare accords with the findings of Ribbens (1994), Dryden (1999), Maushart (2002), Hakim (1996, 2000), Lupton and Barclay (1997) and Warin *et al.* (1999) who have all found that married/cohabiting parents of pre-school children tend to perform parental roles along gendered lines, mothers fulfilling children's embodied and emotional needs, while fathers remain 'primarily anchored in the occupational world' (Parsons and Bales 1956: 14). As with many social 'norms', however, there are exceptions. Before I end this chapter, therefore, I shall touch upon the possibility that, in some circumstances, at least in the UK, men's share of childcare – and the paternal desire to nurture their own children – may be increasing. I argue concurrently, however, that fathers' contribution is carefully defined by themselves and that fathers may leave to women the less attractive child-related tasks (usually involving non-direct contact with children). Thus, 'involved' fatherhood often includes mainly the elements of childcare which men regard as rewarding, both in terms of the enhancement of the father–child relationship, and in relation to the retention of paternal power within heterosexual households where women are in paid work.

In relation to fatherhood and childcare, Lewis (1986), Gershuny *et al.* (1994) Gershuny (1997), Hochschild (1997) and Gatrell (2005) have all remarked upon instances where married/cohabiting fathers' involvement with childcare is more substantial than might have been anticipated. It is noted that paternal contributions to childcare have, often, risen in direct proportion to the number of paid hours worked by employed mothers, who steadily persuade fathers to contribute more. Gershuny *et al.* (1994) have investigated this phenomenon in depth and describe it as 'lagged adaptation'. However, the idea that employed women put pressure on men to do more childcare does not indicate a paternal *desire* to be involved with their children, a trend which I have observed in my own research on parenting and paid work (Gatrell 2007c) and which Smart and Neale (1999) and Neale and Smart (2002) have found in their research on post-divorce parenting.

In my own and in Smart and Neale's research, the centrality of children in fathers' and mothers' lives has contradicted traditional expectations about the gendered nature of parenting. It appears that some contemporary fathers (both married/cohabiting and divorced) are keen to be involved directly in childcare, and are explicit in their wish to share in the embodied nurturing role which has conventionally been mothers' preserve. This may be because childcare which involves embodied contact with children is regarded by men as valuable, in that it strengthens the father–child bond, and consequently the paternal sphere of influence within the household. This may be seen as especially important in situations where mothers are in paid work, regardless of whether the adult relationship has broken down or remains intact. Some mothers welcome fathers' desire to increase their parenting role as a 'healthy' way of doing family, but others resist it, viewing it as a threat to the traditional maternal role. Maternal participants in my own research, and in the work of Smart and Neale (1999) and Neale and Smart (2002), have further observed that the advantages to mothers of sharing childcare with fathers are often offset by the limits which fathers themselves place upon paternal responsibility, particularly with regard to child-related domestic labour.

In my earlier research on dual-earner parenting couples (Gatrell 2007c), while all but one father demonstrated enthusiasm about developing 'direct' relationships with children, the boundaries of paternal involvement were carefully circumscribed by all but one man, and 'involved' fatherhood often included only those tasks which concerned one-to-one contact with children. It did not extend to child-related domestic chores such as washing clothes or packing lunchboxes. Thus, with one exception, all mothers found themselves responsible for managing child-related domestic work. Some mothers were exasperated by fathers' abrogation of responsibility for child-related domestic chores and regarded this as the paternal utilization of debilitative power, eroding mothers' quality time with children. In this context, it is arguable that the heterosexual Victorian notion of women's angelic self-sacrifice, in which male and infant desires are prioritized, and women's own needs are suppressed, remains constant. As men with children develop a new interest in sharing the more rewarding elements of the embodied labour of childcare, many women are still providing, in the background, the physical household labour required to make life comfortable for children and male partners. As one mother, Sarah-Jane, explained:

> The children's time with me is compromised by all these other things I have to do. So I have to find some way of somehow not doing them. But that makes me so frustrated, because I know I've got to do them – I mean I have to cook something for supper because I've got all the children to feed and [they are] demanding my time, but I am trying to cook.

> (Quoted in Gatrell 2007c: 367–8)

Thus, while some fathers are creating quality time which is spent exclusively with children, maternal time with children, which may be very precious when women are in paid work, is more likely to be interrupted by the requirements of child-related domestic tasks.

Conclusions

In this chapter I have considered women's work in relation to the labour of housework and the labour of care. I have discussed how notions of women's embodied sacrifice transfer seamlessly between the home and the labour market in women's work as cleaners and carers. In this context, I have suggested that women who are performing their femininity 'properly' are expected to do such work for others without complaint, regardless of whether this is unpaid or paid (and, if paid, for very low reward). I have also acknowledged that, for some highly paid women, it may be possible to outsource the 'angel' work relating to household chores, especially in the light of what Shove (2003) has observed are increasingly high standards of cleanliness in relation, for example, to laundry. However, these women will be expected to fund and to organize this outsourcing of domestic labour themselves, and may be criticized for handing these responsibilities to others (especially if the outsourcing extends to include childcare and/or elder care).

In conclusion, I would like to make two points. The first is that it is very convenient for society to blame high-earning mothers for situations where the embodied woman's work of housework, childcare and elder care is passed to other women for low pay. However, this situation occurs only because the division of domestic labour continues to be gendered along Parsonian lines, with housework and childcare still articulated as 'women's work'. Responsibility for the situation where housework is undertaken in formal and informal labour markets, usually by working-class women for low pay, should not be laid at the door of one group of women. This responsibility should be shared by society more generally – by men and by governments. In this context, I note that there are some circumstances where government agencies and commissions are trying to address the occupational segregation, low pay and poor work conditions associated with women's care work – for example, in the case of the UK initiative Towards a Fairer Future (Women and Work Commission 2006).

However, in the sense that such initiatives may be successfully implemented, I also suggest the need to further explore and contest essentialist notions of gender and 'biology' in relation to women's responsibility for care work and housework. Here, Judith Butler's ideas about the female body, and notions of performativity are important because Butler's assertion that women's bodies are culturally coded helps to explain how social constructions of 'women's work' are gendered and embodied, while simultaneously opening the door for challenges to traditional and essentialist explanations for gendered inequalities and work. In other words, historical social definitions of women's work continue to produce and reproduce gendered practices, but the notion that 'sex', 'gender' and 'biology' are contested and contestable sites paves the way for the possibility of arguing for change in the way that women's work is perceived.

I end this chapter, however, on a note of caution by raising the prospect that improvements in women's situation may heighten male fears about the erosion of male hegemony – either in the labour market or in the home sphere – and that these fears may be counteracted by paternal strategies to diminish women's sphere of influence both at work and at home.

9 'I'm Mandy, fly me': Sex for sale in formal and informal labour markets

Introduction

In the previous two chapters, I have considered women's economic activities at the high end of the formal labour market, and at the lower ends of formal and informal labour markets. In this chapter, I focus principally on women's work within the informal, or illegal, labour market. Specifically, I consider the position of women prostitutes or sex workers, whose paid work is deemed to be against the law. In this context, I analyse the 'boundaries' in relation to the commodification of women's bodies and suggest that these are often blurred. I identify a 'Catch-22' situation, whereby the ideal situation for women working in the sex industry is seen to be one in which prostitutes are invested with agency and the ability to make rational 'choices' and decisions. I argue, however, that such ideals may, in practice, be undermined by poverty, drugs, and traditional patriarchal systems which formally and informally exclude prostitutes from the rights and benefits afforded to citizens in 'legal' employment.

Before I begin my discussion of sex work, it is important to acknowledge that the commodification of women's bodies, especially in relation to the leisure and travel industries, exists within the formal, 'legal' labour market and has been the subject of feminist scholarship for the last three decades (Hochshild 2003; Adkins 1995). For example, 'I'm Mandy', the title of this chapter, derives from a television advertisement, broadcast in the UK in the 1970s, for air travel. The focus of the advert was a slim, well-made-up woman, dressed in a flight attendant's uniform, inviting passengers – presumably male business travellers (Hochschild 2003) – to 'fly *me* to America'. The implication of the advert was that the body of 'Mandy' the stewardess, or of someone like her, was part of the transaction between passenger and airline. The opportunity to gaze at, and be waited on, by a woman like 'Mandy' was integral to the purchase of a flight ticket.

Notions of women's bodies as commodities in the context of 'legal' employment were introduced by Arlie Hochschild in 1983 in her research on emotion work (Hochschild 2003), and subsequent scholars (e.g. Bolton 2001), have set the agenda for the interpretation of 'emotion work' as a particular form of labour which is often undertaken by women and which may be hidden in essentialist discourses about it being 'natural' for women to adopt caring roles. However, Hochschild (2003), although she focused on emotional labour, began concurrently to raise related questions about the sexualization and commodification of women's bodies in the airline industry.

Sexualization, emotion and 'legal' work

As Hochschild (2003), Sanders (2005a), Wolkowitz (2006) and Brewis and Linstead (2000) have variously suggested, the relationship between women's work which involves elements of sexual labour, and emotion work, may be hard to disentangle. When Hochschild published *The Managed Heart* in 1983, she focused on the requirement for air stewardesses to engage in forms of body work which were often highly sexualized. For example, airlines required women to smile at all times, throughout even lengthy flights, in order to convey the idea that serving (usually male) passengers was a pleasurable activity (Hochschild 2003). During the 1960s and 1970s, more than one major airline adopted advertising strategies similar to the 'I'm Mandy' campaign quoted above. As Hochschild (2003: 93–4) observes:

> The ads . . . [suggest] . . . that the attendant is friendly, helpful and open to requests. But . . . the smile can be sexualized as in . . . 'Fly me, you'll like it'. . . . Such innuendos lend strength to the conventional fantasy that in the air, anything can happen . . . So the sexualized ad burdens the flight attendant with another task . . . she must respond to the sexual fantasies of passengers.

The sexualization of the female flight attendant role, and the legitimization of this approach via television advertising campaigns, assisted airlines in requiring women flight attendants to engage in demanding levels of body work. Women were expected to maintain low body weight and were subjected to physical 'tests' to ensure that they complied with airlines' definitions of physical attractiveness – being obliged, for example, to submit to 'periodic thigh measurements' (Hochschild 2003: 103).

The requirement for flight attendants to engage in sexual role-play as part of their job, regardless of whether they found this intrusive or 'demeaning', illustrates the problems for women working in industries where the female body is utilized as a commodity. Hochschild's (2003) research emphasizes the difficulties of undertaking work of a sexual nature which is not articulated as 'work' or 'recognised as an activity separate from the relationship . . . within which [it is] conducted' (Glucksmann 2005: 19) but is seen as a non-negotiable part of the job. Hochschild's work highlights the constraints experienced by women who are unable to establish, change, or control embodied boundaries in relation to work activities. Similarly, Adkins's (1995) research has shown how, in the workplace, women's bodies at work are often highly sexualized, especially if they are employed in service roles as bar staff, waitresses or junior secretaries. In the leisure industry, in particular, women (especially if they are young) may be expected to perform their tasks while accepting male behaviours verging on sexual harassment, as part of the job. Thus, notions of sex, emotion and subservience are closely bound up (Adkins 1995). Adkins (1995) and Hochschild (2003) explore how women working in sexualized roles within 'legitimate' industries, manage the boundaries between what is required of them by employers and clients, and what feels acceptable to them. The implication, particularly in Hochschild's work, is that women workers draw upon strategies of resistance to set boundaries in relation to how far they are prepared to fulfil the sexual fantasies of customers. As I observe in this chapter, there are some echoes between strategies of resistance employed by the 'legitimate' workers considered by Hochschild (2003) and Adkins (1995) and those drawn upon by women working in the sex trade. For example, in the same way that some of Hochschild's flight attendants manage the emotional and sexual demands of their jobs by viewing these requirements as a 'role', which must be performed but from which they may personally distance themselves, so do many women working in the sex trade (Sanders 2005b; Brewis and Linstead 2000).

Hochschild's focus on embodied boundaries as an issue for research in the context of 'legitimate' paid work, has provided the foundations for more recent studies concerning the boundaries between what is private and what is public in relation to the bodies of sex workers. As Brewis and Linstead (2000: 226) have observed: 'sex work [is] an increasingly important site for the understanding of contemporary self-identity. Here areas traditionally (p)reserved as private, such as the body, are commercially traded and consumed as the boundary with the public sphere is rendered permeable.' The observations of Brewis and Linstead seem particularly relevant to this chapter, in which the main concern is to investigate the notion of 'boundaries' as a source of power in relation to sexuality and paid work. This chapter is concerned with who has the power and the entitlement to define and set boundaries within the informal – and currently criminalized – labour market of prostitution. How far can women who earn money through prostitution – or, as it is termed in this chapter and also by Sanders (2005a) and Brewis and Linstead (2000), 'sex work' – be said to exercise 'choice' in relation to their paid work, and how are these 'illegal' workers treated by the law? It is acknowledged, here, that there are many and varied types of women's activities within the sex trade, and that the boundaries between informal and formal labour market participation may be blurred in relation to some of these. In this chapter, however, the focus is on sex work which falls firmly into the context of 'informal' and, presently criminalized, labour. I thus use the term 'sex worker' in keeping with the definition of Murphy and Venkatesh (2006: 130) in which sex workers are described as 'anyone who exchanges sexual intercourse (including oral sex) for money or some other material good'.

Sex work

I have already observed that one important theme in common between the sexualized nature of work in legitimate industries, and non-legal forms of 'sex work', relates to the issue of boundaries. I suggest, however, that 'boundaries' and notions of 'agency' and 'choice' in relation to sex work are even more complex than in the context of conventional employment. This is for a number of reasons, the main one of which relates to the gendered criminalization of sex work. Sex workers, regardless of whether they are seen as hapless victims or as a decision-making agents, experience higher levels of blame and criminal convictions than do their male clients (Wolkowitz 2006). In the UK, since Victorian times, women prostitutes or sex workers have been treated not only as victims but also as wrongdoers. In her helpful summary of the history of prostitution, Wolkowitz (2006: 122) accounts for how 'draconian nineteenth century legislation put in place particular constructions of the prostitute body'. For example, the Contagious Diseases Act of 1864 permitted the forcible internal examination of female prostitutes by doctors, such inspections often preceding the forcible imprisonment of women to prevent them from spreading sexual diseases. Wolkowitz (2006: 122) suggests that the legislation, which simultaneously criminalized prostitution and socially excluded prostitutes, 'put into place a particular understanding of prostitutes as a distinct, readily identifiable category . . . visibly marked by difference . . . Whereas prostitution had been a temporary reddress for young women at a time of economic hardship, they now became locked into a criminal career and a defining social identity' to be pathologized and treated as a public nuisance.

Many current debates about prostitution or sex work would acknowledge the difficulties, for sex workers, of social exclusion. However, the views of many scholars, policy-makers and activists tend to be polarized between those which regard sex workers as agents making rational decisions to undertake sex work as a preferred form of economic labour in comparison with other (often limited) options, and those which view sex workers as victims.

Sex workers as victims

Among those who regard sex workers as victims, views also tend to differ. Radical feminist writers such as Dworkin (1996) and Pateman (1988) present sex workers as always exploited, and as victims of a patriarchal world. Research by those who hold feminist views about prostitutes as victims of patriarchy tends to portray women sex workers as deeply unhappy individuals who are filled with disgust at their own behaviour and who, consequently, seek to abject themselves from their own bodies. Dworkin and Pateman portray sex workers as incapable of setting their own emotional and physical boundaries, this inability rendering all sex workers, in all circumstances as exploited, non-agentic, vulnerable to abuse and in need of protection from others.

Arguments presented by government agencies and policy-makers, which also construct sex workers as 'victims', are more likely to be motivated by an instrumental desire to reduce levels of sex work (especially street work) for a variety of reasons linked to the assumption that sex work is a criminal activity and that sex workers should be excluded from social interaction with 'respectable' others, unless or until they reform (by leaving the sex trade). Research by policy-makers tends thus to focus on the idea of helping those who cannot help themselves, with the anticipation that this approach will lessen the volume and the visibility of prostitution. Sanders and Campbell (2007) criticize the UK's Coordinated Prostitution Strategy (Home Office 2006) for perpetuating the traditional idea of prostitution as an 'unacceptable' form of employment. This is because while the Prostitution Strategy recommends help for those who give up sex work, it also implies that women who remain in the industry will continue to be criminalized and unprotected on the basis that 'they are not valid citizens' (Sanders and Campbell 2007: 15). In this sense, the policy-makers set, on behalf of society, the boundaries and contexts for what is 'acceptable' in relation to sex work, both in legal and spatial terms. Policy-makers have, in this context, been accused of 'condemning the very people they seek to help' (Harvey 2005). Hubbard (2004: 1688–9), who focuses on attempts by the state to 'promote family-oriented gentrification' in Paris and in London's West End, suggests that government plans to enhance the desirability of cities for those in legitimate, middle-class employment, both as residents and as income-generating tourists, facilitate government agencies in justifying

> strategies of zero tolerance policing. Bolstered by a rhetoric of spatial cleansing and purification . . . such policies enjoy a level of public and political support and . . . female sex workers are currently being identified as a threat to national values in an era when nebulous anxieties about difference and diversity are prompting the state to instigate 'public order' legislation which serves to criminalise specific groups,

[prostitution being] antithetical to the reinvention of city centres as safe, middle class, family oriented consumption spaces.

Although their motivation and strategic approaches may differ, politicians and feminists who write against prostitution both seek the same 'end result' – the total disintegration of the sex industry. In this regard, both groups of 'abolitionists' (Sanders and Campbell 2007: 2) view prostitution as an exploitative, non-legitimate form of work and the 'end result' sought is the same.

Sex workers as agents

The sex-worker-as-victim approach has been criticized by scholars who regard this as patronizing and classed, the portrayal of the sex worker as victim meaning that her voice is suppressed, and hidden by the reforming zeal of feminists and others, who believe they are acting in the her best interests. Jeffrey and MacDonald (2006: 314) describe the nature of such discourse as dominating 'any understanding of the lives of sex workers or the realities they face. Furthermore, it judges sex workers, reinforces their pathological stigmatization and, even in attempts to portray the sex worker as "victim" infantilizes her [and] denies her of agency.'

Critics of the interpretation of sex worker as victim argue that many sex workers make rational (if sometimes circumscribed) decisions to join the sex trade. Some writers view 'sex workers' as agentic beings who do not need to be patronized, either by academics or by government officials. This group argues that many sex workers 'overwhelmingly view sex-work as a job' and assert that, as Jeffrey and MacDonald (2006: 314) suggest, sex work is: 'A social and political resistance [by sex workers] to being constructed as "cheap labour" or the deserving object of managerial of government intervention and control'.

Some writers, such as Brewis and Linstead (2000), write about sex work in positive terms, suggesting that in some circumstances it may be sexually and economically liberating, with sexuality and power inextricably bound up and some power inevitably ascribed to female sex workers. Brewis and Linstead (2000) define sex work as a form of employment, and highlight similarities between the body and emotion work required of sex workers and of workers in other jobs and professions. They cite examples of how sex workers may be highly competent at managing personal boundaries, these strategies enabling them to separate out working life from personal lives – as in the case of the 'legitimate' workers considered by Hochschild (2003) and Adkins (1995).

The concept of sex workers either as victims or as agentic beings who 'choose' sex work is seen as unhelpful by some scholars. Benoit and Shaver (2006: 249) argue the need to move beyond what they describe as the 'flawed' dichotomy which polarizes 'prostitution as one thing or another –

exploitation or work, slavery or freedom'. They argue that such polarized views 'fail to reflect the complex heterogeneity between people who work in the sex industry'.

One means of exploring the debate about whether sex workers are victims or decision-making agents, or something in between, is to examine their ability (or otherwise) to articulate and to maintain personal boundaries when working. In the next part of this chapter, I consider how far decisions about what services to make available, and when and where to work, are the province of individual sex workers. I analyse the similarities and differences between trafficked, outdoor, and indoor groups of sex workers, regarding the setting of personal boundaries. I also compare the relative constraints and opportunities associated with sex work in relation to 'legitimate' employment. In particular, I observe how 'legitimate' jobs within the formal labour market (even when low-waged and exploitative) can enable workers to access support from employers and enforcement agencies, especially in the case of violent crime. Sex-work, by contrast, excludes women from claiming the status of 'citizenship', with its attendant rights to health, safety and protection from crime, both in policy and in practice.

The global trafficking industry

Although more research into the sex industry has been recommended (Benoit and Shaver 2006), it is important to acknowledge that sex work is a challenging and complex field to research, given its 'illegitimate' status in most countries (McKeganey and Barnard 1996) and with the attendant pressures on sex workers to maintain secrecy (Sanders 2006). Even though researchers have gained access to some arenas of the sex industry, others are more difficult to enter. This is especially the case with regard to the sex trafficking industry which, Seager (2005: 56) suggests, 'is sustained by . . . coercion, torture, rape and systematic violence' and draws in women and children under false pretences, through the offering of bogus overseas jobs. The coercive and violent nature of trafficking means that extent of the sex trafficking industry can only be estimated, and that qualitative research on global trafficking is rare. Brewis and Linstead (2000: 250) observe the considerable range of 'debates about the definition of trafficking, as well as . . . myth-making around the phenomenon and its extent which makes it more difficult to recognize those workers who do move freely and autonomously'. However, Brewis and Linstead (2000) and Seager (2005) acknowledge that trafficking is widespread.

The problem of access makes it difficult to establish accurately how far trafficked sex workers can define their own personal boundaries. At the same time, however, it seems reasonable to assume that the articulation of boundaries and choice, for trafficked sex workers, is very limited. Seager (2005) suggests that trafficked women have little protection or autonomy, are often under age, and are subject to aggression and brutality from managers and customers. In addition, trafficked sex workers are vulnerable to bullying from the law enforcement agencies which, in attempts to break up sex rings, may imprison women sex workers and confiscate their possessions (Ditmore 2007). It therefore appears (despite limited knowledge about the scale and operational details of the industry) that trafficked sex workers have limited ability to articulate any personal boundaries at all. In this respect, ideas about decision-making and agency are optimistic, especially in the case of trafficked minors, and the 'prostitute as victim' approach of feminist 'abolitionists' such as Dworkin (1996) and Pateman (1988) seem to be depressingly apposite.

Scholars of the sex-work industry are effectively denied access to the everyday lives of trafficked sex workers. However, there is an increasing wealth of research on (apparently) non-trafficked sex work. This does not mean that information on the lives of sex workers is easy to obtain. Even where researchers are granted access (perhaps through health initiatives directed at sex workers: McKegany and Barnard 1996), research on the sex trade may be challenging because the environments can be hostile and frightening (Sanders 2006). Thus, despite the fact that women have engaged in sex work for thousands of years, and although there are an estimated 64,000 women sex workers in Britain (Wolkowitz 2006), our knowledge about sex work remains limited in comparison to other industries. Nevertheless, important empirical work by McKegany and Barnard (1996), Benoit and Shaver (2006), Murphy and Venkatesh (2006), Sanders (2005a), Sanders and Campbell (2007), Jeffrey and MacDonald (2006) and Hubbard (2004) has opened a window on the experiences of non-trafficked sex workers. For example, Sanders (2005a) and Benoit and Shaver (2006) reveal important differences between outdoor (street) sex work and indoor (massage parlour and escort) sex work. The work of Sanders (2005a) and others allows for a research-based discussion around the issue of 'agency versus victimhood' in relation to sex work. In order to understand better the position of sex workers in relation to choice, and the formal and informal labour market, I now focus on the experiences of outdoor and indoor sex workers, in relation to debates about boundaries and citizenship.

Outdoor sex work

Sex work on the streets, or 'outdoor' sex work, is considered to be the 'low end' of the sex-work market. For women performing sex work on the streets, life is a strange mix of freedoms and constraints. Women who work the streets may do so intermittently (McKegany and Barnard 1996) and usually make the decision to do this due to short-term and extreme financial need. In Jeffrey and MacDonald's (2006) study, most outdoor sex workers 'had weighed sex work and its advantages and disadvantages against other forms of work and found that sex work, overall, was an optimal choice'.

This view implies that outdoor sex work may enable women to set their own boundaries and make autonomous decisions about the best form of paid work for them. On this basis, it would appear that outdoor sex work may have some advantages over low-paid 'legitimate' jobs and indoor sex work, offering the chance of flexible work without the need for job applications or interviews, and providing instant cash reward which is likely to be higher than anything else on offer from local employers and (possibly) no need to 'fit in' with rules stipulated by massage parlour managers (Murphy and Venkatesh 2006). In addition, outdoor sex work involves few set-up costs. Unlike indoor sex work, street work does not require investment in working premises or computer technology, and outdoor sex work may also allow for better use of time. For example, if sex workers have been allocated space in an indoor venue, this may involve paying for access to rooms and reception services during 'quiet' times when clients are few. Street workers, however, may move on to seek clients elsewhere, or go home, and return later without financial obligations to massage parlour owners for access to workplace space and so on.

In the context of notions about outdoor sex work and 'choice', however, the 'choices' available to street workers are constrained and gendered, For example, Murphy and Venkatesh (2006) suggest that women 'who are starting their lives anew' (which might initially sound like an inviting prospect) often enter the outdoor sex trade as an 'escape from ... domestic violence', or because they are desperate for money. This implies that, while it might open the door to a 'new' life, the decision to become an outdoor sex worker has been made in the context of very limited and unattractive alternative options. Often, for women engaging in outdoor sex work, the opportunities available within 'legal' labour markets consist only of low-waged unskilled jobs which offer little or no flexibility, and which are consequently incompatible with many women's lifestyles. Thus, in Jeffrey and MacDonald's study of sex workers in the Maritimes in Canada, many women (especially those with children) became sex workers because they were unqualified for skilled labour of any kind, and were unable to combine inflexible low-paid employment with childcare responsibilities. In the context of flexibility, outdoor sex work is more manageable than indoor sex work which might involve inconvenient shifts and (unless women are working singly from their own premises) regulations 'set' by parlour owners and managers. Thus, women who work the streets often take this route because it lends itself to flexible working and offers higher short-term earnings than other jobs (Murphy and Venkatesh 2006). Women undertaking 'outdoor' sex work could, thus, be said to have a level of personal autonomy in that they can develop their own routines and may not be 'answerable' to others. As Jeffrey and MacDonald (2006: 321) explain: 'It is not only the money that makes sex work a viable option; it also provides that other key ingredient: flexibility'. They note how, especially for women with children, 'the combination of time constraints and minimum wages makes for particular economic hardship'. They go on to observe how for mothers supporting dependent children, plus in some cases older and ailing relatives, 'Sex work, which in comparison with other types of work, can allow women to make relatively large amounts of money in relatively short amounts of time and which can fit their own schedule, clearly furnished a way around the constraints of minimum-wage work.'

In the case of the Canadian Maritimes, however, it is observed by Jeffery and MacDonald (2006) that unqualified men have access to a wider range of more attractive options within the formal labour market than women. Men living in the area studied were less likely to be caring for children (so did not need to worry about flexibility) and, assuming they could find a job, would be better paid than women. Thus, 'the conclusion that women disproportionately bear the burden of low-wage work in Atlantic Canada is inescapable' (Workman 2003, quoted in Jeffery and MacDonald 2006: 320). On this basis, while women could be said to have 'chosen' sex work in preference to other jobs within the formal labour market, it is apparent that this choice has been made in a situation where unskilled women are offered a much narrower range of options than are available to unskilled men.

Furthermore, in relation to 'choice', research by McKegany and Barnard (1996) and Sanders (2005a) indicates that many women working on the street are drug users, and may be working partly because they require money to support their habit. Both McKegany and Barnard's (1996) ethnography of street workers in Glasgow, and Sanders's (2005b) research highlight the benefits of thinking of sex workers as rational agents, rather than as hapless victims. However, both these studies also acknowledge that, among drug-using sex workers, notions of 'choice' are often more limited than for those who are not using drugs, recognizing that outdoor workers are more likely to have a habit than indoor workers. McKegany and Barnard's study of outdoor sex workers in Glasgow in the 1990s suggested that 72–76% of women were likely to be injecting drug users, and Degenhardt *et al.* (2006) have also noted the links between injecting drug use and street-based sex work in Australia, especially if this is combined with cocaine use. A survey of sex workers in Bristol, UK, revealed that 60 out of 71 outdoor interviewees used heroin, compared with only four out of 71 'parlour' or indoor 'respondents' (New Scientist 2007). Noting that the relationship between drug use and outdoor sex work is not 'unique to Glasgow' but has also 'been noted in countries throughout the world', McKegany and Barnard (1996: 36) observe how a serious drug habit develops in a relatively short time. This, in its turn, may place outdoor sex workers under increased pressure to work more often and for lengthier periods. McKegany and Barnard (1996: 41) quote the experiences of one outdoor sex worker, Elaine, who says: 'The more money you make the more you spend, you just get a bigger habit, that's all . . . you do it cos you need the money but then you get a big habit so you have to keep coming out'.

The writers express uncertainty about whether, initially, women join the outdoor sex industry in order to support drug habits, or whether they use drugs to block out their experiences on the street. However, once working as an outdoor sex worker, it appears that women require drugs to assist in blanking out the experiences of providing sex to clients. One worker is quoted (McKegany and Barnard 1996: 42) as explaining:

> If I've no had a hit [injected drugs] I just want the work over and done with, if you've had a hit you can stand the work . . . But if you're straight you start to think about it, it keeps flooding back intae your mind.

When drugs are involved in sex work, I would suggest that the setting of boundaries becomes even more difficult than in other circumstances. Sanders and Campbell (2007) underline the importance, for those in the sex trade, of being able to set personal boundaries, insisting, for example, on the use of condoms by clients. McKegany and Barnard's (1996) study suggests that on some occasions, the level of intoxication through alcohol and drugs means that some outdoor sex workers are left uncertain as to whether they have had a 'quiet' evening, or whether they may have serviced clients without condoms, without payment and/or been robbed of what money they had on their person. This situation suggests that rational decisions about personal boundaries, such as insisting that clients wear condoms throughout sex, may be difficult to achieve. Furthermore, some women who are injecting drug users may be working to pay debts owed to drug dealers for heroin previously supplied, and the notion that these workers might have a 'choice' about whether to pay these debts seems idealistic, to say the least. The idea that outdoor sex workers may be working to pay drug dealers and/or, as McKegany and Barnard suggest, to support male partners who accompany them while they work in order to 'protect' them is suggestive of pimping – even if some sex workers prefer not to use that term. The concept of 'pimping' implies some level of coercion and indicates that, for some women, 'choices' about how often to work, and whether to stay in or move out of the outdoor sex trade, may be very limited – as may the prospect that monies earned will be for the benefit of the sex worker herself.

Finally, I think it is important to note that, for outdoor sex workers, while some ideas about sexual liberation may cut the ice in relation to hypotheses of sex workers as rational and agentic beings, the performing of outdoor sex work (whether by 'choice' or otherwise) comes at a great cost to social freedoms. As Sanders (2005a) points out, sex workers – and in particular, outdoor sex workers – are criminalized. They may consequently, therefore, be excluded from much needed health and social services. The criminalization of sex work may be unfair, but reports on current political attitudes towards sex work in the UK, the USA, France, Australia and the previously more liberal Netherlands suggest that change is unlikely to occur in the immediate future (Saunders and Cambell 2007; Hubbard 2004; Harvey 2005). In practice, this means that outdoor workers are often obliged to hide from view, performing their 'illegitimate' work alone, in risky circumstances and in out-of-the-way places where violence is most likely to occur. In addition, because they are stigmatized and afraid of the 'authorities', sex workers are far less likely to report to the police acts of violence against them than would other workers who were assaulted as part of their employment. This indicates that the autonomy of sex workers to set embodied boundaries in relation to their personal safety is limited, because both sex workers and clients are aware that 'back-up' from enforcement agencies such as the police is not available to street workers in the same way that it may be to employees within the formal labour market. Thus, the level of violence experienced by sex workers is far greater than that suffered by workers in other occupations. As Sanders and Campbell report, well over 50% of outdoor sex workers encounter violence in their jobs, and can do little to prevent it. Consequently, in the UK, street sex workers are 12 times more likely to die from violence at work than other women their own age.

On this basis, notions of agency and choice in relation to outdoor sex work may seem preferable to what Jeffrey and MacDonald (2006) refer to as the 'infantilization' of sex-workers. This is especially relevant in situations where narratives of victimhood are utilized as reasons for excluding sex workers from social benefits which are available to workers employed in the formal labour market (Harvey 2005; Sanders 2005a). However, ideas about outdoor sex work and 'choice' must also be moderated by the recognition that viable alternatives to sex work appear limited – especially when sex work is combined with drug addiction. Thus, the picture of sex workers as rational and agentic beings may be more accurate than the idea of sex workers as victims and/or immoral persons who require redemption, in that outdoor sex work may be 'chosen' as the best alternative among other (often unattractive) available options. However, the level of autonomy which outdoor sex work confers upon women workers in relation to setting boundaries, both in relation to their bodies and more widely in terms of their working conditions, appears in most cases to be pretty bleak. In the next section, I examine how far this can be said of indoor sex work, and observe how the problems faced by indoor sex workers are different, but are also challenging.

Indoor sex work

The description 'indoor sex work' encompasses a wide range of working practices. 'Indoor sex work' might involve renting space in a brothel (often termed 'massage parlour'), which will be managed (but not necessarily owned) by a house manager or 'madam' (Murphy and Venkatesh 2006). Massage parlours will often employ a receptionist to organize bookings and provide back-up if sex workers are faced with challenging clients, as well as installing security cameras around the building (Sanders and Campbell 2007). Massage parlour work will thus require the sex worker to pay a percentage of her earnings as rent (Murphy and Venkatesh 2006). In the UK, especially in provincial locations, indoor sex work may allow sex workers to establish regular business with some clients, and the installation of video cameras means that they may also be able to exclude clients from the premises (Sanders 2005b; Sanders and Campbell 2007). At what Murphy and Venkatesh (2006: 138) term the 'high end' of the market, indoor sex work might involve escort agency or call-girl work, well paid and usually involving servicing a business clientele. Sex workers involved at this level may find that sex work 'affords them the ability to live a life of relative luxury', and may consequently think of sex work as a 'profession' or 'career' (Murphy and Venkatesh 2006). This group of workers may be able to work independently from their own premises, assisted by new technologies such as the internet which enable them to source and liaise with clients.

It has been suggested that in the UK (Sanders and Cambell 2007; Brewis and Linstead 2000) and in the USA (Murphy and Venkatesh 2006) 'indoor' sex workers are less likely than outdoor workers to be drug users. Drug use is often forbidden in massage parlours where space is rented, and sex workers are obliged to adhere to rules and regulations relating to safety if they wish to trade there (Sanders and Cambell 2007). However, the focus on safety in massage parlours, combined with reduced drug use, does appear to offer indoor workers greater opportunity for setting and maintaining personal boundaries than is the case among street workers. Many women at all levels within the sex trade seek to distance themselves from the work they do, and from their clients, by adopting roles and dressing the part (Sanders 2005b; Brewis and Linstead 2000). However, among indoor sex workers, especially those who establish regular clients, the opportunity for developing and maintaining a manufactured identity which simultaneously hides the 'inner self from the audience' or client (Sanders 2005b), as well as functioning as a business strategy for attracting and keeping high-paying customers, appears greater than for outdoor workers. Women working in massage parlours may find it easier to maintain personal boundaries because these accord with 'house rules', meaning that if a paying customer attempts to contravene these rules (by, for example, refusing to wear a condom) the assistance of a receptionist may be summoned (Sanders and Campbell 2007).

For women working independently, however, perhaps soliciting customers through the internet and working alone in a house or flat, there are dangers of isolation and exclusion from important communications about, for example, bad clients or sympathetic doctors. Furthermore, while it may be assumed that indoor work means that women are less likely to be exposed to violent crime from clients, there is also evidence to suggest that some parlours are less well run and less 'safe' than others (Sanders 2007). In addition, while women themselves 'perceive themselves to be at less risk of encountering violence . . . while working indoors . . . they are in no way immune to such dangers' (Murphy and Venkatesh 2006: 139). In Murphy and Venkatesh's study of sex work in New York, 27% of sex workers reported having been robbed by a client on at least on occasion, 48% had been forced by clients to engage in sexual acts for which they had refused permission and 43% had been beaten up. While these figures may be less than corresponding figures for outdoor sex workers (80% of whom may experience violence, and 60% of whom are forced by clients to do something against their will) the numbers of indoor workers who experience violent and bullying treatment are still high. This is probably because, as Sanders and Campbell observe, the criminalization of the sex trade means that sex workers themselves feel marginalized by the legislation which protects other employees. Thus, indoor workers may be just as reluctant as outdoor workers to report violence, and this increases in areas where there is a 'zero tolerance' attitude towards sex work.

Thus, while indoor sex work may appear to offer more security and better opportunities to set personal boundaries in comparison with outdoor sex work, the 'illegitimate' nature of the work, especially when combined with notions of 'crack-down' and the 'demonization of those who sell sex' (Sanders and Campbell 2007: 16), means that workers do not report violent and/or sexual crimes against them.

In addition, research has suggested that those sex workers who do report violent crime will not receive the same treatment as women who are not in the sex trade. Instead, sex workers are treated in a dismissive manner, especially if the violent crimes committed against them are sexual in nature. This is due firstly to assumptions that violent and sexual crimes against women sex workers are somehow less distressing for this group of women than they are for women who are not in the sex trade. Brewis and Linstead (2000), for example, recount the recommendation of a court judge that rape should carry a lighter sentence when committed against a sex worker than when committed against a non-prostitute. Secondly, the exclusion of sex workers from state protection against violent crime occurs due to the belief that women should themselves be held accountable for (especially sexual) violent crimes committed against them. It is argued that women are expected to demonstrate supposedly virtuous personal behaviour before the authorities will designate them fit to be protected from violent and sexual assault. In this respect, Sanders and Campbell (2007) observe that, 'by making . . . all women responsible for . . . avoiding sexual danger, women are blamed for putting themselves in a position to be attacked, rather than the cause and subsequently the violence [being located] with the perpetrator'. Such discriminatory attitudes disadvantage sex workers in comparison with workers in the formal labour market – even those for whom sexualization is seen as 'part of the job'. Hochschild's flight attendants, for example, may have been expected to smile at passengers, but their status as 'legitimate' workers would have enabled them to seek legal protection and recompense in the event of sexual assault.

In relation to the disadvantaged legal and social position of sex workers, compared with workers in 'legitimate' jobs, the reluctance of some scholars to position sex workers as prostitutes or victims is understandable. The concept of sex work as prostitution (and consequently as illegal) immediately positions women sex workers either as victims or criminals, or both, and separates them from workers in the formal labour market. This makes it easier for politicians and anti-prostitution enforcement agencies to construct arguments which exclude women from the protective and legislative rights (health services, employment law and criminal law) which are available to other workers. The reframing of prostitution as a legitimate form of 'work', 'chosen' by rational agents in preference to other forms of work, would make it much harder for governments and other agencies to defend the social exclusion and criminalization of sex workers. Thus, it could be seen as beneficial to invest the role of sex worker with the concept of agency and choice, in the hopes that this will assist in legitimizing sex work and enhancing the social position of sex workers. On this basis, research on the sex industry provides some examples where sex workers have formed support groups, this assisting them in maintaining personal and embodying boundaries. For example, Hubbard (2004) cites instances of sex workers resisting government attempts to oust them from areas where they have traditionally worked, and Ditmore (2007) claims that sex workers have facilitated the escape of those 'trafficked' unwillingly into the sex industry.

Conclusions

Despite these examples of resistance, however, the legal positioning of sex workers as second-class citizens makes the concept of sex work and 'choice' problematic, in comparison with the choices on offer to other workers. I acknowledge that the idea of sex workers as abject victims could undermine hopes of attaining improved social circumstances for sex workers. However, I find it difficult to regard sex workers, particularly those working in the most impoverished circumstances, as agents whose opportunities for 'choice' can be compared with the options available to other workers, unless looking through rose-coloured spectacles. Thus, while I can see the logic behind arguments regarding the need to view sex workers as rational agents, I also fear that such views may underplay the narrow choices and limited social protection available to women sex workers – especially women with no qualifications, who are injecting drug users and who are working the streets.

More explicitly, I would like to join with Sanders (2005b) and others in protesting about those who create and enforce law (often men) abrogating responsibility for their own role in the sex industry through the criminalization of sex work, thereby effectively stripping women sex workers of their rights as citizens. In arguing that sex workers may have less autonomy, and less ability to set boundaries, than other workers, I would also like it to be recognized that society colludes with this problem by excluding sex workers from social and legal benefits which would facilitate the opportunity for sex workers to themselves establish and maintain boundaries. Thus, whether or not sex work is legitimized, I argue that sex workers should be afforded the same rights as workers within formal labour markets in relation to health and social services, and protection from crime. Furthermore, I would like to relate to the notion of women's 'choosing' to become sex workers, the problems of horizontal occupational segregation and the gender pay gap (discussed in Chapter 6). Especially at the lower ends of the formal labour market, low pay and a lack of workplace flexibility might combine to effectively make sex work seem like the only viable 'choice' for impoverished and unqualified women, especially if they are supporting children.

In conclusion, I recognize that the 'boundaries' in relation to the commodification of women's bodies are often blurred. However, for women whose bodies are sexualized as part of their paid work within the formal economy (e.g. flight attendants and bar staff), their position as 'citizens' with rights to access health and legal services is clear. The same cannot be said to apply to sex workers. Thus, although the 'ideal' definition of sex work is seen by some scholars to invest sex workers with agency and the ability to make rational 'choices', such ideals may, in practice, be diminished by poverty, drugs and traditional patriarchal systems which undermine the notion that prostitutes are citizens with 'rights'.

10 Working women – a force to be reckoned with? Conclusions and futures

Introduction

In this final chapter, I draw some conclusions about women's work and women's bodies in late modern society, and share some thoughts about the future. I answer the question 'what did I find?' and I attempt to define the contribution of this book. In doing this, I first summarize the three main arguments made in the book, and the related contributions to debates about women and work. I then assess what these findings might mean for women, both now and in the future.

What of the main arguments? The purpose of this book has been to investigate the relationship between women's bodies and women's work. I have suggested that women's bodies are central to gendered power relations, and I maintain that the reproductive 'maternal' body, regardless of whether a woman has children or not, remains a disputed site of power between women and men in late modern society.

I have undertaken this investigation from three different, but closely related, perspectives. The first of these focused on the labour of pregnancy and birth, and I have argued that the social understanding of 'women's work' should be extended to include reproductive as well as productive labour. On this basis, I observe how women's potential for maternity involves them in (often poorly rewarded) forms of labour which are less likely to affect men, women with no children being expected, for example, to possess essentialist nurturing qualities commonly associated with the maternal body, while being required to offer employers 'spare' and available time which may not be required of either men or mothers.

In relation to actual maternity, I have observed that the labour involved in pregnancy, birth and motherhood can be intensive, requiring bodily conformity to complex and exacting standards. At the same time, I have argued that the labour of reproduction is often obfuscated by the narrative of 'good motherhood'. On this basis, I am arguing that notions of women's work should be reconceptualized. Referring back to the issues raised in Chapter 1, about how 'work' should be defined and articulated, I believe that the definition of 'work' should be broadened and should encompass reproductive as well as productive labour. Reproductive labour, I suggest, is a central component of women's work and should be explicitly included in debates about 'work', 'opportunity' and 'choice' – not as something which occurs 'off-stage' and is simply 'part of the job' for a maternal body. The argument that reproductive labour should be conceptualized as a form of 'work' has been presented principally through the lens of radical feminism. The application of a historical theoretical approach to a late modern dilemma has, I believe, enabled me to contribute a fresh and contemporary perspective on some of the important observations made during the 1970s in relation to policy and women's potential for reproduction.

Having reconceptualized reproductive labour as 'work', I moved on to consider women's reproductive labour in the context of women's paid employment. I surfaced the tensions between the Taylorist goals set by health professionals with regard to pregnancy, birth and infant feeding, and the embodied demands of the workplace, which often require the concealment of the pregnant body, the minimizing of children's needs, and the foregrounding of the exigencies of employers. Drawing upon the arguments of writers such as Tyler (2000), Longhurst (2001), Grosz (1994), and Shildrick (1997) to facilitate these discussions, I have suggested that women's reproductive bodies are regarded with fear and abjection within the labour market. This fear of the womanly body – that it has the potential for pregnancy, that it might change shape and/or 'leak' both in the material and the metaphorical sense – is, I have argued, one important reason for the continued existence of occupational segregation, the gender pay gap, and the barriers which still exist to prevent women from attaining equal economic status with men. I have further suggested that the association of women with mothering (regardless of whether or not they have children) is also seen as an explanation for the ghettoizing of women in low-paid health, social and service sectors where the roles of carer and domestic labourer remain the preserve of women, who are expected to perform the same roles as employees as they are assumed to undertake within the home.

Finally, I have explored women's position specifically in relation to productive work, both unpaid and paid, in the context of contemporary formal and informal labour markets. My quest to analyse the boundaries between paid and unpaid work, and formal and informal sectors, via the lens of the body has enabled me to draw together a range of ideas about, and research on, women's work, which have tended previously to fall within separate disciplines. I have reviewed a range of interdisciplinary ideas about women's work which previously have often been considered either in specialist journals – for example, the *International Small Business Journal* (Hamilton 2006) – or in the context of a particular subject area – for example, management, economics or sociology. The combining of this cross-disciplinary approach with the concept of women's work as embodied has facilitated the drawing together of a range of viewpoints such as Hakim's (1995, 1996, 2000) work on the economics of women's employment decisions; Puwar's (2004) feminist and cultural exploration of the gendered and racialized body within leadership; Singh and Vinnicombe's (2004) business and management perspectives on the gender pay gap; Sanders's (2005b) sociological research on women working in illegal labour markets as sex workers; and the radical feminist approaches of Oakley (1981) and Kitzinger (2005) in relation to birth. The pulling together of these and other sources has allowed me, in the latter part of this book, to analyse the impact of radical feminist arguments, and equal opportunities initiatives and policies, on women's productive work during the post-war years from a range of perspectives. I have thus revisited the questions posed by writers such as Rich (1977) and Firestone (1970) regarding how far women are able to establish and maintain embodied boundaries and in what sense ideas about opportunity and choices available to women have changed.

In the context of women's progress within the labour market, focusing initially on career opportunities for women and how far contemporary female workers have joined men, on equal terms, within the labour market, I have observed how women are still poorly represented in the powerhouses of Parliament (especially at senior ministerial level) and on executive boards, where places continue to be reserved for (usually white) male bodies, and women are still few enough in number to be considered as 'space invaders' (Puwar 2004). I have noted how, in a professional capacity, women are tolerated to some degree, but only if they are prepared either to play supporting roles (often without the status and remuneration afforded to equivalent males) or to undertake the functions which senior male colleagues deem suitable for women to perform. So, for example, women in family businesses struggle to be treated on equal terms with male kin, and in professional and/or executive situations women are channelled at an early stage in their careers into 'velvet ghettos' – positions within professional arenas which offer less power, pay and resource than may be available to equivalent male colleagues. Thus, in corporate institutions, the most senior women on the staff are often to be found in human resources roles, supporting the male executives on the board. In professions such as law, women solicitors are steered towards labour-intensive but less prestigious areas such as conveyancing and family law, while men are directed towards lucrative fields such as litigation, which are more likely to lead to partnership status (Bacik *et al.* 2003).

I have observed how, despite women's increased labour market participation, the unpaid productive labour of housework continues to be regarded as principally women's responsibility, and women in heterosexual relationships undertake consistently more housework than men, especially if they are married. In the context of domestic and care work, I have considered how forms of women's productive (but often unpaid) labour such as housework and care work have transferred into the contemporary labour market and I have suggested that these forms of labour, all involving intensive forms of physical work, are undervalued, just as they have traditionally been in the private sphere. Jobs such as cleaning and care work remain largely the province of women, are low-paid and carry few prospects of promotion or opportunity.

In the penultimate chapter of the book, I considered the experiences of sex workers and explored how far ideas about embodied boundaries and choice extended to this group. I concluded that, while the idea of female sex workers as 'victims' may be unhelpful in promoting the notion of women as autonomous and agentic beings, the idea of 'choice' could also not be easily applied to this group who were often, arguably, making decisions about how to manage their bodies and their paid work in the context of sometimes very limited and/or uninviting alternatives.

Women, work and 'choice'

What are the implications of these findings for women and work, both now and in the future? In relation to the three main themes of this book – the categorization of reproductive labour as 'work'; the tensions between the Taylorization of the reproductive labour and expectations about appropriate embodied workplace behaviour; and the continued inequalities within the labour market – I would like to make two points about the constraining of women's opportunities and the hidden nature of women's work.

Opportunity and the limitations of policy

The first point relates to the extent of women's 'choice' in relation to productive and reproductive work. 'Choice' is a concept which I have interpreted via the notion of the body and bodily boundaries. Throughout the text I have observed the disparity between policy and practice, in terms of how the opportunities and choices offered to women in theory are much wider than women's choices are in practice, in the context of both reproductive and productive labour. I have noted how the boundaries (often set by others) dictating women's embodied behaviour are often hidden from view, but may be more powerful than paper policies purporting to offer to women opportunity and choice. So, for example, UK pregnant and birthing women are presented with theoretical 'choices' in relation to how and where to give birth. However, expectant mothers are in practice unlikely to be able to 'choose' either a home birth or a Caesarean section, especially if giving birth for the first time.

In the context of women's paid, productive labour, it remains an issue that women's child-bearing years correspond with the time when they are most likely to be developing their paid work or career. Employed women – in the UK, the USA, Australia and parts of Europe – are offered equality of opportunity in the workplace on paper. Often, however, they still find themselves the subject of limited opportunities and/or explicit discrimination if they combine motherhood with paid work. As I have shown in Chapters 4 and 5, many employed women who do have children find themselves obliged to conceal and even to disavow their maternity in the context of their paid work (even if they are concurrently labouring to meet the health standards required of the reproductive maternal body in late modern society). Policies claiming to protect women from pregnancy-related discrimination appear to be ineffective, and women who work part-time at any stage during their years of employment because of childcare responsibilities find that their choices and opportunities, both in the present and in the future, are sharply circumscribed.

Women also still experience constrained career choices on the basis of their maternal bodies and their *potential* for maternity. This level of discrimination is often subtle and begins early in women's lives – remember the women medical students at the start of this book who were directed away from surgery and specialties and into general practice, on the basis of their capacity for possible future motherhood? For this group the 'choice' was not about which area of medicine to specialize in, but remained centred upon the notion that women must 'choose' between having children and a career as a hospital consultant – a decision which was apparently not imposed on their male student colleagues. In this case, the boundaries about what was acceptable at consultant level were not set through 'official' policy, but appeared nevertheless to be firmly established via unwritten conventions about opportunities and medical careers, which were imposed on women trainees before any of them had made decisions about motherhood.

Women thus remain caught in a double bind which leaves them disadvantaged in comparison with men. Professional women, at least, are still expected to 'choose' between family and career, and if they remain in paid work, they must subjugate the requirements of the lived maternal body, and the needy bodies of small children, to workplace expectations about suitable embodied behaviour – 'norms' which are based upon studies of male embodied behaviour dating back as far as the early twentieth century. Women's 'choice' about whether or not to have children is in itself related to age and class, and may be highly circumscribed, depending on age, lifestyle and economic circumstances. For professionally employed women, the more senior they become, the more likely it is that they will be denied career progress due to their potential or actual maternity, and the more likely it is that they will be criticized if they do combine paid work with motherhood (especially if they have a heterosexual partner who is also employed). This suggests that women's choices are restricted in comparison with those of most men – as Bates Gaston (1991: 69) points out, 'few would question paternal employment in the context of the birth of a child', but the debate about maternal employment still poses a 'dilemma for mothers'.

'Choice' as a form of social resistance

For women, then, 'choices' about embodied labour – for example, how they give birth, and/or whether they combine breastfeeding with employment – are often more about the 'choice' between conformity and resistance than about 'choice' as a no-cost opportunity. The way in which women are expected to comport their bodies, and the decisions they make in relation to reproductive and productive labour, are continually subject to the social demands and embodied boundaries set by late modern society. Thus – no matter how inviting and open the offers professed by legislation and policies may *appear* to be, women's experience of 'choosing' is likely to be constrained, with conflicting boundaries imposed on women by health services, politicians and employers.

Furthermore – regardless of what might be promised in equal opportunities policies – when women make productive and reproductive 'choices' which fail to fit in with conventional social expectations, such behaviour is likely to be interpreted as a form of resistance which may be challenged by employers and colleagues and others. For example, as discussed in Chapter 6, women who 'choose' careers more usually associated with men, such as firefighting, flying and the armed and police forces, may find themselves the subject of intensive surveillance as their activities are observed by colleagues (and sometimes the national media). They may also be subject to harassment and discrimination. Women who challenge unwritten (and sometimes unlawful) social conventions which privilege men, in order to claim their entitlements to equality of opportunity and choice (by, for example, demanding equal pay), may find this expensive in both financial and career terms.

Accessing 'choice' therefore, is likely to come at a cost both financially and in terms of 'hidden' work. Women often have to fight hard in order to access the social and embodied 'choices' which are in theory supposed to be freely on offer to them. Thus, women of particular age groups and income levels will find themselves under pressure to have children, especially if they are in heterosexual partnerships, while post-menopausal women will be seen as inappropriate candidates for motherhood. Women seeking a home birth (especially for a first birth) would be unlikely to obtain this without strenuous effort on their part (e.g. being au fait with recent research on home birth before starting negotiations with health providers). Thus women are required to undertake a good deal of hidden work in order to access the choices that appear to be freely on offer. Comparably, women who 'choose' to combine motherhood with paid work are likely to 'pay a price' in relation to job prospects especially if they decide to work part-time, in which case they may be expected to accept demotion as a trade-off for the chance to work less than full-time – as one door opens, another is closed firmly shut! This appears to be linked to the maternal body for, as noted in Chapter 7, men with portfolio or consultancy careers, who work part-time for more than one employer, do not appear to be similarly affected.

Finally, in relation to notions of 'choice', I would argue that, where women are seen to have made 'choices' in relation to paid work, these decisions are often made in the context of narrow choices compared with what is on offer to equivalent men. I have considered the boundaries between different forms of work – paid and unpaid, formal and informal. In this respect, I have extended the idea that the boundaries of women's work should be more explicitly articulated by investigating how, and by whom, boundaries are established. I have suggested that if boundaries and standards relating to women's productive and reproductive labour are set and measured by others (using systems of measurement designed around men), the range of 'choice' on offer to women must necessarily be limited, regardless of attempts to offer women more social freedoms through policy. For example, a woman's decision to be a sex worker may appear to be her 'choice' but this decision might have been made in the face of few other, viable, options. She may, for example, have 'chosen' to undertake sex work in a setting where occupational segregation allows men to access reasonably well-paid manual work, while the equivalent jobs available to women involve long, inflexible hours and low pay. Furthermore, as discussed in the previous chapter, her disadvantaged position within the informal labour market relates to legislative and political decisions made by others.

Choice and radical feminism

Thus, it appears that the relationship between women's work, women's bodies and notions of choice is hard to disentangle. However, it is apparent that women's 'choices', in relation to how they manage their maternal bodies and their paid work, are still constrained. The notion of the maternal body and its supposed incompatibility with paid work continues to be used by those in power (often men) as an excuse for restricting women's opportunities in the labour market. And in the arena of reproductive labour (while it is acknowledged that maternal and infant mortality are much less of a threat than in the pre-war years, and that this partly due to medical advances), it remains that case that the reproductive body is subject to the constraints of obstetric guidelines, and that obstetricians are mainly male. This suggests that that the radical feminist arguments of the 1970s and early 1980s, which ascribed women's limited career options to social attitudes towards the maternal body, remain acutely relevant to contemporary women. Even though there are more women in the formal labour market than there were 30 years ago (especially at professional and managerial levels), and even though the opportunities for women to be educated are more open now than in the past, the argument put forward by feminist scholars such as Firestone (1970), Rich (1977) and Oakley (1981) – that women's actual or potential maternity should not limit their opportunities for paid employment any more than the potential for fatherhood limits men's choices – still applies to contemporary women.

Thus, the embodied freedoms which the radical feminists of the 1970s and 1980s were fighting for are a long way from being achieved, and the problems about which radical feminists expressed concern remain pertinent to contemporary women. The way in which women's productive and reproductive choices are restricted and the social attitudes which constrain women's embodied behaviour still have the ring of 'tyranny' (Firestone 1970: 270), of 'devaluation' of the maternal body (O'Brien 1981), observed by radical feminist writers over 30 years ago. Women remain oppressed by embodied workplace and reproductive conventions which continue to privilege masculine norms and 'male control' (Rich 1977:13), and which may be hidden from view. It appears, therefore, that patriarchy continues to operate quite smoothly behind the cover of policies purporting equality of opportunity and choice.

'Hidden' work and the discourse of 'natural' motherhood

Just as some elements of good old fashioned discrimination may be subtle, and hidden, so are many aspects of women's work. The second observation deriving from the findings of this book relates to the consequences, for women, of the continued obfuscation of women's work (both productive and reproductive) behind discourses of 'natural' and/or 'good' motherhood. This observation relates to the maternal body, but is not confined specifically to actual motherhood. For example, as noted in Chapter 2, assumptions that women are imbued with essentialist, 'natural' maternal qualities may be instrumental in workplace decisions to allocate pastoral labour to female personnel, perhaps *especially* if these women are not raising small children, as it may then be presumed that they have 'spare' nurturing capacity available. Essentialist assumptions about women's 'natural' potential for maternity and nurturing or care work can lead not only to allocation to women of care work, but also to the discounting of the labour involved in this. This is because the tasks that are supposed to come 'naturally' to women are not counted as 'work', in the same way that might occur if the same jobs were undertaken by men. This could provide part of the explanation for why male nurses often rise quickly through nursing hierarchies, and are statistically more likely to gain promotion than equivalent women nurses, because men's caring work is noticed and rewarded, while for women this is regarded as a 'natural' role for a maternal body and counts, therefore, for less.

Surfacing reproductive labour

As I have observed in Chapter 4, the labour of pregnancy, birth and the mothering of small children requires women to perform to a set of highly prescribed and complex standards, but is often not 'counted' as a form of work. The discounting of reproductive labour, on the basis that this is (or should be) a 'natural' part of 'good mothering' has two implications for women. The first is that, if reproductive labour is regarded as 'natural', women are unlikely ever to be given social recognition for achieving some or all of the goals set for 'good mothers' to achieve by late modern health services – though conversely, women will be accused of failure if they fall short of the standards expected of a 'good mother'. The lack of acknowledgement of the work involved in reproductive labour has a further and possibly more damaging consequence in relation to women's paid work. If the labour involved in reproduction – of pregnancy, birth and new motherhood – is metaphorically 'hidden' behind the narrative of 'natural' mothering, then it becomes very easy for employers to demand of women that they should conceal and obscure the labours of maternity in practice. The fact that the work of reproduction goes unrecognized and unacknowledged makes it very convenient for employers to insist that such work is kept out of sight. Thus, women's hidden work is doubled as they struggle to meet the exacting standards of contemporary motherhood and the everyday needs of infants, while keeping this maternal labour out of the employment arena.

Women's bodies, women's futures

What of the future? The above analysis of women's choice seems rather bleak, and I feel it is important to end this text by looking at some positive changes in working practices which may improve the prospects for women's work – both productive and reproductive – in the future. In this respect, I end with an examination of women's resistance to the male-dominated conventions which exclude them from paid work, as well as a consideration of how women's networks – both face-to-face and on the internet – may be improving the situation for women with regard both to productive and reproductive labour. The discussion about choice and opportunity has surfaced the prospect that many women, in a variety of ways, are resisting the social boundaries which constrain their agency and autonomy in relation to embodied choices regarding the maternal body, paid work and discrimination.

Fighting fire with fire: women resisting inequality

Some women are facing workplace discrimination head-on, and while it must be acknowledged that many cases fail to produce results (either because the case is lost or settled out of court), there have been several instances where women's unfair treatment in the workplace has been exposed and recompensed to a high level. Sex discrimination cases involving highly paid women in the banking industry, who may be treated shabbily when it comes to opportunities for pay and promotion, have, since the 1990s, received a good deal of press attention – often because the sums of money involved in pay and bonuses are so large (Bowers 2004). Since 2000, however, an increasing number of cases have been reported in relation to women employed in jobs where pay and conditions are more in keeping with national averages. Clusters of successful challenges to discrimination appear to be emerging in uniformed occupations such as the armed and/or police forces, firefighting and the aviation industry. Perhaps this is because equal opportunities policies, offering promises of fair treatment and equal choice, are prominent and easily available to employees given the size of these organizations and the links to government and policy-makers. Thus, where policy does not reflect practice, employees may be able to establish clear grounds for their case. Furthermore, as noted in Chapter 6, many uniformed occupations which have previously been the province of men are seeking explicitly to attract women employees, who may feel let down and prepared therefore to take action, if they consider themselves to be treated unfairly in comparison with (or by) male colleagues. It has been acknowledged that this is not an easy course of action. Baigent and O'Connor (2007: 1), speaking at the Seventh International Conference on Diversity in Organisations, observe how many women who experience harassment are so 'weakened' by this experience that 'they cannot face an official hearing and . . . accept a severance payment in return for their silence'.

For those who do speak out, however, there is a possibility of public recognition that such gender discrimination is illegal. The success of some public challenges to workplace discrimination has sent shockwaves through employer communities, and may, hopefully, influence not only policy but also behaviour and attitudes towards the maternal body in the workplace in the future. In 2007, for example, Brenda Lee, a black woman firefighter in Los Angeles who was harassed at work because of her gender, race and sexual orientation (she was also a lesbian), was awarded in court $7.2 million dollars in damages (Casey 2007: 1). Brenda Lee's case is described as one of several settlement cases regarding unfair treatment of women against the Los Angeles Fire Department (Casey 2007), and the result will, hopefully, persuade Los Angeles and other fire departments to think seriously about the consequences of offering equal opportunities policies which are not implemented in practice.

Similarly, in 2005, Jessica Starmer, a pilot and first officer with the UK airline British Airways, won a three-year battle with her employer to work 50% part-time, so that she could combine mothering her 1-year-old daughter with 'continuing a career in which myself and my employer have invested lots of money' (BBC News 2005). Ms Starmer is further quoted as telling the tribunal that 'BA's family-unfriendly working practices' reinforced male-dominated traditions (BBC News 2005). Despite British Airways' protestations that their refusal to allow Ms Starmer to work 50% was based on safety issues, the tribunal found in Ms Starmer's favour. She was allowed to reduce her working hours to 50% while continuing as a first officer, and the implications of her victory were seen by the UK's Equal Opportunities Commission as having positive implications for other women in the future.

Sex discrimination cases involving harassment are regularly reported in specialist journals, as well as the national press. For example, *Personnel Today*, recounting the employment hearing of Lance Bombadier Kerry Fletcher, who had been sexually harassed by her commanding officer, described in detail how 'her life was made a misery after she ignored [the harasser] and complained that she was being victimised' to the point where she 'did not want to go to work' (Vorster 2007).

It is to be hoped that such detailed commentaries of events, combined with the negative impressions these give about the institutions concerned (perhaps to men as well as women), will act as an incentive for employers in the future to ensure that policies aimed at 'actively encouraging' women to join uniformed occupations (Stephenson 2007) are followed up by working practices to actively support women once they have joined their respective institutions.

Caring and closing the gender pay gap

Encouragingly, successful challenges to sex discrimination have not been confined to women in professional or uniformed occupations. At the beginning of 2008, it was reported that Rosalind Wilson, a UK care worker with supervisory responsibilities employed by the local council at a rate of £6.50 per hour, led a group of 26 other women in an equal pay case, and won an individual settlement of £32,000 (Brindle and Curtis 2008). One might have expected workers such as Wilson to have turned to their union for support on equal pay claims, but Wilson chose to lead her own battle, retaining her own legal adviser, on the basis that her union was not prepared to 'rock the boat' in order to fight the women's case (Brindle and Curtis 2008). As noted in Chapter 6, feminist writers such as Morris (1990) and Bruley (1999) have linked the gender pay gap to the suggestion that union representation has historically prioritized and privileged the interests of men, thus perpetuating the notion that the male employed body should be afforded a greater economic value than an employed female body in an equivalent role. In this respect, it is interesting to observe how 5,000 women in the UK are, at the time of writing, bringing a class action against their own union on the basis of its failure to fight for their right to equal pay. The union is accused by its female members of sex discrimination, having 'encouraged them to agree to a settlement that seriously undervalued their claims and prioritised protection for their male colleagues' (Brindle and Curtis 2008: 11).

It is possible to speculate that the determination of women such as Brenda Lee, Jessica Starmer, Kerry Fletcher, Rosalind Wilson and the 5,000 women involved in the union case may make a significant difference to working conditions for women in the future. It is to be hoped that women such as these – and the many unknown women who attempt to fight their corner but fail to win a settlement – may be the harbingers of positive change. The institutions and individuals who have previously considered it acceptable to value women less highly than men, and who have treated women employees with less respect than men in equivalent jobs, may think twice about their attitudes and their actions. The thought of damage to their finances and to their reputation may be the incentive they need to ensure that steps are taken to improve working practices, so that what is promised in equal opportunities policies bears more relation to women's everyday experience than it does at present.

Jobs for the girls? Women's work and women's networks

Arguably, legal action in the face of explicit discrimination is only one part of women's resistance to unequal treatment and restricted choice – both in the workplace and in respect of women's reproductive labour. Since the 1980s, women in paid work have increasingly drawn upon the established idea of formal networking to enable them to challenge the gender politics of big organizations or professional institutions. In this way, women's networks may provide a powerful means of challenging male hegemony in the public and private sectors and this might, in turn, enhance the changes which have been achieved through legislation and government policy.

The advent of the internet has seen a rapid growth of networks created by women, for women, to provide mutual career support. It is acknowledged that some women's networks have existed for many years, the purpose of these having been, historically, to support women's unpaid labour in relation to their domestic or caring responsibilities (for example, the Women's Institute, founded in the nineteenth century in Canada). It is also acknowledged that not all women have access to the internet, meaning that those with the least resources are less able than others to join networks which provide both online support plus the possibility of joining face-to-face meetings with other women in the same geographical area. However, it is also the case that (as noted in Chapter 4 in relation to pregnancy and birth) internet use by women, seeking support and information from specialist websites and/or other women, is growing fast and become increasingly inclusive.

In respect of paid work, the Aurora Women's Network, founded by Australian entrepreneur Glenda Stone on International Women's Day 2000 (and formerly known as the Busygirl Network), has over 16,000 members and exists 'to advance the economic status of women' through 'business and career'. Aurora has no government funding but has attracted sponsorship from commercial organizations and generates revenue by providing services that:

- assist organisations to attract and advance women
- accelerate corporate women's career advancement . . .
- support the growth of women-owned businesses. (Aurora Network 2007)

Similarly, the National Black Women's on-line network exists specifically to support the interests of black women and is a 'non-profit organisation dedicated to raising the position of black women in all walks of life'. This network aims to promote the contribution of black women within all fields, ensuring that black women gain recognition for their achievements. Support is offered by the network to women from 'diverse backgrounds and occupations to develop strong professional and social contacts; high quality training and . . . leadership and national recognition' (National Black Women's Network Online 2007).

In relation to reproductive labour, as noted in Chapter 4, women can and do access support and advice not only from 'official' or 'expert' sources such as the UK's National Childbirth Trust, but also from other women on maternity message boards. Women use message boards and chat rooms to seek advice from others when support from official sources (such as human resources departments, unions and health services) is felt to be inadequate. Women seeking guidance from other correspondents on internet message boards do not hesitate to recognize the value of the quality of support and information offered, which often appears to derive from women with personal expertise. On Babyworld, for example, in response to a request for help from 'lovely HR people', one pregnant mother, querying her employers' decision to reduce her holiday entitlement, received by return three helpful and clearly articulated responses from well-informed women, outlining legal rights and suggesting useful contacts for further information (Babyworld 2006a).

Likewise, women who seek information on health issues such as the possibility of home birth, bleeding, sickness and exhaustion during pregnancy, plus advice on the care and nourishment of small children, acknowledge the help given by other women, who offer assistance from both professional and lay experiences (Madmums 2007).

Conclusions

It would be lovely to end this book on a positive note, with the suggestion that society is changing and that things look brighter for women in the future. However, the optimism raised by the idea of women's resistance, via networks and legal processes, to negative social attitudes towards the maternal body, especially in a labour market context, must be moderated. Resistance – whether explicitly feminist and/or as part of a group action, or in response to individual constraints and inequities – is positive. The attempts of some women to campaign for equality with men in the workplace and/or to gain and share with other women information on the internet, may well be a catalyst which facilitates social change.

However, it must be remembered that resistance is only necessary in situations where problems exist. If employed women were offered the same choices and opportunities as men, and if women's reproductive labour was counted as 'work', resistance would be less of a requirement. Furthermore, for those women who do refuse to give in to particular and traditional sources of gendered power relations (e.g. refusing to accept union advice not to 'rock the boat'), life is difficult. Women who fight for their beliefs are treated either as failing to perform their femininity to an appropriate standard, or as foolish and irresponsible, and women who insist on their 'rights' to equality and/or choice may be punished as a result of their determination. In the context of productive labour, for example, in the case of the women fighting for equal pay without union backing, threats of job losses for both themselves and colleagues were issued, and the women were constructed by both unions and employers as rashly threatening their own 'interests [plus those] of their colleagues' (Brindle and Curtis 2008: 11). In relation to reproductive labour, where women question the judgement of (often male) obstetricians and seek, for example, to avoid hospital screening or medical interventions, they are likely to be dissuaded from their chosen course of action via warnings that they must accept hospital protocols or risk the baby's life, such prospects usually serving to 'legitimise obstetric power' (Kitzinger 1992: 73).

Arguably, challenges by institutions and powerful individuals to women's defiance of conventional boundaries relate to fears that women's resistance threatens traditional sources of male hegemony. Women's resistance may, therefore, alter conventional ways of doing and being that are very comfortable for those holding the most powerful roles (Baigent and O'Connor 2007). Thus, through attempts to access the opportunities apparently on offer to them in policy, women who withstand the social conventions that restrict their 'choice' may face retaliation. Resistance to the status quo, therefore (even if women are only claiming their official entitlements), can be a risky business. Women who are resisting the social constraints imposed upon them thus require much broader and more reliable support from those who create policies which supposedly offer women greater opportunity and more 'choice'. The experiences of women engaged in all forms of work, paid and unpaid, productive and reproductive, suggests, however, that such support is unlikely to be forthcoming in the near future.

In the meantime, it is important to keep hold of the notion that women's work remains undervalued. During the three decades since equal opportunities legislation came into being, we have seen some improvements in the situation of women – but these have been limited. This is due, at least in part, to negative social attitudes towards the maternal body. Arguments that women now 'have it all' are not substantiated by evidence in relation to women's choice or women's pay. The radical feminist argument that women should have as much control over their own bodies, and in relation to their working lives, as do men, remains as strong and as valid today as it did thirty years ago. Women's work thus needs to be reconceptualized and re-evaluated, so that, in forthcoming decades, hidden aspects of women's labour – both reproductive and productive – are recognized and esteemed. In the workplace, women must be valued both economically and socially, so that their wages and opportunities in the labour market no longer lag behind those of men. Women need resources and support so that we may establish our own boundaries, so that our potential for motherhood is valued and respected, and so that we may at last access the opportunities and entitlement apparently on offer to us without disadvantage.

We must not settle for less.

References

Adkins, L. (1995) *Gendered Work: Sexuality, Family and the Labour Market*. Buckingham: Open University Press.

Anderson, B. (2000) *Doing the Dirty Work? The Global Politics of Domestic Labour*. New York: Zed Books.

Anleu, S.R. (2006) Gendered bodies: Between conformity and autonomy. In K. Davies, M. Evans and J. Lorber (eds) *Handbook of Gender and Women's Studies* (pp. 357–75). London: Sage.

Anstruther, I. (1992) *Coventry Patmore's Angel: A Study of Coventry Patmore, His Wife Emily and 'The Angel in the House'*. London: Haggerston Press.

Arber, S. and Ginn, J. (1995) The mirage of gender equality: Occupational success in the labour market and within marriage. *British Journal of Sociology*, 46(1): 21–43.

Association of University Teachers (2003) *The Unequal Academy, UK Academic Staff 1995–96 to 2002–03*. London: AUT.

Atkins, L. (2004) 'I was so completely traumatised by the fact that I hadn't given birth'. *The Guardian*, Health section, 23 March: 10–11.

Aurora Network (2007) About the Aurora Women's Network. www.network. auroravoice.com/about.asp (accessed 19 December 2007).

Babcock, L. and Laschever, S. (2003) *Women Don't Ask: Negotiation and the Gender Divide*. Princeton, NJ: Princeton University Press.

Babyworld (2006a) Pregnant and working. www.babyworld.co.uk (accessed 14 June 2007).

Bacik, I., Costello, C. and Drew, E. (2003) *Gender Injustice*. Dublin: Trinity College Law School.

Baigent, D. (2007) One more last working class hero: A cultural audit of the UK fire service. www.fitting-in.com (accessed 14 January 2008).

Baigent, D. and O'Connor, S. (2007) Women firefighters: seeking ways of reducing their harassment. In *Proceedings of The Seventh International Conference on Diversity in Organisations*, Amsterdam. http://d07.cgpublisher.com/ (accessed 7 December 2007).

Bailey, C. and Pain, R. (2001) Geographies of feeding and access to primary health care. *Health and Social Care in the Community*, 9(5): 309–17.

Barton, F. (2005) Oh Mummy, what big wrinkles you've got! *Daily Mail*, 9 April: 34–5.

Bates Gaston, J. (1991) The female reproductive system and work. In J. Firth-Cozens and M.A. West (eds) *Women at Work* (pp. 66–83). Buckingham: Open University Press.

BBC News (1998) Cambridge women return for their rights. http://bbc.news.co.uk, 4 July (accessed 8 April 2008).

BBC News (2005) BA pilot wins discrimination case. http://bbc.news.co.uk, 22 April (accessed 19 December 2007).

Beasley, C. (1999) *What is Feminism? An Introduction to Feminist Theory*. London: Sage.

Beck, U. and Beck-Gernsheim, E. (1995) *The Normal Chaos of Love*. Cambridge: Polity.

Bell, E. and Nkomo, S. (2001) *Our Separate Ways: Black and White Women and the Struggle for Professional Identity*. Boston: Harvard University Press.

Benoit, C. and Shaver, F.M. (2006) Critical issues and new directions in sex work research. *Canadian Review of Sociology and Anthropology*, 43(3): 243–64.

Berger, L.M., Hill, J. and Waldfogel, J. (2005) Maternity leave, early maternal employment and child health and development in the US. *The Economic Journal*, 115: 29–47.

Bernandes, J. (1997) *Family Studies, An Introduction*. London: Routledge.

Berrington, A., Diamond, I., Ingham, R., Stevenson, J., Borgoni, R., Hernandez, I. and Smith, P. (2005) *Consequences of Teenage Parenthood: Pathways which Minimise the Long Term Negative Impacts of Teenage Childbearing*. Final Report, University of Southampton.

Bewley, S., Davies, M. and Braude, P. (2005) Which career first? *British Medical Journal*, 331(7517): 588–9.

Biggs, H. (2002) The ageing body. In M. Evans and E. Lee (eds) *Real Bodies: A Sociological Introduction* (pp. 167–85). Basingstoke: Palgrave Macmillan.

Birnie, J., Madge, C., Pain, R., Raghuram, P. and Rose, G. (2005) Working a fraction and making a fraction work: a rough guide for geographers in the academy. *Area*, 37(3): 251–9.

Blair-Loy, M. (2003) *Competing Devotions: Career and Family among Women Executives*. Cambridge, MA: Harvard University Press.

Bolton, S. (2001) Changing faces: nurses as emotional jugglers. *Sociology of Health and Illness*, 23(1): 85–100.

Bosanquet, N., Ferry, J., Lees, C. and Thornton, J. (2005) *Maternity Services in the NHS*. London: Reform.

Boston Women's Health Collective (1973) *Our Bodies, Ourselves: A Book by and for Women*. New York: Simon and Schuster.

Boswell-Penc, M. and Boyer, K. (2007) Expressing anxiety? Breast pump usage in American wage workplaces. *Gender, Place and Culture*, 14(5): 551–67.

Bosworth, H. (2004) Depression increases in women during early to late menopause but decreases after menopause. *Evidence-Based Mental Health*, 7: 90.

Bowers, S. (2004) Investment bank's European manager was 'bullied and belittled' – and told to serve drinks. *The Guardian*, 9 June: 3.

Bowles, H., Babcock, L. and Lai, L. (2007) Social incentives for gender differences in the propensity to initiate negotiations: Sometimes it does hurt to ask. *Organizational Behavior and Human Decision Processes*, 103.1 (May): 84–103.

Bradley, H., Erickson, M. Stephenson, C. and Williams, S. (2000) *Myths at Work*. Cambridge: Polity Press.

Brannen, J. and Moss, P. (1991) *Managing Mothers: Dual Earner Households after Maternity Leave*. London: Unwin Hyman.

Brewis, J. and Linstead, S. (2000) *Sex, Work and Sex Work*. London: Routledge.

Brewis, J. and Linstead, S. (2004) Gender and management. In S. Linstead, L. Fulop and S. Lilley (eds) *Management and Organization: A Critical Text*. Basingstoke: Palgrave Macmillan.

Brindle, D. and Curtis, P. (2008) Fight for equality that could put jobs at risk. *The Guardian*, 2 January: 11.

Broad, R. and Fleming, S. (eds) (2006) *Nella Last's War, The Second World War Diaries of Housewife, 49*. Exmouth: Profile Books.

Brown, J. and Ferree, M. (2005) Close your eyes and think of England: Pronatalism in the British print media. *Gender and Society*, 19(1): 5–24.

Bruley, S. (1999) *Women in Britain since 1900*. Basingstoke: Macmillan.

Bryson, V. (1999) *Feminist Debates: Issues of Theory and Political Practice*. Basingstoke: Macmillan.

Bunce, J. (2006) Fears for older mothers. *Daily Telegraph*, 19 December. www.news.com.au/dailytelegraph/story (accessed 6 April 2008).

Butler, J. (1990) *Gender Trouble: Feminism and the Subversion of Identity*. London: Routledge.

Butler, J. (1993) *Bodies that Matter: On the Discursive Limits of 'Sex'*. London: Routledge.

Casey, C. (2007) Massive discrimination award for black lesbian firefighter. *Pink News*, 5 July. www.pinknews.co.uk/news/articles/2005-4855.html (accessed 8 April 2008).

Centers for Disease Control and Prevention (2005) *Having a Healthy Pregnancy*. www.cdc.gov/ncbddd/bd/abc.htm (accessed 8 August 2007).

Chira, S. (1998) *A Mother's Place: Choosing Work and Family without Guilt or Blame*. New York: Harper Perennial.

Channel 4 (2006) *Extraordinary Breastfeeding*. TV broadcast, 1 February, 9 p.m.

Cheung, N.F., Mander, R., Cheng, L., Chen V.Y. and Yang, X.Q. (2006) Caesarean decision-making: Negotiation between Chinese women and healthcare professionals. *Evidence Based Midwifery*, 4(1): 24–30.

Cockburn, C. (2002) Resisting equal opportunities: the issue of maternity. In S. Jackson and S. Scott (eds) *Gender: A Sociological Reader* (pp. 180–91). London: Routledge.

Code, L. (1991) *What Can She Know? Feminist Theory and the Construction of Knowledge*. New York: Cornell University Press.

Collins, G. (2007) Cleaning and the work-life balance. *International Journal of Human Resource Management*, 18(3): 416–29.

Collinson, D. (2000) Strategies of resistance: Power, knowledge and subjectivities in the workplace. In K. Grint (ed.) *Work and Society: A Reader*. Cambridge: Polity Press.

Collinson, D. and Collinson, M. (2004) The power of time: Leadership, management and gender. In C.F. Epstein and A.L. Kalleberg (eds) *Fighting for Time: Shifting the Boundaries of Work and Social Life* (pp. 219–46). New York: Russell Sage Foundation.

Connell, R.W. (1995) *Masculinities*. Cambridge: Polity Press.

Cooper, C.L. and Davidson, M. (1982) *High Pressure: Working Lives of Women Managers*. Glasgow: Fontana.

Cosslett, T. (1994) *Women Writing Childbirth: Modern Discourses of Motherhood*. Manchester: Manchester University Press.

Crompton, R. (1997) *Women and Work in Modern Britain*. Oxford: Oxford University Press.

Crossley, N. (2001) *The Social Body: Habit, Identity and Desire*. London: Sage.

Crossley, N. (2005) *Key Concepts in Critical Social Theory*. London: Sage.

Cusk, R. (2001) *A Life's Work: On Becoming a Mother*. London: Fourth Estate.

Dahle, R. (2003) Shifting boundaries and negotiations in knowledge: Interprofessional conflicts between nurses and nursing assistants in Norway. *International Journal of Sociology and Social Policy*, 23(4/5): 139–59.

Dahle, R. (2005) Men, bodies and nursing. In D. Morgan, B. Brandth and E. Kvande (eds) *Gender, Bodies and Work* (pp. 127–38). Aldershot: Ashgate.

Davidson, J. (2001) Pregnant pauses: agoraphobic embodiment and the limits of (im)pregnability. *Gender, Place and Culture*, 8: 283–97.

Davidson, M.J. and Cooper, C.L. (1992) *Shattering the Glass Ceiling: The Woman Manager*. London: Paul Chapman Publishing.

Davis, J. (2004) Bad breastfeeders/good mothers: Constructing the maternal body in public. *Berkeley Journal of Sociology*, 46: 49–75.

Daycare Trust (2002) News from Daycare Trust. www.daycaretrust.org.uk (accessed 5 July 2002).

Defago, N. (2005) *Childfree and Loving It*. London: Fusion Press.

Degenhardt, L. Day, C., Conroy, E. and Gilmour, S. (2006) Examining links between cocaine use and street-based sex work in New South Wales, Australia. *Journal of Sex Research*, 43(2): 107–14.

Delphy, C. and Leonard, D. (1992) *Familiar Exploitation: A New Analysis of Marriage in Contemporary Western Societies*. Cambridge: Polity Press.

Department for Business Enterprise and Regulatory Reform (2007) *Maternity Entitlements and Responsibilities: A Guide. Babies Due on or after April 2007*, URN NO: 07/983/A. London: Department for Business Enterprise and Regulatory Reform.

Department of Health (1993) *Changing Childbirth*, Report of the Expert Maternity Group. London: HMSO.

Department of Health (2004a) *Infant Feeding Recommendations*. London: Department of Health.

Department of Health (2004b) *Good Practice and Innovation in Breastfeeding*. London: Department of Health.

Department of Health (2007) *Maternity Matters: Choice, Access and Continuity of Care in a Safe Service*. London: Department of Health.

Desmarais, S. and Alksnis, C. (2005) Gender issues. In J. Barling, K. Kelloway and M. Frone (eds) *Handbook of Work Stress* (pp. 445–87). Thousand Oaks, CA: Sage.

Ditmore, M. (2007) I never want to be rescued again. *New Internationalist* (September): 15–16.

Dobson, R. and Waite, R. (2007) Men opt out of the housework after marriage. *The Times*, 12 August. www.timesonline.co.uk (accessed 24 August 2007).

Doucet, A. (1995) Gender equality and gender differences in household work and parenting. *Women's Studies International Forum*, 18: 271–84.

Dryden, C. (1999) *Being Married, Doing Gender*. London: Routledge.

Dunne, G. (1999) A passion for 'sameness'? Sexuality and gender accountability. In E. Silva and C. Smart (eds) *The New Family?* (pp. 66–82). London: Sage.

Dworkin, A. (1996) Pornography. In S. Jackson and S. Scott (eds) *Feminism and Sexuality*. Edinburgh: Edinburgh University Press.

Dyhouse, C. (2006) *Students: A Gendered History*. London: Routledge.

Dykes, F. (2005). 'Supply' and 'demand': Breastfeeding as labour. *Social Science & Medicine*, 60: 2283–94.

Earle, S. (2002) Factors affecting the initiation of breastfeeding: Implications for breastfeeding promotion. *Health Promotion International*, 17(3): 205–14.

Economist (2003) Be a man. *The Economist*, 28 June: 64–5.

Economist (2005) Special report: women in business, the conundrum of the glass ceiling. *The Economist*, 23 July: 67–9.

Edmond, W. and Fleming, S. (1975) *All Work and No Pay: Women, Housework, and the Wages Due*. Bristol: Power of Women Collective, Falling Wall Press.

Edwards, P. and Wajcman, J. (2005) *The Politics of Working Life*. Oxford: Oxford University Press.

Ehrenreich, B. and Hochschild, A. (2003) *Global Women: Nannies, Maids and Sex Workers in the New Economy*. London: Granta.

Elliott, C. and Stead, V. (2008) Learning from leading women's experience: Towards a sociological understanding. *Leadership*, 4(2).

Equal Opportunities Commission (2004) *Pregnant and Productive: An Update on Our Investigation*. Glasgow: Equal Opportunities Commission Scotland.

Equal Opportunities Commission (2005a) *Greater Expectations*. Manchester: Equal Opportunities Commission.

Equal Opportunities Commission (2005b) *Sex and Power, Who Runs Britain?* Manchester: Equal Opportunities Commission.

Equal Opportunities Commission (2007a) *Sex and Power, Who Runs Britain*. Manchester: Equal Opportunities Commission.

Equal Opportunities Commission (2007b) Final EOC report warns sex equality still generations away (press release). Manchester: Equal Opportunities Commission.

Evans, M. (2002) Real bodies: An introduction. In M. Evans and E. Lee (eds) *Real Bodies: A Sociological Introduction* (pp. 1–13). Basingstoke: Palgrave Macmillan.

Evertsson, M. (2006) The reproduction of gender: housework and attitudes towards gender equality in the home among Swedish boys and girls. *British Journal of Sociology*, 57(3): 415–36.

Family Education (2007) Announcing your pregnancy at work. http://life.familyeducation.com/working-parents/pregnancy/40389.html (accessed 28 March 2008).

Fernandes, H. (2007) Move over boys! Surgery is women's work. *Daily Mail*, 31 July: 50.

Fielden, S. and Cooper, C.L. (2001) Women managers and stress: a critical analysis. *Equal Opportunities International*, 20(1): 3–16.

Finch, J. and Mason, J. (1993) *Negotiating Family Responsibilities*. London: Tavistock/ Routledge.

Firestone, S. (1970) *The Dialectic of Sex*. New York: William Morrow.

Frances, B. (2002) Relativism, realism, and feminism: An analysis of some theoretical tensions in research on gender identity. *Journal of Gender Studies*, 11(1): 39–53.

Freeman, E., Sammel, M., Liu, L., Gracia, C., Nelson, D. and Hollander, L. (2004) Hormones and menopausal status as predictors of depression in women in transition to menopause. *Archives of General Psychiatry*, 61(1): 62–70.

Friedan, B. (1965) *The Feminine Mystique*. Harmondsworth: Penguin. First published in 1963.

Friese, C., Becker, G. and Nachtigall, R. (2006) Rethinking the biological clock: Eleventh-hour moms, miracle moms and meanings of age-related infertility. *Social Science and Medicine*, 63(6): 1550–1560.

Gagg, M.E. (1961) *Helping at Home: A Ladybird Learning to Read Book*. Loughborough: Ladybird.

Galtry, J. (1997) Suckling and silence in the USA: The costs and benefits of breast-feeding. *Feminist Economics*, 3: 1–24.

Gatrell, C. (2005) *Hard Labour, The Sociology of Parenthood*. Maidenhead: Open University Press.

Gatrell C. (2006a) *Managing Part-time Study, A Guide for Undergraduates and Post-graduates*. Maidenhead: Open University Press.

Gatrell, C. (2006b) Interviewing fathers – feminist dilemmas in fieldwork. *Journal of Gender Studies*, 15(3): 237–53.

Gatrell C. (2006c) Managing maternity. In D. McTavish and K. Miller (eds) *Women in Leadership and Management*. Cheltenham: Edward Elgar.

Gatrell, C. (2007a) A fractional commitment? Part-time working and the maternal body. *International Journal of Human Resource Management*, 18(3): 462–75.

Gatrell, C. (2007b) Secrets and lies: Breastfeeding and professional paid work. *Social Science & Medicine*, 65: 393–404.

Gatrell, C. (2007c) Whose child is it anyway? The negotiation of paternal entitlements within marriage. *Sociological Review*, 55(2): 352–72.

Gatrell, C. and Cooper, C.L. (2007) (No) cracks in the glass ceiling: Women managers, stress and the barriers to success. In D. Bilimoria and S. Piderit (eds) *The Handbook of Women in Business and Management* (pp. 55–77). Cheltenham: Edward Elgar.

Gatrell, C. and Swan E. (2008) *Gender and Diversity in Management: A Concise Introduction*. London: Sage.

Gatrell, C. and Tyler, I. (2005) Maternal Bodies Workshop (unpublished). Lancaster University.

Gershuny, J. (1997) Sexual divisions and the distribution of work in the household. In G. Dench (ed.) *Rewriting the Sexual Contract* (pp. 141–52). London: Institute of Community Studies.

Gershuny, J. (2002) Service regimes and the political economy of time. In G. Crow and S. Hearth (eds) *Social Conceptions of Time*. Basingstoke: Palgrave Macmillan.

Gershuny, J., Godwin, M. and Jones, S. (1994) The domestic labour revolution: A process of lagged adaptation? In M. Anderson, F. Bechhofer and J. Gershuny (eds) *The Social and Political Economy of the Household*. Oxford: Oxford University Press.

Giles, F. (2004) 'Relational and strange': A preliminary foray into a project to queer breastfeeding. *Australian Feminist Studies*, 19: 301–14.

Gilman, C.P. (2002) *The Home: Its Work and Influence*. Reprint of the 1903 edition with an introduction by Michael Kimmel. Oxford: Altamira Press.

Glucksmann, M. (1990) *Women Assemble: Women Workers and the New Industries in Inter-war Britain*. London: Routledge.

Glucksmann, M. (2005) Shifting boundaries and interconnections: Extending the 'total social organisation of labour'. *Sociological Review*, 53(Supplement 2): 19–36.

Goldberg, A.E. and Perry-Jenkins, M. (2007) The division of labor and perceptions of parental roles: Lesbian couples across the transition to parenthood. *Journal of Social and Personal Relationships*. 24(2): 297–318.

Graham, H. (1993) *Hardship and Health in Women's Lives*. Hemel Hempstead: Harvester Wheatsheaf.

Greer, G. (2006) *The Female Eunuch*. London: Harper Perennial. First published in 1970.

Gregson, N. and Lowe, M. (1994) *Servicing the Middle Classes: Class Gender and Waged Domestic Labour in Contemporary Britain*. London and New York: Routledge.

Griffin, Z. (2004) Gallery visitor told not to breastfeed by nudes. *Daily Telegraph*, 10 July: 5.

Griffiths, S. (2008) The new mum battleground. *Sunday Times*, New Review section: 13 January: 10.

Grint, K. (1998) *The Sociology of Work*. Cambridge: Polity Press.

Grint, K. (2005) *The Sociology of Work*. Cambridge: Polity Press.

Grosz, E. (1994) *Volatile Bodies: Toward a Corporeal Feminism*. Bloomington: Indiana University Press.

Hakim, C. (1979) *Occupational Segregation: A Comprehensive Study of the Degree and Pattern of the Differentiation between Men and Women's Work in Britain, the United States and other Countries*, Research Paper. London: Department of Employment.

Hakim, C. (1995) Five feminist myths about women's employment. *British Journal of Sociology*, 46: 429–55.

Hakim, C. (1996) The sexual division of labour and women's heterogeneity. *British Journal of Sociology*, 47: 178–88.

Hakim, C. (2000) *Work-Lifestyle Choices in the 21st Century: Preference Theory*. Oxford: Oxford University Press.

Hamilton, E. (2006) Whose story is it anyway? Narrative accounts of the roles of women in founding and establishing family businesses. *International Small Business Journal*, 23(3): 1–16.

Harvey, P. (2005) Prostitution versus constitution. *The Economist*, 376(8440): 62.

Hausman, B.L. (2004) The feminist politics of breastfeeding. *Australian Feminist Studies*, 19: 273–85.

Hewlett, S. (2002) *Baby Hunger: The New Battle for Motherhood*. London: Atlantic Books.

Hirst, J., Formby, E. and Owen, J. (2006) *Pathways into Parenthood: Reflections from Three Generations of Teenage Mothers and Fathers*. Sheffield: Sheffield Hallam University.

Hochschild, A. (1997) *The Time Bind: When Work Becomes Home and Home Becomes Work*. New York: Henry Holt.

Hochschild, A.R. (2003) *The Managed Heart: The Commercialization of Human Feeling*, 20th anniversary edition. Berkeley, CA: University of California Press.

Holiday, R. and Hassard, J. (2001) Contested bodies: An introduction. In R. Holiday and J. Hassard (eds) *Contested Bodies* (pp. 1–18). London: Routledge.

Holland, C.C. (2007) The five dangers of parental leave. www.bnet.com/2403-13068_23-67231.html (accessed 14 June 2007).

Holland, J. and Ramazanoğlu, C. (1994) Coming to conclusions: Power and interpretation in researching young women's sexuality. In M. Maynard and J. Purvis (eds) *Researching Women's Lives from a Feminist Perspective* (pp. 125–48). London: Taylor & Francis.

Home Office (2006) *Coordinated Prostitution Strategy*. London: HMSO.

hooks, b. (1981) *Ain't I a Woman*. Boston: South End Press.

hooks, b. (1986) Sisterhood: Political solidarity between women. *Feminist Review*, 23: 125.

hooks, b. (1991) Sisterhood: Political solidarity between women. In S. Gunew (ed.) *A Reader in Feminist Knowledge* (pp. 29–31). London: Routledge.

Höpfl, H. (2000) The suffering mother and the miserable son: Organizing women and organizing women's writing. *Gender, Work and Organization*, 17(2): 98–105.

Höpfl, H. and Hornby Atkinson, P. (2000) The future of women's careers. In A. Collin and R. Young (eds) *The Future of Career* (pp. 130–43). Cambridge: Cambridge University Press.

Hopkins, N. (2005) Women as advertising executives? No, they'll just wimp out and go and suckle something. *The Times*, 21 October: 43.

Howorth, C., Rose, M. and Hamilton, E. (2006) Definitions, diversity and development: Key debates in family business research. In M. Casson, B. Young and N. Wadeson (eds) *The Oxford Handbook of Entrepreneurship* (pp. 225–47). Oxford: Oxford University Press.

Howson, A. (2005) *Embodying Gender*. London: Sage.

HRM Guide Canada (2001) *Women Still Working More Than Men*. www.hrmguide.net/canada/diversity/gender_gap.htm, 12 March (accessed 18 February 2004).

Hubbard, P. (2004) Cleansing the metropolis: Sex work and the politics of zero tolerance. *Urban Studies*, 41(9): 1687–702.

Hughes, C. (2002) *Women's Contemporary Lives: Within and Beyond the Mirror*. London: Routledge.

Isaksen, L. W. (2005) Gender and care: The role of cultural ideas of dirt and disgust. In D. Morgan, B. Brandth and E. Kvande (eds) *Gender, Bodies and Work*. Aldershot: Ashgate.

Jackson, S. (1997) Women, marriage and family relationships. In V. Robinson and D. Richardson (eds) *Introducing Women's Studies*, 2nd edn. Basingstoke: Macmillan Press.

Jackson, S. and Jones, J. (1998) *Contemporary Feminist Theories*. Edinburgh: Edinburgh University Press.

Jackson, W. (2004) Breastfeeding and type 1 diabetes mellitus. *British Journal of Midwifery*, 12(3): 158–65.

Jacobson, J.P. (2007) *The Economics of Gender*, 2nd edn. Oxford: Blackwell.

Jayson, S. (2007) Married women unite! Husbands do far less housework. *USA Today*, 29 August: 7.

Jeffrey, L.A. and MacDonald, G. (2006) 'It's the money, honey': The economy of sex work in the Maritimes. *Canadian Review of Sociology and Anthropology*, 43(3): 313–27.

Jervis, L.L. (2001) The pollution of incontinence and the dirty work of caregiving in a US nursing home. *Medical Anthropology Quarterly*, 15(1): 84–99.

Judge, E. (2003) Women on board: Help or hindrance? *The Times*, 11 November: 21.

Kelly, L. (1988) *Surviving Sexual Violence*. Cambridge: Polity Press.

Kerfoot, D. and Knights, D. (1993) Management, masculinity and manipulation: From paternalism to corporate strategy in financial services. *Journal of Management Studies*, 30(4): 659–77.

Kilby S. (2007) I'm pregnant, not mad, bad and dangerous. www. babyworld.co.uk/information/pregnancy/pregnancyandwork.asp (accessed 14 June 2007).

Kitzinger, S. (1992) Birth and violence against women: Generating hypotheses from women's accounts of unhappiness after childbirth. In H. Roberts (ed.) *Women's Health Matters*. London: Routledge.

Kitzinger, S. (2003) *The New Pregnancy and Childbirth: Choices and Challenges*. London: Dorling Kindersley.

Kitzinger, S. (2005) *The Politics of Birth*. London: Elsevier Butterworth Heinemann.

Kitzinger, S. (2006) *Birth Crisis*, London: Routledge.

Kmietowicz, Z. (1998) Women warned to avoid peanuts during pregnancy and lactation. *British Medical Journal*, 316(7149): 1926.

Knight, I. (2006) Think again, old girl. *Sunday Times*, News Review section: 7 May.

Kohl, J., Mayfield, M. and Mayfield, J. (2005) Recent trends in pregnancy discrimination law. *Business Horizons*, 48(5): 421–9.

Lagan, B., Sinclair, M. and Kernohan, W.G. (2006) Pregnant women's use of the internet: a review of published and unpublished evidence. *Evidence Based Midwifery*, 4(1): 17–23.

Laurance, J. (2005) Mother in plea for breastfeeding law. *The Independent*, 10 August: 10.

Laws, S. (1983) The politics of pre-menstrual tension. *Women's Studies International Forum*, 6(1): 19–31.

Lea, R. (2001) The work life balance and all that. The re-regulation of the labour market. Policy Paper, Institute of Directors, London.

Leifer, M. (1980) Pregnancy. *Journal of Women in Culture and Society*, 5(4): 754–65.

Leonhardt, D. (2006) Gender pay gap, once narrowing, is now back in place. *New York Times*, 24 December.

Letherby, G. and Shiles, J. (2001) Isn't he good but can we take her seriously? Gendered expectations in higher education. In P. Anderson and J. Williams (eds) *Identity and Difference in Higher Education: Outsiders Within* (pp. 121–32). London: Ashgate.

Lewis, C. (1986) *Becoming a Father*. Milton Keynes: Open University Press.

Lewis, M. and Langley, C. (2007) I am giving birth up the hill: will you come? *RCM Midwives Journal*, 10(9): 428–9.

Lewis, S. and Cooper, C.L. (1999) The work-family agenda in changing contexts. *Journal of Occupational Health Psychology*, 4(4): 382–93.

Longhurst, R. (2001) *Bodies: Exploring Fluid Boundaries*. London: Routledge.

Longhurst, R. (2008) *Maternities: Gender, Bodies and Space*. New York: Routledge.

Longworth, L., Ratcliffe, J. and Boulton, M. (2001) Investigating women's preferences for intrapartum care: Home versus hospital births. *Health and Social Care in the Community*, 9(6): 404–13.

Lupton, D. and Barclay, L. (1997) *Constructing Fatherhood: Discourses and Experiences*. London: Sage.

Macones, G.A. (2004) Medical care during pregnancy. http://kidshealth.org/parent/pregnancy_newborn/pregnancy/medical_care_pregnancy.html (accessed 8 August 2007).

Madmums (2007) Bleeding in pregnancy: Advice please. Madmums Pregnancy and Parenting Forum. www.madmums.com/forum 07/04.2007 (accessed 25 June 2007).

Malthouse, T.-J. (1997) *Childcare, Business and Social Change*. London: Institute of Directors.

Marshall, A. (1994) Sensuous sapphires: A study of the social construction of black female sexuality. In M. Maynard and J. Purvis (eds) *Researching Women's Lives from a Feminist Perspective*. London: Taylor & Francis.

Marshall, H. (1991) The social construction of motherhood: An analysis of childcare and parenting manuals. In A. Phoenix, A. Woollett and E. Lloyd (eds) *Motherhood: Meanings, Practices and Ideologies* (pp. 66–85). London: Sage.

Marshall, J. (1995) *Women Managers Moving On: Exploring Career and Life Choices*. London: Routledge.

Martin, E. (1989) *The Woman in the Body: A Cultural Analysis of Reproduction*. Boston: Beacon Press.

Martin, N. (2007) When it comes to housework, women are better off single. *Daily Telegraph*, 23 February: 3.

Maternity Alliance (2004) *Experiences of Maternity Services: Muslim Women's Perspectives*. London: Maternity Alliance.

Maushart, S. (2002) *Wifework: What Marriage Really Means for Women*. London: Bloomsbury.

Mayhew, E. (2006) The parental employment context. In J. Bradshaw and A. Hatland (eds) *Social Policy, Employment and Family Change in Comparative Perspective* (pp. 37–60). Cheltenham: Edward Elgar.

Maynard, M. and Winn, J. (1997) Women, violence and male power. In V. Robinson and D. Richardson (eds) *Introducing Women's Studies*, 2nd edn. Basingstoke: Macmillan Press.

McIntyre, E., Pisaniello, D., Gun, R., Saunders, C. and Frith, D. (2002) Balancing breastfeeding and paid employment: A project targeting employers, women and workplaces. *Health Promotion International*, 17(3): 215–22.

McKeganey, N.P. and Barnard, M. (1996) *Sex Work on the Streets: Prostitutes and Their Clients*. Buckingham: Open University Press.

McKinlay, N.M. and Hyde, J.S. (2004). Personal attitudes or structural factors? A contextual analysis of breastfeeding duration. *Psychology of Women Quarterly*, 28: 388–400.

Miles, A. (1992) *Women, Health and Medicine*. Buckingham: Open University Press.

Miller, T. (2005) *Making Sense of Motherhood: A Narrative Approach.* Cambridge: Cambridge University Press.

Mollen, D. (2006) Voluntarily childfree women: Experiences and counselling considerations. *Journal of Mental Health Counseling,* 28(3): 269–82.

Moore, S. (2006) Baby strike? Blame the invisible man. *Mail on Sunday,* 26 February: 31.

Moorhead, J. (2004) For decades we've been told that Sweden is a great place to be a working parent but we've been duped. *The Guardian,* 22 September: 10–11.

Morgan, D. (1996) *Family Connections: An Introduction to Family Studies.* Oxford: Polity Press.

Morgan, D. (2005) Gender, bodies, work: Re-reading texts. In D. Morgan, B. Brandth and E. Kvande (eds) *Gender, Bodies and Work* (pp. 19–30). Aldershot: Ashgate.

Morgan, D., Brandth, B. and Kvande, E. (eds) (2005) *Gender, Bodies and Work.* Aldershot: Ashgate.

Morgan, G. (1986) *Images of Organisation.* London: Sage.

Morris, L. (1990) *The Workings of the Household.* Cambridge: Polity Press.

Mothers 35 Plus (2007) Older mothers – facts and figures.
www. mothers35plus.co.uk/intro.htm (accessed 7 April 2008).

Mullin, A. (2005) *Reconceiving Pregnancy and Childcare: Ethic, Experience and Reproductive Labour.* New York: Cambridge University Press.

Mulholland, K. (1996) Gender, power and property relations within enterpreneurial wealthy families. *Gender Work and Organisation,* 3(2): 78–102.

Murphy, A.K. and Venkatesh, S.A. (2006) Vice careers: The changing contours of sex work in New York City, *Qualitative Sociology,* 29: 129–54.

Murphy, E. (2003) Expertise and forms of knowledge in the government of families. *Sociological Review,* 51: 433–62.

Murray, W. (1964) *Things We Like,* Ladybird Key Words Reading Scheme. Loughborough: Ladybird.

Nash, B. (1980) *St Michael: The Complete Book of Babycare.* London: Octopus Books.

National Black Women's Network Online (2007) About us.
www.nbwn.org/about_us.htm (accessed 9 April 2008).

National Statistics Online (2004) Lifestyles: Women do more chores than men. www.statistics.gov.uk/cci/nugget.asp?id=440 (accessed 27 March 2008).

Neale, B. and Smart, C. (2002) Caring, earning and changing: Parenthood and employment after divorce. In A. Carling, S. Duncan and R. Edwards (eds) *Analysing Families, Morality and Rationality in Policy and Practice* (pp. 183–99). London and New York: Routledge.

Nettleton, S. (2006) *The Sociology of Health and Illness,* 2nd edn. Cambridge: Polity Press.

New Scientist (2007) Street sex work takes its toll. *New Scientist,* 194(2608): 40.

NHS Direct (2008) Which foods should I avoid during pregnancy?
www.nhsdirect.nhs.uk/articles/article.aspx?articleId=917 (accessed 23 March 2008).

Oakeshott, I. (2007) The battle over birth. *Sunday Times*, 25 March: 16.

Oakley, A. (1974) *Housewife: High Value Low Cost*. London: Allen Lane.

Oakley, A. (1981) *From Here to Maternity: Becoming a Mother*. London: Penguin.

Oakley, A. (1984) *The Captured Womb*. Oxford: Blackwell.

Oakley, A. (1993) *Essays on Women, Medicine and Health*. Edinburgh: Edinburgh University Press.

Oakley, A. (2002) *Gender on Planet Earth*. Cambridge: Polity.

O'Brien, M. (1981) *The Politics of Reproduction*. London: Routledge & Kegan Paul.

Odent, M. (2003) *Birth and Breastfeeding: Rediscovering the Needs of Women During Pregnancy and Breastfeeding*. Forest Row: Clairview.

Olesen, V. (1994) Feminisms and models of qualitative research. In N. Denzin and Y. Lincoln (eds) *Handbook of Qualitative Research* (pp. 158–74). London: Sage.

Ortiz, A., Harlow, S., Sowers, M. and Romaguera, J. (2006) Age at natural menopause and factors associated with menopause state among Puerto Rican women aged 40–59 years. *Journal of North American Menopause Society*, 13(1): 116–24.

Ortiz, J., McGilligan, K. and Kelly, P. (2004) Duration of breast milk/expression among working mothers enrolled in an employer-sponsored lactation program. *Pediatric Nursing*, 30: 111–19.

Padavic, I. and Reskin, B. (2002) *Women and Men at Work*. Thousand Oaks, CA: Pine Forge Press.

Parsons, T. and Bales, R. (1956) *Family and Socialization and Interaction Process*. London: Routledge & Kegan Paul.

Parsons, T. (1971) The normal American family. In B. Adams and T. Weirath (eds) *Readings on the Sociology of the Family* (pp. 53–66). Chicago: Markham.

Pateman, C. (1988) *The Sexual Contract*. Oxford: Blackwell.

Patient UK (2004) Pregnancy – screening tests. www.patient.co.uk/pdf/pilsL.722.pdf (accessed 29 August 2002).

Patmore, C. (1856) *The Angel in the House*. Boston: Ticknor and Fields.

Peterson, M. J. (1972) The Victorian governess: Status incongruence in family and society, in Victorian women and menstruation. In M. Vicinus (ed.) *Suffer and Be Still: Women in the Victorian Age* (pp. 3–19). Bloomington: Indiana University Press.

Phillips, M. (2004) *The Ascent of Woman: A History of the Suffragette Movement and the Ideas behind It*. London: Abacus.

Pollock, D. (1999) *Telling Bodies Performing Birth*. New York: Columbia University Press.

Porter, S. (1998) *Social Theory and Nursing Practice*. London: Macmillan Press.

Powell, H.F. (2005) Birth rates are down across Europe so 'middle class' mums in France are to get £500 a month to have a third child. Should Britain follow suit? *Sunday Times*, 5 September.

Pringle, R. (1998) *Sex and Medicine*. Cambridge: Cambridge University Press.

Purdy, L.M. (1997) Babystrike! In H. Nelson (ed.) *Feminism and Families* (pp. 69–75). New York: Routledge.

Puwar, N. (2004) *Space Invaders: Race, Gender and Bodies out of Place.* Oxford: Berg.

Ramazanoğlu, C. and Holland, J. (2002) *Feminist Methodology: Challenges and Choices.* London: Sage.

Ramsay K. and Letherby, G (2006) The experience of academic non-mothers in the gendered university. *Gender Work and Organisation*, 13(1): 25–44.

Raymond, J. (2005) Another reason for you to breastfeed. *Working Mother*, 28(4): 70–4.

Reynolds, F. (1999) Distress and coping with hot flushes at work: implications for counsellors in occupational settings. *Counselling Psychology Quarterly*, 12(4): 353–9.

Ribbens, J. (1994) *Mothers and Their Children: A Feminist Sociology of Childrearing.* London: Sage.

Rich, A. (1977) *Of Woman Born: Motherhood as Experience and Institution.* London: Virago.

Roberts, H.E. (1972) Marriage, redundancy or sin: The painter's view of women in the first twenty five years of Victoria's reign. In M. Vicinus (ed.) *Suffer and Be Still: Women in the Victorian Age* (pp. 45–76). Bloomington: Indiana University Press.

Rogers, L. (2006) Decade long quest of the oldest mother: Pregnancy of 63 year old sparks new inquiries from menopausal women. *Sunday Times*, 7 May: 10.

Romito, P. (1997) Damned if you do and damned if you don't: Psychological and social constraints in motherhood in contemporary Europe. In A. Oakley and J. Mitchell (eds) *Who's Afraid of Feminism?* London: Hamish Hamilton.

Rooks, J.P., Weatherby, N.L. and Ernst, E.K.M. (1992) The National Birth Centre study, Part II. Intrapartum and immediate post-partum and neo-natal care. *Journal of Nurse Midwifery*, 37(5): 301–30.

Rothman, B.K. (1982) *In Labour: Women, and Power in the Birthplace.* New York: W.W. Norton.

Rowbotham, S. (1997) *A Century of Women: The History of Women in Britain and the United States.* London: Penguin.

Royal College of Obstetricians and Gynaecologists (2001) *The National Sentinel Caesarean Section Audit Report.* London: RCOG Press.

Ryan, M.K. and Haslam, S.A. (2005) The glass cliff: Evidence that women are over-represented in precarious leadership positions. *British Journal of Management*, 16(2): 81–90.

Ryan, M. and Haslam, S.A. (2007) *Change Agenda: Women in the Boardroom, the Risks of Being at the Top.* London: CIPD.

Sanders, T. (2005a) *Sex Work: A Risky Business.* Cullompton: Willan.

Sanders, T. (2005b) 'It's just acting': Sex workers' strategies for capitalizing on sexuality. *Gender Work and Organization*, 12(4): 320–42.

Sanders, T. (2006) Sexing up the subject: Methodological nuances in researching the female sex industry. *Sexualities*, 9(4): 449–68.

Sanders, T. and Campbell, R. (2007) Designing our vulnerability, building in respect: Violence, safety and sex work policy. *British Journal of Sociology*, 58(1): 1–19.

Scott, J. (1999) Family change: Revolution or backlash? In S. McRae (ed.) *Changing Britain, Families and Households in the 1990s*. Oxford: Oxford University Press.

Scott, J. and Duncombe, J. (1991) A cross-national comparison of gender-role attitudes: Is the working mother selfish? Working Papers of the ESRC Centre on Micro-social Change, No. 9.

Seager, J. (2005) *The Atlas of Women in the World*. London: Earthscan.

Shaw, R. (2004) The virtues of cross-nursing and the 'yuk factor'. *Australian Feminist Studies*, 19: 288–99.

Shildrick, M. (1997) *Leaky Bodies and Boundaries: Feminism, Postmodernism and Bio-ethics*. London: Routledge.

Shove, E. (2003) *Comfort, Cleanliness and Convenience: The Social Organization of Normality*. Oxford: Berg.

Showalter, E. and Showalter, E. (1972) Victorian women and menstruation. In M. Vicinus (ed.) *Suffer and Be Still: Women in the Victorian Age* (pp. 38–44). Bloomington: Indiana University Press.

Singh, V. and Vinnicombe, S. (2004) Why so few women directors in top UK boardrooms? Evidence and theoretical explanations. *Corporate Governance*, 12(4): 479–88.

Singh, V. and Vinnicombe, S. (2005) *The Female FTSA Report 2005*. Centre for Developing Women Business Leaders, Cranfield University School of Management.

Siskos, C. (2004) It pays to haggle for that first check. *Kiplingers Personal Finance*, April: 29–30.

Skeggs, B. (1995) *Feminist Cultural Theory: Production and Process*. Manchester: Manchester University Press.

Smart, C. and Neale, B. (1999) *Family Fragments?* Cambridge: Polity Press.

Stephenson, D. (2007) Women wanted for the fire brigade. *The Londoner*. www.london.gov.uk/londoner/07may (accessed 18 December 2007).

Stoppard, M. (2005) Family Health Guide. London: Dorling Kindersley.

Summerfield, P. (1998) *Reconstructing Women's Wartime Lives*. Manchester: Manchester University Press.

Summers, L. (2005) Remarks at NBER Conference of Diversifying the Science and Engineering Workforce. Office of the President, Harvard University. www.president.harvard.edu/speeches (accessed 29 May 2008).

Swan, E. (2005) On bodies, rhinestones and pleasures: Women teaching managers. *Management Learning*, 36(3): 317–33.

Sullivan, O. (1997) Time waits for no (wo)man: An investigation of the gendered experience of domestic time. *Sociology*, 31: 221–39.

Tahmincioglu, E. (2007) Pregnancy discrimination is on the rise, EEOC seeing more complaints. www.msnbc.msn.com/id/18742634/ (accessed 29 May 2008).

Thomas, C. (1999) *Female Forms: Experiencing and Understanding Disability*. Buckingham: Open University Press.

Thomas, C. (2002) The 'Disabled body'. In M. Evans and E. Lee (eds) *Real Bodies*. Basingstoke: Palgrave.

Thomas, C. (2007) *Sociologies of Disability and Illness, Contested Ideas in Disability Studies and Medical Sociology*. Basingstoke: Palgrave.

Tooley, J. (2002) *The Miseducation of Women*. London: Continuum.

Truman, C. (1996) Paid work in women's lives: Continuity and change. In T. Cosslett, A. Easton and P. Summerfield (eds) *Women, Power and Resistance: An Introduction to Women's Studies*. Buckingham: Open University Press.

Turner, B. (1984) *The Body and Society*. Oxford: Basil Blackwell.

Turner, B. (1996) *The Body and Society*, 2nd edn. London: Sage.

Tyler, I. (2000) Reframing pregnant embodiment. In S. Ahmed, J. Kilby, S. Lury, M. McNeil and B. Skeggs (eds) *Transformations: Thinking through Feminism* (pp. 288–301). London: Routledge.

Tyler, I. (2006) 'Welcome to Britain'. The cultural politics of asylum. *European Journal of Cultural Studies*, 9: 185–202.

Tyler, I. (2007) The selfish feminist: Public images of women's liberation. *Australian Feminist Studies*, 22(53): 174–90.

US Department of Health and Human Services (2007) Older mothers more likely than younger mothers to deliver by Caesarean. *National Institutes of Health News*, 8 March. www.nih.gov/news (accessed 29 May 2008).

US Department of Labor (2005) Employment status of women and men in 2005. www.dol.gov/wb/factsheets (accessed 23 August 2006).

Valeska, L. (1984) If all else fails I'm still a mother. In J. Trebilcot (ed.) *Mothering: Essays in Feminist Theory*. Totowa, NJ: Rowman and Allanheld.

Vendantam, S. (2007) The truth about why women are paid less – even if they ask for more. *Guardian Unlimited*, 21 August. www.guardian.co.uk.

Verybestbaby (2007) Announcing your pregnancy at work. www. verybestbaby.com/MyPregnancy/SecondTrimester.aspx?ArticleId= 39922 (accessed 29 May 2008).

Vorster, G. (2007) Lesbian soldier claims she was harassed for sex by male sergeant, *Personnel Today*, 8 November. www.personneltoday.com/articles/2007/11/08/43182/lesbian-soldier-claims-she-was-harassed-for-sex-by-male.html (accessed 27 March 2008).

Wajcman, J. (1998) *Managing Like a Man: Women and Men in Corporate Management*. Cambridge: Polity Press.

Walby, S. (1990) *Theorising Patriarchy*. Blackwell: Oxford.

Walker, M.B. (1998) *Philosophy and the Maternal Body: Reading Silence*. London: Routledge.

Walsh, D. (2006) Subverting the assembly line: Childbirth in a free-standing birth centre. *Social Science and Medicine*, 62: 1330–40.

Warren, S. and Brewis, J. (2004) Matter over Mind? Examining the experience of pregnancy. *Sociology*, 38: 219–236.

Warin, J., Solmon, Y., Lewis, C. and Langford, W. (1999) *Fathers, Work and Family Life*. Family Policy Studies Centre.

Watson, T.J. (1994) *In Search of Management: Culture, Chaos and Control in Managerial Work*. London: Routledge.

Watson, T.J. (2008) *Sociology, Work and Industry*, 5th edn. London: Routledge.

Webb, M.S. (2007) *Love Is Not Enough: The Smart Woman's Guide to Making and Keeping Money*. HarperPress.

WebMD (2000) Older mothers have higher risk of miscarriage. www.webmd.com/news/20000626/older-mothers-have-higher-risk-of-miscarriage (accessed 8 April 2008).

Wharton, E. (1997) *The House of Mirth*. Ware: Wordsworth Editions. First published in 1905.

What To Expect (2007) Work issues: when to tell your boss. www.whattoexpect.com/pregnancy/workissues.

Williams, A. (2001) Home care re-structuring at work: the impact of policy transformation on women's labor. In I. Dyck, N.D. Lewis and S. McLafferty (eds) *Geographies of Women's Health* (pp. 107–27). London: Routledge.

Williams, J. (2000) *Unbending Gender: Why Work and Family Conflict and What to Do about It*. New York: Oxford University Press.

Witters-Green, R. (2003) Increasing breastfeeding rates in working mothers. *Families, Systems and Health*, 21: 415–34.

Wolf, J. (2006). What feminists can do for breastfeeding and what breastfeeding can do for feminists. *Signs: Journal of Women in Culture and Society*, 31: 397–424.

Wolkowitz, C. (2006) *Bodies at Work*. London: Sage.

Wollstonecraft, M. (2004) *A Vindication of the Rights of Woman*. London: Penguin Books (first published 1792).

Womack, S. (2008) Men taking over from women in the child care 'Daddy Wars', *Daily Telegraph*, 22 January: 14.

Women's Work Commission (2006) *Shaping a Fairer Future*. London: Women and Equality Unit, Government Equalities Office. www.equalities.gov.uk (accessed 8 April 2008).

Woolf, V. (1979) *Women and Writing*. London: Women's Press.

Young, I.M. (2005) *On Female Body Experience: 'Throwing Like a Girl' and Other Essays*. Oxford: Oxford University Press.

Index

Locators shown in *italics* refer to illustrations.